An Aook

# Human Performance and Limitations for the Professional Pilot

**Airlife**
England

*Nothing in this text supersedes any legislation, rules, regulations or procedures contained in any operational document issued by The Stationary Office, the Civil Aviation Authority, the manufacturers of aircraft, engines and systems, or by the operators of aircraft throughout the world.*

Copyright © 2001 Aviation Theory Centre

ISBN 1 84037 332 6

First edition (UK) September 2001

This handbook was developed from the original Air Pilot's Manual. For that text the Aviation Theory Centre would like to thank the editorial team. For subsequent development, we gratefully acknowledge the advice given by Dr Adrian Zentner and by Dr Sarina Lococo.

Cover Photo – Aviation Theory Centre Archives

Graphics and Typesetting – Aviation Theory Centre

Printed in England by MPG Books Ltd, Bodmin, Cornwall

**Airlife Publishing Ltd**
101 Longden Road, Shrewsbury SY3 9EB, Shropshire, England
Email: airlife@airlifebooks.com
Website: www.airlifebooks.com

# The **Airlife** Pilot's Handbooks

To complement the very popular and highly regarded Air Pilot's Manuals, Airlife has commissioned this new, more advanced series of reference texts – the Airlife Pilot's Handbooks. These books prepare and progress the student beyond the simple, single-engine, private pilot standard to advanced flight operations. Following volumes then lay the theoretical foundations for the operation of complex systems – essential for a professional career as a pilot, controller or flight despatcher in a demanding air traffic environment.

The books also place the airline applicant in a position whereby he or she is already familiar with the technology, terminology and principles of operation of the systems on a modern wide-body jet.

The books are written in plain language and are superbly illustrated.

To explain the functions, modes and operation of the systems of a typical jet, we have selected the Boeing 767 300 ER as the reference aeroplane. There is a great deal of commonality with other US types, and the principles are also applicable to Airbus and other European aircraft. Any significant differences are highlighted.

The first volumes of this series include:
- *Multi-Engine Piston;*
- *Aerobatics – Principles and Practice;*
- *Avionics and Flight Management Systems for the Professional Pilot;*
- *Aerodynamics, Engines and Systems for the Professional Pilot;* and
- *Human Performance and Limitations for the Professional Pilot.*

*WINGS*
by David Robson, 1996

*How Proudly*
*they stood*
*uniformed and winged*
*young – yet not so*
*confident, ready*
*and eager to go*
*forward and upward*
*higher and faster*
*than we would ever know*
*but we knew*
*that they went*
*with the knowledge and skill*
*of all that we,*
*who went before,*
*could instil*
*and so,*
*in our hearts and souls,*
*we, in our way,*
*could also go,*
*and therefore stay,*
*with them –*
*forever*

# Editor – Author

## David Robson

David Robson is a career aviator having been nurtured on balsa wood, dope (the legal kind) and tissue paper. As an Air Training Corps cadet he was awarded a flying scholarship and made his first solo flight in a Chipmunk, with the Surrey and Kent Flying Club at Biggin Hill, shortly after his seventeenth birthday. He made his first parachute jump with the British Parachute Club at Fairoaks at the age of sixteen.

His family returned to Australia in 1962. He joined the Royal Australian Air Force in 1965 and served for twenty-one years as a fighter pilot and test pilot. He flew over 1,000 hours on Mirages and 500 on Sabres. He completed a tour in Vietnam, as a Forward Air Controller, with the United States Air Force.

He was a member of the *Deltas*, a seven-aircraft formation aerobatic team, which flew his favorite aircraft, the Mirage fighter. This team was specially formed to celebrate the fiftieth anniversary of the RAAF in 1971.

He completed the Empire Test Pilot's course at Boscombe Down in 1972, flying everything from gliders, through the Chipmunk, Argosy and Canberra, to the magnificent Hunter and English Electric Lightning. Memorable moments include passing the Concorde test aircraft in flight, inverted spinning in the Hunter and in-flight refuelling the Lightning from a Victor tanker over the North Sea.

After retiring from the Air Force, David became a civilian instructor and lecturer. During 1986–8 he was the editor of the *Aviation Safety Digest* which won the Flight Safety Foundation's prestigious international award.

He spent over ten years at the Australian Aviation College at Parafield as the Director of Pilot Training and Manager, Business Development. He holds a First Class Airline Transport Pilot's Licence and a Grade 1 Instructor's Rating. He was awarded the Australian Aviation Safety Foundation's Certificate of Air Safety for 1998.

He has completed the KLM Human Factors (KHUFAC) introductory course developed by Captain Frank Hawkins. He was recently awarded the Australian Aviation Safety Foundation's Certificate of Air Safety.

David Robson (right) with Roger Green of the Institute of Aviation Medicine, Farnbourough, to whom this volume is dedicated. Roger spent his life researching and promoting the role of the human in aviation safety but sadly succumbed to terminal cancer in 1998

# Contributors

### Captain Trevor Thom

Trevor was a training Captain on Boeing 757 and 767 aircraft and has also flown the Airbus A320, Boeing 727, McDonnell Douglas DC-9 and Fokker F-27. He was active in the International Federation of Airline Pilots' Associations (IFALPA) and a member of the IFALPA Aeroplane Design and Operations Group. He also served as IFALPA representative to the Society of Automotive Engineers (SAE) S7 Flight-Deck Design Committee, a body that makes recommendations to the aviation industry, especially the manufacturers. Prior to his airline career, Trevor was a lecturer in mathematics and physics, and an aviation ground instructor and flying instructor. He is a double-degree graduate from the University of Melbourne, and also holds a Diploma of Education.

### Peter Godwin

Chief instructor at Bonus Aviation, Cranfield, Peter has amassed over 13,000 instructional flying hours as a fixed-wing and helicopter instructor. As a member of the CAA Panel of Examiners, he is a CAA Authorised Examiner (AE), Instrument Rating and Type Examiner, and is currently training flying instructors and candidates for the basic commercial pilot's licence and instrument rating.

### Dr Sarina Lococo

Sarina is a qualified biochemist, nutritionist, naturopath and fitness instructor operating her own healthy lifestyle centre in Melbourne. Sarina's business *Naturally Fit* specialises in guiding individuals in attaining their nutrition and fitness goals. She also travels Australia giving public and corporate lectures in health and nutrition. Her work crosses into other media where she has spoken on radio and is author of numerous health and fitness articles, as well as two books, *Fat Loss for Life* and *Your Supplement Guide to Vitality, Energy, Health, Wellbeing.*

# Contents

# Introduction

> 'To see oursels as others see us'
> *Robbie Burns*

This book is designed to serve several purposes:
- to encompass the theoretical knowledge required by pilots studying for flight crew examinations on *Human Performance and Limitations*;
- to harmonise internationally, so as to be relevant to all ICAO-compliant licences and associated human factors training programs;
- to serve as a standard reference text for competency-based training at all levels of flight training, including airline CRM; and, most importantly
- to broaden knowledge and to promote discussion and further reading into this vital and fascinating topic.

Knowledge about our human machine is *the* most important information needed for the modern flight and ground crew to perform effectively the multi-functional tasks required by a modern jet in its complex operational environment.

Traditionally, we were trained to allocate priorities in the following order – aviate, navigate and then communicate. No longer. The aircraft and systems are highly reliable and largely fly and navigate themselves – they are better at routine operations than we are. The systems also self-monitor. What has been neglected in training is the importance of human relationships and needs, and the importance of internal and external communications. Further, the most important factor of team management was omitted. For modern aircraft, pilot training is incomplete. It must address the total person and include:
- skills (the *wright* stuff);
- knowledge (the *write* stuff);
- attitudes (the *right* stuff); and
- habits (the *rite* stuff).

*Automation*

There are now fewer demands for strength and manipulative skill. Mental, social, management and leadership skills are paramount. Certainly the pilot still needs to manipulate the controls and to navigate, but these abilities alone are insufficient. Current training is not preparing us well for the essential task of wise decision-making. This book proposes that our training priorities should now be to *manage, communicate, aviate* and *navigate*.

Aircraft and systems design represents leading-edge technology. We have reached the point where they far exceed the capabilities and capacity of the human body and the human data processor. While careful design of those systems and procedures can enhance the bodies and minds of the crew, there are many circumstances in which the human has to take control and rely on raw data. Knowledge of his or her own limitations allows better observations and safer decisions to be made.

The growing realisation of the crucial role of human factors can be seen in recent changes in terminology. For example, the old term *pilot error* has been replaced by *human error* as a causal factor in aircraft accidents. As a subject for study, *aviation medicine* (Avmed) has become *physiology of flight,* which, with the addition of individual and collective psychological aspects, has become known as *human factors.* At the moment the subject is formally titled *Human Performance and Limitations* – the generally accepted, international term.

It was our intention to cover the syllabus for both the commercial pilot and the air transport pilot, but it has not been possible at this stage to positively define the boundary between the two. Ultimately the information in this book is relevant to all of us and so we have combined the material into one volume, which we hope will not only serve a formal purpose but be of extremely practical value. Even the single pilot will benefit from an understanding of crew resource management as it affects the total operation rather than within the cockpit. We rarely operate in total isolation – all activities depend on interaction with some other humans.

The fact that 80% of aircraft accidents are attributable to, or could have been prevented by, human intervention suggests that the greatest impact on flight safety has to be achieved by improving human potential – the competencies a crew member brings to his or her duties. This book offers a lifetime reference, both for initial and continuing study. All accidents are avoidable – in retrospect. We need to avoid accidents in their formative stage. The human is sometimes portrayed as the weak link in the chain. We disagree – strongly. The human is, in fact, the strong link in 99,999 cases out of 100,000 – the strong link that detects and corrects a deteriorating situation before it becomes serious – not a bad performance by any standard. While the stories about the occasional rogue pilot will always get the most attention, the untold story is really about the thousands of true pros who are out there quietly and safely going about their job. All readers are invited to join the *pro club* through such measures as self-management and commitment to gaining and maintaining important aviation knowledge, such as is presented in this book. Learn it thoroughly, not just for the examinations, but to become a real professional.

To maintain and hopefully improve our performance, and therefore our value as pilots and as members of a crew, we need to understand our role, our capabilities and our limitations. Armed with this knowledge we can build buffers of safety to accommodate our weaknesses and to exploit our strengths. Machines can be tailored to assist, and procedures can be designed to be more tolerant of human limitations and error.

This book has been written, by pilots for pilots, by a team with in excess of 140 years of collective aviation experience and more than 45,000 flying hours – including military, civil, GA, RPT, instruction, single-pilot and multi-crew. Most have personally experienced the situations and conditions described in this book and thus can speak with authority. They have been there and done that, and fortunately survived – so far. We hope that new pilots will accept some of the advice that is truly given here in good faith. For now, forget that you are studying for an examination. Come into the fascinating world inside the human body and the human mind. Let's explore ourselves.

## Chapter 1

# Human Physiology and Flight

## Our Human Condition

An aircraft is specifically designed for flight; the human body is not. To ensure safe travel by air, we have to develop systems that provide a comfortable travelling environment. In doing so, we must develop an awareness of the limitations of the human body (in the case of the crew), and go through a training/learning process to adapt the body to the airborne environment.

The body (and mind) needs:
- food (fuel);
- water;
- oxygen;
- sleep;
- exercise (mental and physical);
- warmth and comfort; and
- love and reward.

The body consists of several major systems, of which we will consider:
- the nervous system;
- the circulatory system; and
- the respiratory system.

## Nervous System

The body contains a vast network of cells that carry information in the form of nerve impulses to and from all of its parts. These impulses are the means by which all bodily activity occurs. The brain – the master controller – and the spinal cord together form the *central nervous system*, which is responsible for the integration of virtually all nervous activity in the body.

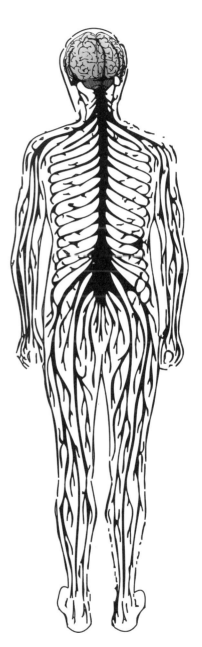

Figure 1-1

There are several levels of mental (nervous) activity:
- reflex or instinctive (knee-jerk) reaction;
- autonomic (breathing, heartbeat, etc);
- motor-programs and conditioned responses (trained or learned skills, routines or processes such as riding a bike, kicking a football); and
- consciously controlled actions and decisions.

The remaining nervous tissue – the *peripheral nervous system* – includes the *autonomic nervous system*, which controls various bodily functions that are autonomically regulated, including:
- the beating of the heart (and responding to demand);
- digestion and intestinal movements;
- breathing;
- temperature control by perspiration; and
- salivation.

Other functions, such as the need to move the arm, hand and fingers to turn the pages of this book, require our conscious intervention, or, if repetitive, they could be learned unconscious responses and triggered by conscious decisions or rehearsed situations.

## Circulatory System

The *circulatory*, or *cardiovascular*, system moves blood around the body, carrying oxygen and nutrients to the cells, and takes away waste products, such as carbon dioxide. Blood is composed of plasma carrying red and white blood cells, or *corpuscles*. The red blood cells contain the iron-rich pigment *haemoglobin*, the principal function of which is to transport oxygen around the body. The white blood cells, of which there are various types, protect the body against foreign substances and are involved in the production of antibodies. The antibodies attack any substance that the body regards as foreign or dangerous. *Platelets* in the blood function to form clots when necessary to stop loss of blood from an injury.

### Heart

The heart is a muscular pump, about the size of a closed fist, that is divided into two sides, each with two chambers. The muscles of the heart contract in a double-action pulse, forcing blood through the one-way heart valves and on through the network of arteries. This pump stroke causes a pressure pulse that can be felt at various parts of the body where the arteries are near the surface (such as the wrist and the side of the neck).

The amount of blood pumped by the heart depends upon the size of the heart, the heart rate (or *pulse* rate), and the strength of the heart contraction. This is controlled principally by the autonomic nervous system, and so requires no conscious thought.

## Blood Pressure

Blood pressure is a measure of the pressure of the blood against the walls of the main arteries. It is highest during the period when the lower heart chambers are contracting, known as *systolic* pressure, and is lowest when the chambers are relaxing and refilling with blood, known as *diastolic* pressure.

The normal range varies with age, but a healthy young adult will typically have a systolic pressure of about 120 millimetres of mercury (mm Hg), and a diastolic pressure of 80 mm Hg – written as 120/80. An elevation of the lower figure indicates the heart is under high pressure all the time, and in the longer term damage can occur.

## Blood Vessels

The blood vessels form a system of arteries, capillaries and veins known as the *vascular system. Arteries* carry blood into the body, away from the heart, and *veins* carry blood back to the heart. The walls of the veins are thinner and less elastic than the walls of the arteries, and the veins contain valves to prevent the reverse flow of blood. The smallest blood vessels are the *capillaries*, which enable an exchange of oxygen and other matter with individual cells in the body tissues

The circulation of blood through the vessels and the tissues is known as the *systemic circulation*. A second system – the *pulmonary circulation* – diverts the blood that returns to the heart into capillaries situated in the walls of two air sacs – the lungs.

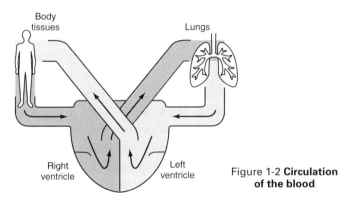

Body tissues

Lungs

Right ventricle

Left ventricle

Figure 1-2 **Circulation of the blood**

The bloodstream passes through the lungs, which exchange the carbon dioxide from the blood and add oxygen to it. The lungs also act as a filter to remove small blood clots. The oxygenated blood then returns to the heart, where it is pumped into the *aorta* – the main artery – and then carried around the body through the systemic circulation. On reaching the heart, the deoxygenated blood is again pumped through the lungs to remove the carbon dioxide that has accumulated in its journey through the body (including the brain), and to obtain a fresh charge of oxygen.

It is necessary for the blood to be continuously replenished with oxygen, which has been given out during the systemic circulation, and at the same time rid itself of the carbon dioxide that is acquired from the tissues.

## Respiratory System

The process of respiration brings oxygen into the body and removes carbon dioxide. It happens in two stages: the first stage occurs in the lungs – *external* respiration – and the second stage takes place in the body tissues – *internal* respiration.

The body has a permanent need for oxygen; it is used in the energy-producing 'burning' process that goes on in every cell of the body tissues. The body is unable to store oxygen permanently – hence the need for continuous breathing– and so any interruption to breathing lasting more than a few minutes may lead to permanent physical damage, especially of the brain, and to possible death.

### Breathing Rate

The autonomic nervous system detects both the need for more blood to certain parts of the body, and the amount of carbon dioxide ($CO_2$) in the blood. The carbon dioxide in the blood returning to the heart, and then to the lungs, is a waste product from the consumption of oxygen ($O_2$) in the tissues to produce energy.

Chemical sensors in the lungs detect the level of waste carbon dioxide and, to a lesser extent, the level of oxygen, and send messages to the brain. A high level of carbon dioxide (or a low level of oxygen) returning to the lungs in the blood is interpreted autonomically by the brain as a need for more oxygen. A lot of carbon dioxide means that a lot of oxygen has been burned in the body tissues. The brain then responds autonomically by speeding up the respiration rate to increase the supply of oxygen.

Each breath when we are resting is about one half-litre, which is only one-tenth of the lung capacity of five litres. This means that a lot of used air remains in the lungs. With the constant transfer of oxygen into the bloodstream and of carbon dioxide out of the bloodstream, the air in the lungs have a much higher concentration of carbon dioxide and a lower concentration of oxygen than the surrounding atmospheric air. This difference in concentration increases as altitude is gained. The air in the lungs is also saturated with water vapour (as witnessed by the fog it forms when we breathe out on a cold day).

Another way in which a high level of $CO_2$ can be present in the lungs is through the body becoming inactive, or 'winding down', getting sleepy. There is little demand for oxygen, so the breathing rate slows. That lessens the rate of $CO_2$ being 'flushed' from the lungs and the $CO_2$ concentration therefore increases. That, in turn, activates the same 'switch' – the 'get more oxygen' signal. But this time, the command is processed as a yawn. The yawn is another example of an autonomic or reflex reaction.

A higher than normal amount of carbon dioxide means that a lot of oxygen has been burned, and therefore there is a need for more replacement oxygen around the body. As a result of a high carbon dioxide content in the blood, the breathing rate is autonomically increased to bring more oxygen into the lungs for the bloodstream to absorb.

## External Respiration

Two processes occur in the lungs:

- Energy-giving oxygen, breathed in the air from outside the body, diffuses through the thin walls of the lungs and into the blood, the red blood cells of which carry it to the body tissues.
- Waste carbon dioxide, returned to the lungs, is diffused through the lung walls and is breathed out (expired) with unused air.

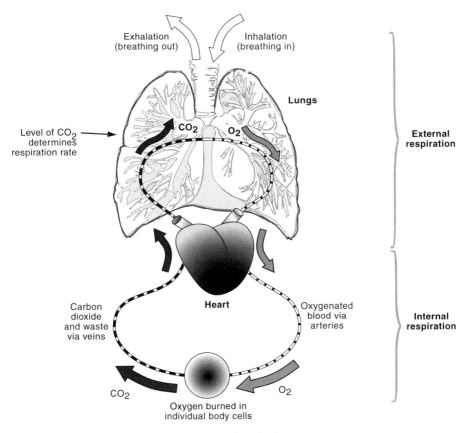

Figure 1-3 **Respiration**

### Internal Respiration

These processes also occur in the body tissues:

- Oxygen, brought to the body tissue by the red blood cells, diffuses through the very thin capillary and body cell walls into the body tissue, where it is burned up to produce energy.
- Carbon dioxide, a waste product from the burning of oxygen, diffuses back into the capillaries and is carried away in the bloodstream back to the lungs for external expiration.

### Lungs

Two separate lungs are housed within the chest cavity, being protected by the rib cage, and having a muscular, curved diaphragm beneath them. The diaphragm can be flattened by contraction of the muscles, which expands the chest cavity, and draws fresh air in through the mouth and/or nose.

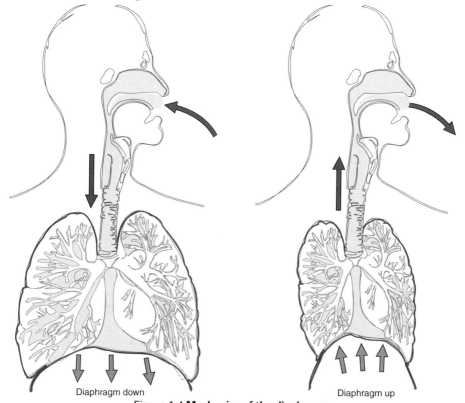

Diaphragm down                                 Diaphragm up

Figure 1-4 **Mechanics of the diaphragm**

This function is normally controlled by the autonomic nervous system being triggered by the $CO_2$ level, without our conscious intervention, although we can consciously increase the rate and depth of our breathing.

The lowered pressure in the chest cavity draws the air down through the bronchial passage, which divides into two tubes, one going to each lung. The two tubes divide into smaller and smaller tubes, ending in millions of small sacs with very thin walls known as *alveoli*, which are surrounded by blood capillaries.

Oxygen molecules that diffuse through the walls of the alveoli sacs and into the bloodstream attach themselves to the *haemoglobin* in the red blood cells, which have a high affinity for oxygen, and are transported to the body tissues requiring oxygen. The oxygen attached to the haemoglobin causes the blood to look very red, whereas the oxygen-deficient blood returning through the veins looks somewhat bluer.

# Environment of Flight

## Atmosphere

The earth is surrounded and protected by a life-giving layer called the atmosphere. The atmosphere consists of a transparent mixture of gases which we call *air*. The atmosphere is held to the earth by the force of gravity and, because air is compressible, it packs in around the earth's surface. As altitude is gained, the air thins out, with fewer and fewer molecules in the same volume, but the percentage composition of the air does not change. Total air pressure falls with altitude, as does the partial pressure of each of the gases in the air. (Total air pressure is a sum of all of the partial pressures.)

### International Standard Atmosphere

So that we have a common reference, scientists have agreed on average atmospheric conditions called the International Standard Atmosphere (ISA). Like the average person, it never exists but it is an essential yardstick for comparisons, especially of aircraft performance.

The International Standard Atmosphere is as follows:

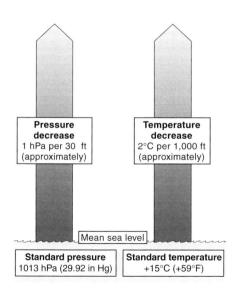

Figure 1-5 **ISA parameters**

| | |
|---|---|
| Sea level temperature | +15°C |
| Lapse rate | −2°C per 1,000 ft |
| Freezing level (0°C) | 7,500 ft |
| Sea level pressure | 1,013.2 hPa |
| Tropopause | 36,080 ft |
| Tropopause temperature | −56°C |

Figure 1-6 **ISA**

## Composition of Air

Air is a mixture of various gases. Because it has mass, it is pulled to the earth by the force of gravity. The main gases are oxygen (21%), nitrogen (78%), with small quantities of carbon dioxide (0.03%) and ozone, and an extremely variable percentage of water vapour (which is not counted as a component of the atmosphere).

| | |
|---|---|
| **Nitrogen** **Oxygen** | 78% 21% |
| **Other gases** **(argon, carbon dioxide, neon, helium, etc.)** | 1% |
| **Total** | 100% |

Figure 1-7 **Composition of air by volume**

## Oxygen (O$_2$)

The presence of oxygen in the atmosphere is mainly due to the process of photosynthesis in plants. This process, triggered by sunlight, uses carbon dioxide and water for the purposes of the plant – one of the resulting by-products being oxygen. In this way, the plant world supports the animal world, providing it with oxygen, as well as being a source of food. Oxygen is essential for animals because it is a necessary component of the combustion (energy and heat productions) process that produces energy in the body tissues.

## Nitrogen (N$_2$)

Nitrogen is the most plentiful gas in air, but it is not directly used by the body in the respiration process. It is used in the building of cells in both plants and animals, and saturates the body cells and tissues. Excess nitrogen in the tissues can cause problems, under certain circumstances (e.g. the bends).

## Carbon Dioxide (CO$_2$)

Carbon dioxide is produced in the combustion process, when oxygen combines with carbon, and forms about 0.03% of the atmosphere. Since the industrial revolution beginning in the late eighteenth century, the enormous consumption of fossil fuels (timber, coal, peat and coke, oil, diesel, petrol) has led to a significant increase in the amount of carbon dioxide present in the atmosphere. This is a major contributor to the warming of our planet. Carbon dioxide is also produced in the body tissues and expelled in animal and human breath.

**Water Vapour**

Water vapour is carried in the air and plays a significant role in the weather. When the saturation point for water is reached, the water vapour condenses out as liquid water droplets and forms cloud, fog, rain, or dew. The percentage of water vapour in the air varies from almost none over dry, desert areas to as much as 95% in warm, humid air. At high altitudes, above the tropopause, there is little water vapour. The humidity of the air (or lack of it) affects the human pilot and the performance of the aircraft.

**Ozone**

Ozone is a molecule containing three oxygen atoms ($O_3$), whereas normal oxygen contains two ($O_2$). Ozone is formed when air or oxygen is subjected to electrical discharges, and is poisonous if breathed in large amounts. It is found in the stratosphere, and prevents most of the sun's damaging ultraviolet radiation from reaching the earth's surface (hence the concern about holes in the ozone layer). Depletion of the ozone in the earth's atmosphere and consequent exposure to cancer-causing ultraviolet rays is a concern when flying at high altitudes – as well as at the beach.

## Flying at Altitude

The human body is designed to function in the lower levels of the atmosphere, where the air is fairly dense. Aircraft may operate at quite high altitudes where the air density is very low, exposing the pilot to possible oxygen deficiency and other problems such as low ambient temperatures. There are three major effects of altitude on the human body that are brought about by pressure changes:
* Lower external pressure causes gases inside body cavities to expand.
* Lower oxygen pressure causes hypoxia.
* Dissolved gases come out of solution, due also to decreased external pressure.

An understanding of gas laws will help us understand the effects of flight at altitude on the human body.
* *Boyle's law* states that volume is inversely proportional to pressure at constant temperature.
* *Charles's law* states that volume is proportional to temperature at constant pressure.

These laws relate the variables of temperature, pressure and volume, all of which change with altitude, causing considerable effects on the body.
* *Dalton's law* states that total pressure of a mixture of gases is the sum of the partial pressure of each of the gases, so that atmospheric pressure is made up of the partial pressure of nitrogen, oxygen, and to a small extent other gases.

Whilst atmospheric pressure falls to half by 18,000 ft, oxygen partial pressure is halved at around 9,000 ft. Also, oxygen pressure in the lungs is lower than in the atmosphere due to the increase in partial pressure of water vapour and carbon dioxide in the lungs. Human life depends on oxygen. The amount of oxygen passing through the lung membrane depends on the partial pressure of oxygen at the alveolar surface.

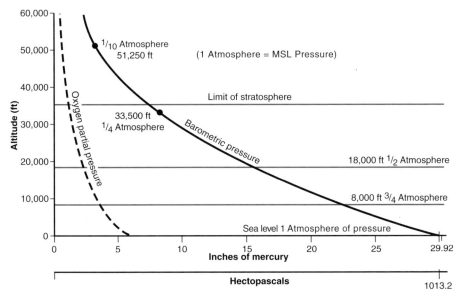

Figure 1-8 **The atmosphere**

- *Graham's law* states that gas will defuse through a membrane from high to low pressure. Oxygen pressure at the lung membrane at sea level is 103 mm Hg. This gives a maximum oxygen saturation of the blood. By 10,000 ft this has dropped to 55 mm Hg, causing the blood to be only 90% saturated and hypoxia already present. Normal performance can be regained by increasing oxygen pressure to 103 mm Hg using an oxygen/air mix. By progressively increasing the percentage of oxygen, oxygen pressure can be maintained at 103 mm Hg until at 33,700 ft, at which point the subject would be breathing pure oxygen. Increasing altitude above 33,700 ft, even when breathing pure oxygen, the oxygen pressure falls to 55 mm Hg at 40,000 ft. Any increase of altitude above this would require breathing oxygen under pressure (pressure breathing).
- *Henry's law* states that the weight of gas in solution is proportional to the partial pressure of the gas above the liquid. In the case of a human body with, say, nitrogen dissolved in the body, it is obvious that with increased altitude, and consequent decreased pressure, eventually an altitude will be reached where pressure in the body exceeds that outside and bubbles will form, just like a bottle of soft drink, as is the case with decompression sickness (discussed later). This is unlikely below 18,000 ft. If a height of 63,000 ft (referred to as *Armstrong's line*) is reached, all body fluids will bubble off.

## Hypoxia

*Hypoxia* is a condition where oxygen concentration in the tissues is less than normal. Total absence of oxygen is called *anoxia*.

Air pressure and density decrease with altitude. As an aeroplane climbs, the density of the air in which it is flying gradually reduces. The less dense the air, the lower the mass of oxygen taken into the lungs in each breath. Also, because of the lower partial pressure of oxygen at altitude (i.e. fewer molecules), less oxygen will diffuse across the alveoli membranes into the bloodstream. A high cabin altitude, therefore, means that less oxygen will be transported around the body, and less energy will be generated (including in the brain).

In this oxygen-deficient condition, a pilot is less able to think clearly and less able to perform physically. The body attempts to compensate by increasing pulse, and rate and depth of ventilation. Pilots between 25 and 50 years who are in good physical condition, and regularly exposed to low oxygen levels, have a higher tolerance. Above about 8,000 ft cabin altitude, the effects of oxygen deprivation may start to become apparent in some pilots, especially if the pilot is active or under stress. At 10,000 ft, most people can still cope with the diminished oxygen supply, but above 10,000 ft supplementary oxygen is required (i.e. oxygen supplied through a mask), if a marked deterioration in performance is not to occur.

The effects of oxygen deprivation are very personal in that they may differ from person to person and become apparent at different cabin altitudes. In general, night vision, for instance, will start to deteriorate above 4,000 ft cabin altitude. The effects of oxygen deprivation will eventually be the same, but some people are more resilient than others. In general terms, 10,000 ft cabin altitude is considered to be the critical cabin altitude above which flight crew should wear an oxygen mask.

The preference of haemoglobin for carbon monoxide (CO), as opposed to oxygen, means that a person who has been smoking has less oxygen circulating than would have been the case had CO, a component of cigarette smoke, not been absorbed. The onset of symptoms of hypoxia will occur at a lower altitude in that person. However, a smoker is acclimatised to being hypoxic and may be more tolerant – to a degree. At 14,000 ft without supplementary oxygen, performance will be very poor, and at 18,000 ft the pilot may become unconscious; this will occur at lower altitudes if the pilot is a smoker, or is unfit or fatigued. Rapid rates of ascent can allow higher altitudes to be reached before severe symptoms occur. In these circumstances, unconsciousness may occur before any or many of the symptoms of hypoxia appear.

The initial symptoms of hypoxia may hardly be noticeable to the sufferer, and in fact they often include feelings of euphoria. The brain is affected quite early, so a false sense of security and well-being may be present. Physical movements will become clumsy, but the pilot may not notice this. Difficulty in concentrating, faulty judgement, moodiness, drowsiness, indecision, giddiness, physical clumsiness, headache, deterioration of vision, high pulse rate, blue lips and fingernails (cyanosis), and tingling of the skin may all follow, ending in loss of consciousness. Throughout all of this pilots will probably feel euphoric and as if doing a great job.

Hypoxia is subtle and it sneaks up on you, like the effects of that extra glass of wine. Susceptibility to hypoxia is increased by anything which reduces the oxygen available to the brain, such as a high cabin altitude (of course), high or low temperatures, illness, stress, fatigue, physical activity, or smoke in the cockpit.

## Pressurised Cabins

Pressurised cabins maintain a higher pressure than the outside atmosphere. For instance, an aeroplane flying at 35,000 ft may have a cabin that is pressurised *(pumped up)* to the same pressure level found at 5,000 ft in the outside atmosphere.

The situation, of course, changes if the aeroplane depressurises at high altitudes. The cabin air escapes, reducing the partial pressure of oxygen in the air available to the pilot. The sudden lower pressure surrounding the body in a rapid depressurisation causes a sudden exhalation of breath (as the air pressure in the lungs tries to equalise with the external air pressure). The same volume in the lungs will now contain fewer oxygen molecules. Supplementary oxygen then becomes vital, hence quick-donning oxygen masks. There isn't much time to waste.

Pressure loss within seconds is called a *rapid decompression*; within milliseconds, it is called an *explosive decompression*. Not only is hypoxia a concern, but also the risk of barotrauma, shock, anxiety, decompression sickness and even physical injury due to flying debris. Often decompression is accompanied by noise, rapid air movement and cabin misting. The cabin may temporarily reach an altitude higher than the actual aircraft altitude due to a venturi effect. Conversely, slow depressurisation is insidious. However, when cabin altitude reaches a predetermined level, audible and visual warnings activate.

## Time of Useful Consciousness

If a person is deprived of an adequate supply of oxygen, unconsciousness will ultimately result. The cells of the brain are particularly sensitive to a lack of oxygen, even for a brief period. Total cessation of the oxygen supply to the brain results in unconsciousness in 6 to 8 seconds and irreversible damage ensues if the oxygen supply is not restored within 4 minutes. The time available for pilots to perform useful tasks without a supplementary oxygen supply, and before severe hypoxia sets in, is known as the *time of useful consciousness* (TUC), or *effective performance time* (EPT). TUC reduces with increasing altitude (see Figure 1-9 on page 13).

## Types of Hypoxia

Hypoxia caused by a lack of oxygen in the air is called *hypoxic hypoxia*. Hypoxia caused by an inability of the blood to carry oxygen is called *anaemic hypoxia*, and may be due to a medical condition (anaemia) or to carbon monoxide poisoning in the blood (from a faulty engine exhaust system or from smoking). A person with heart or circulatory problems may have *stagnant hypoxia*, and *hystoxic hypoxia* is where poisoning of the cells or tissues renders them unable to use oxygen.

| Altitude above sea level | Time from failure of oxygen supply | |
|:---:|:---:|:---:|
| | Moderate activity | Minimal activity |
| 18,000 feet | 20 minutes | 30 minutes |
| 22,000 feet | 5 minutes | 10 minutes |
| 25,000 feet | 2 minutes | 3 minutes |
| 28,000 feet | 1 minute | 1½ minutes |
| 30,000 feet | 45 seconds | 1¼ minutes |
| 35,000 feet | 30 seconds | 45 seconds |
| 40,000 feet | 12 seconds | 15 seconds |

Figure 1-9 **Time of Useful Consciousness
(Effective Performance Time)**

The reduction of the oxygen-carrying capacity of the blood by smoking has the same effect as increasing the cabin altitude by 4,000–5,000 ft; the effect on you will worsen as the aeroplane climbs to higher altitudes. Hypoxia can also be aggravated by a loss of blood: for instance, after a person has made a blood donation.

## Avoiding Hypoxia
To minimise the effects of hypoxia, be reasonably fit, have no cigarette smoke in the cockpit, and ensure that oxygen is used at the higher cabin altitudes, definitely above 10,000 ft. The oxygen mask must be donned as a matter of procedure when the cabin altitude approaches 10,000 ft.

## Middle Ear Infection
The common cold, hay fever, sinusitis, tonsillitis or similar condition can lead to blocked ears. This can mean trouble for a pilot because the equalisation of pressure on either side of the eardrum is not possible when the *Eustachian tubes*, which connect the ears and the nasal passages, are blocked by a cold or similar infection.

In the training environment, problems are more likely to occur on descent than when climbing, as even low-powered aircraft can change altitude rapidly on descent, giving rise to rapid pressure changes.

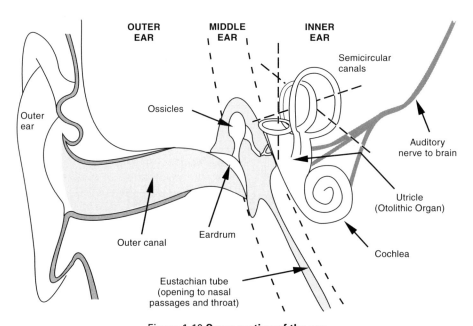

Figure 1-10 **Cross-section of the ear**

Blocked ears can normally be cleared by holding your nose and blowing hard (a technique known as the *Valsalva manoeuvre*), by chewing, swallowing or yawning. The safest advice is, however, if you have a cold, do not fly. Problems can also arise in the sinuses, which are cavities in the head connected by narrow tubes to the nasal/throat passages. Such blockages can cause great pain, especially during descent. Even though pressure changes in a pressurised cabin will be less as the aircraft changes altitude (compared with an unpressurised cabin), there is always the risk of a sudden depressurisation, in which case the pressure changes can be dramatic. Note also that the pressure changes per thousand feet of altitude is greatest at the lower levels.

## Barotrauma

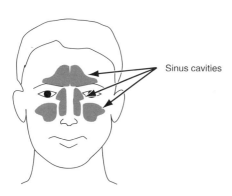

Figure 1-11 **Barotrauma**

Another effect of increasing cabin altitude is that gases trapped in parts of your body – such as the stomach, intestines, sinuses, middle ear, or in a decaying tooth – will want to expand as external pressure decreases. Either they will be able to escape into the atmosphere, or they may be trapped and possibly cause pain, known as *barotrauma*. Pain is most severe on ascent with teeth and intestines and on descent with ears and sinus. Foods such as legumes and leafy greens known to produce gas should be avoided when flying.

## Decompression Sickness (The Bends)

Gas bubbles in the body will cause great pain and some immobilisation in the shoulders, arms and joints. This serious complaint is known as *decompression sickness*. The remedy is to subject the body to a region of high pressure for a lengthy period of time (in a *recompression chamber*, for example), and then gradually return it to normal pressures over a period of hours or days. In an aircraft, the best you can do if the bends is suspected is to descend to a low altitude, where air pressure is greater. Even landing may not provide a sufficient pressure increase to remedy the problem, in which case seek medical assistance without delay. Sometimes low altitude pressure will cause nitrogen to form bubbles; however, this is unlikely below 18,000 ft.

### Scuba Diving

Decompression sickness can result from flying after scuba diving. When the body is deep under water it is subjected to strong pressures, and certain gases, such as nitrogen, are absorbed into the blood under pressure, because the air cylinders have to be pressurised above the local water pressure so that the lungs can inhale. The deeper and longer the dive, the more this absorption occurs. If the pressure on the body is then reduced too quickly – for example, by rapidly returning to the surface from a great depth or, even worse, then by flying in an aeroplane at high cabin altitudes – the gases (especially nitrogen) will come out of solution and form bubbles in the bloodstream and tissues, especially the joints.

Figure 1-12 **Time your dives**

(You can see the same effect caused by a suddenly reduced pressure when the top is removed from gaseous drinks and bubbles of gas come out of solution.)

Rules regarding diving and flying vary slightly from country to country. In Australia, it is recommended that you do not fly for 4 hours after a dive not requiring decompression stops. Do not fly for 12 hours after a dive of less than 4 hours requiring decompression stops, and if the dive is greater than 4 hours with required decompression stops, then you must not fly for 48 hours. Decompression stops are necessary if a dive is deeper than 33 ft. At this depth the pressure is twice that at sea level and the amount of nitrogen dissolved increases appreciably. Snorkelling will not cause decompression sickness as you are not taking in air under pressure. The risk of suffering decompression sickness increases with the depth to which you dive, the rate at which you resurface, how soon you fly and how high you fly, how quickly the cabin altitude increases, your age, obesity, fatigue, and re-exposure to decompression within 24 hours.

## Hyperventilation

Hyperventilation can occur when the body overbreathes due to some psychological distress such as fear or anxiety (gasping for breath). It is most likely to occur with inexperienced pilots in new situations. It is a self-perpetuating cycle, in which a feeling of breathlessness develops – one is unable to catch one's breath and so one becomes more stressed – and continues even if the triggering influence is removed.

Even though the person is now overbreathing, he or she still feels breathless, which tends to add to the anxiety and so promote the overbreathing further. Hyperventilation flushes the carbon dioxide out of the blood, disturbing its chemical balance; this produces symptoms of light-headedness, numbness and tingling in the lips, fingertips and toes. The further effects may include palpitations, an increased pulse rate, sweating, chest pain, blurred vision, dizziness, fainting, ringing in the ears, muscle spasms, drowsiness, and unconsciousness. Donning an oxygen mask will not help treat hyperventilation.

### Treating Hyperventilation

It may be difficult to establish whether the problem is hyperventilation or hypoxia. Hypoxia is the more urgent situation to treat. You will know the circumstances and the likelihood of either. The best procedure to deal with hyperventilation is to try and calm the person – by being calm yourself, by talking normally to them and by encouraging them to talk. Allocating simple distracting tasks in the cockpit may also help the person to relax.

- Hyperventilation can be remedied by consciously slowing down the breathing rate (talking is a good way of doing this).
- A suggested direct remedy for hyperventilation is to breathe into and out of a paper bag (to restore the carbon dioxide level in the blood).
- If recovery is not evident, then assume that hypoxia rather than hyperventilation is the problem.

## Carbon Monoxide Poisoning

Carbon monoxide is produced during combustion. It is present in engine exhaust gases and in cigarette smoke, both of which can sometimes be found in the cockpit. It can enter the cockpit from a faulty heating system. Carbon monoxide is a colourless, odourless, tasteless and poisonous gas for which haemoglobin in the blood has an enormous affinity. If carbon monoxide molecules are inhaled, then the haemoglobin will transport them in preference to oxygen, causing the body and the brain to suffer oxygen starvation, even though oxygen is present in the air. Carbon monoxide poisoning is insidious and can be ultimately fatal. Hence, the first cigarette can cause light-headedness. Recovery, even on pure oxygen, may take several hours.

Susceptibility to carbon monoxide poisoning increases as the cabin altitude increases because there is already an oxygen deficiency. Many cabin heating systems use warm air from around the engine and exhaust manifold as their source of heat. Any leaks in the engine exhaust system can allow carbon monoxide to enter the cabin in the heating air and possibly through open windows and cracks. To minimise the effect of any carbon monoxide that enters the cockpit in this way, fresh air should always be used in conjunction with cabin heating. Regular checks and maintenance of the aircraft are essential. Even though carbon monoxide is odourless, it may be associated with other exhaust gases that do have an odour. Engine smells in the cabin are a warning that carbon monoxide may be present.

Many operators place carbon monoxide detectors in the cockpit. The most common type contains crystals that change colour when carbon monoxide is present. These detectors are inexpensive and are a wise investment, but they do have a limited life, so check the expiry date. If the detector is date-expired it is not reliable. Indeed, the crystal-type detector may not be as reliable as first thought. Increasingly, the more costly but effective electronic detectors are being recommended.

Symptoms of carbon monoxide poisoning include:
- headache, dizziness and nausea;
- deterioration in vision;
- impaired judgement;
- personality change;
- impaired memory;
- slower breathing rate;
- cherry red complexion.
- loss of muscular power; and
- convulsions.

If left untreated, coma and eventually death results.

Actions if carbon monoxide is suspected in the cabin:
- shut off the cabin heat;
- stop all smoking;
- increase the supply of fresh air through vents (except exhaust ones) and windows; and
- land as soon as possible.

Be aware that carbon monoxide is not the only toxic chemical to which you may be exposed in aircraft operation (agricultural pilots especially). Vapours and fumes from fuels and lubricants, poorly packed dangerous goods and other products of combustion may produce a range of symptoms including skin, eye and lung irritation, dizziness, drowsiness, confusion and loss of consciousness.

| Condition | Cause/Altitude | Common Symptoms | Notes | Actions |
|---|---|---|---|---|
| Hypoxia | Rare below 10,000 ft. | Euphoria. Visual disturbances. Dizziness. Light headedness. Confused thinking. Apprehension. Sense of well-being. | May be unaware of condition due to decreased partial pressure of oxygen. | Descend. Use oxygen. 10,000–33,700 ft, air-oxygen mix. 33,700–40,000 ft, 100% oxygen. |
| Hyper-ventilation | Anxiety. (Any altitude. Hypoxia if above 10,000 ft.) | Light-headedness. Dizziness. Tingling. Tremors. Visual disturbances. Confused thinking. Faintness. Numbness. | Overbreathing, reduces carbon dioxide level in the blood. | Control breathing rate. Breathe into hand. If above 10,000 ft suspect hypoxia. |
| Carbon monoxide poisoning | Faulty exhaust/heating. Smoking. Any altitude. | Headache. Breathlessness. Sluggishness. Impaired judgment. Feeling of warmth. Cherry red skin. | Haemoglobin has greater affinity for CO than for oxygen. (Smoking makes night vision poor.) | Immediate fresh air. Oxygen. Land and seek medical attention. |
| Decompression sickness | Flying after diving. Unlikely below 18,000 ft. | Headache. Pain (joints). Paralysis. Choking. Skin irritation. | Nitrogen comes out of solution and forms bubbles in lungs (chokes), joints (bends), skin (creeps), and central nervous system (paralysis). | Do not fly for 4 hours for dive less than 30 ft; longer if deeper. |

Figure 1-13 **Summary of Symptoms**

**Chapter 2**

# Vision and Visual Illusions

The eyes provide us with a visual image of the environment. Each eye acts as a natural and very sophisticated digital camera. Its basic function is to collect light rays reflected from an object, using the lens to focus these rays into an image on a screen (the *retina*), and then converting this image into electrical signals that are then sent via the optic nerve to the brain. In this way we see. The brain then matches the image to previously stored data so that we then recognise (perceive) the object. The connection of the optic nerve to the brain is so close and integral, and the importance of the messages sent to the brain is so dominant, that the eyes can almost be considered an extension of the brain.

## Structure of the Eye

The main components of the eye are the *cornea* and *lens*, the *retina*, and the *optic nerve*.

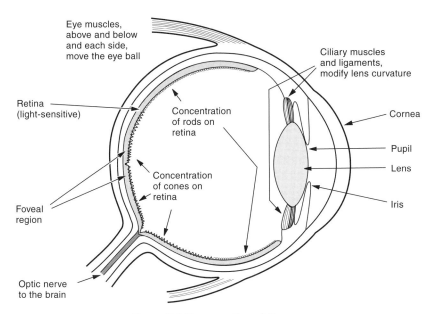

Figure 2-1 **Cross-section of the eye**

## Cornea

The cornea is a transparent cap over the lens, through which the light rays first pass. Its surfaces are curved and some refraction (bending) of the light occurs as it passes through the cornea. Unlike the lens, whose edge is surrounded by the *ciliary* muscles, there are no muscles attached to the cornea, and so we cannot alter its shape and refractive abilities. However, it provides the coarse focus (about 70%). The eye has eyelids that can close over the cornea for protection and assist in spreading lubrication. Most of the movement comes from the large upper eyelid, and less movement from the smaller and weaker lower eyelid.

## Iris

Between the cornea and the lens is a coloured membrane known as the *iris*. The colour of the iris determines the colour of the eye. At the centre of the iris is a small round aperture known as the *pupil*. The pupil changes its size to restrict the amount of light entering the lens. In very bright light, the pupil becomes quite small; in very dim conditions, the pupil widens to allow more light to enter.

## Lens

The lens, like the cornea, is transparent to light, but we change its shape with the ciliary muscles surrounding it, allowing us to focus the light rays. It provides the fine focus for vision. When the muscles are relaxed, the lens tends to flatten, and the reduced curvature of its surfaces means less refraction of the light rays, i.e. less focusing. The muscles can be used to squeeze the lens, which increases the curvature of the lens surfaces, thereby increasing the amount of refraction and the amount of focusing – the greater the curvature, the greater the focusing. This occurs when you focus on a very near object.

The ability of an eye to change its focus, e.g. from a far object to a near object, is known as *accommodation*. The power of the eyes to accommodate varies, especially with tiredness and age. When a person is fatigued, accommodation diminishes, the result being blurred images. Also, with increasing age, the lens becomes less flexible and less able to modify its curvature. This reduced focusing capability is noticed by middle-aged people, and reading glasses are usually necessary. The condition is called *presbyopia*.

## Retina

The *retina* is a light-sensitive layer located at the back of the eye. It is the screen onto which the lens focuses images, and these images are converted into electrical signals that pass along the optic nerve to the brain. The retina contains two types of light-sensitive (or photosensitive) cells: *cones* and *rods*.

### Cones

Cones are concentrated around the central section of the retina, especially the *foveal region* directly opposite the lens. Cones are sensitive to colour, details, and distant objects. They are most effective in daylight, and less effective in darkness. They provide the best *visual acuity* (the ability to resolve fine detail). The foveal region is where we focus most objects and it is this area of the retina that provides our central colour vision in good light conditions. Objects focused on the foveal region in very dim light (as at night) will not stimulate the cones to transmit a message along the optic nerve, so the image will therefore not be seen.

## Rods

Rods are concentrated in a band outside the central foveal area. They are sensitive to movement, but not to detail or colour, and so see only in black, white, and shades of grey, rather than the colours seen by the cones. Rods are effective in both daylight and darkness, and are responsible for our *peripheral* vision (i.e. off-centre vision), which helps our orientation and night vision. Objects in dim light are therefore most easily noticed when their image falls somewhere on the peripheral area of the retina where the rods are concentrated. You can achieve this by deliberately looking slightly to the side of an object at night, rather than directly at it as you would during daylight.

### Eyes Sookotc

The eye is approximately spherical, hence it is often called an eyeball. Each eye has a series of muscles that rotate the ball in its socket, thereby allowing it to follow a moving object without your having to move your whole head. Conversely, they allow you to keep the eyes directed at a stationary object even though your head might be moving.

To track a moving object with both eyes, they must act in harmony, and this means coordinated control of the two sets of muscles by the brain. In a fatigued person, this coordination sometimes fails, and the result is quite different images from each eye, known as *double vision*. When focusing on near objects, the visual axis of each eye will be turned-in slightly; when focusing on distant objects, say more than six metres away, the visual axes of your two eyes will be nearly parallel.

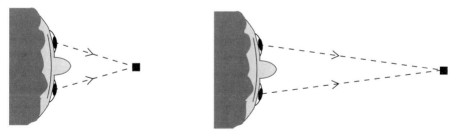

Figure 2-2 **Binocular vision**

When you are *not* trying to focus on any particular object and you are, for instance, just gazing out the window into an empty blue sky, the tendency is for the eyes to relax focus, and both focus and accommodate in the range of one to two metres. This is referred to as *empty field myopia* (empty field short-sightedness).

## Binocular Vision

A person normally has two functioning eyes that together provide binocular vision. *Binocular* is the adjective used to describe the use of both eyes, as against *monocular*, which describes the use of one eye only. Two eyes are better than one for a number of reasons.

### Estimation of Distance

Relative distance to an object is estimated by:
- change of focus from near to far (accommodation);
- clarity of the image relative to the surroundings;
- contrast and colour brilliance of close objects compared to diffused images of distinct objects (called *atmospheric perspective*); and
- apparent, relative and known size of recognised objects.

Absolute distance can only be established by triangulation (convergence of sight lines). This is the prime reason for binocular vision.

*Relax your arms and wrists and hold a pencil in each hand at mid-distance – arms not fully extended. With one eye closed, try to bring the points together. You can see how information through monocular vision presents a far less reliable reference than binocular.*

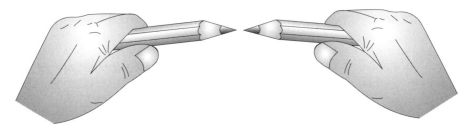

Figure 2-3 **Estimating distance**

### Focus

When the eyes are focused at infinity, they look straight ahead (i.e. they are parallel). Closer distances are estimated by the convergence angle of the eyes when focusing on a nearer object. Light from a particular object, especially a near one, will also enter each eye at a slightly different angle, causing the images formed by each eye to be different. This is called *stereopsis*. The brain uses these two different images as one means of estimating the distance of nearby objects: the difference in the two images being greater for near objects than for far objects.

You can observe this effect by holding a pencil or a finger up against a distant background, closing one eye at a time and viewing it through the other. Each eye will provide a different image – the pencil or finger will be seen from different angles, and its relationship to the background will be different.

With normal two-dimensional photographs or films projected onto a screen, each eye receives an identical image, so the impression of depth and reality is lost to some extent. Attempts have been made to artificially replicate binocular vision and its three-dimensional (3-D) effect by using 3-D (stereoscopic) films and 3-D photographs.

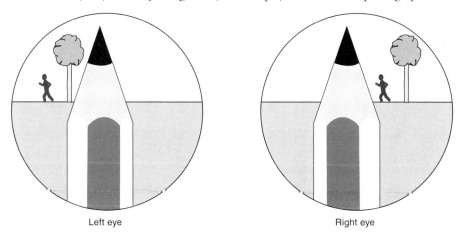

|                Left eye                 |                Right eye                |

Figure 2-4 **Stereoscopic vision**

This is done, not by presenting a real three-dimensional situation, but by presenting a slightly different two-dimensional picture to each eye, with objects seen from slightly different angles and in slightly different positions relative to the background. The brain then forms a more realistic three-dimensional picture than is possible when each eye receives an identical picture. This proved very effective in interpreting wartime reconnaissance photographs.

### Blind Spot

Binocular vision counters the *blind spot* in each eye. The blind spot is the small area on the retina of the eye where the *nerve fibres* from the light-sensitive cells on the retina lead into the optic nerve. There are no rods or cones at this spot on the retina, and hence it is blind. However, it is not possible for an image of an object to fall on the blind spot of *both* eyes simultaneously. Even

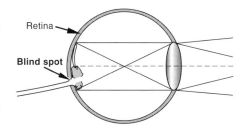

Figure 2-5 **The blind spot**

when an image falls on the blind spot of one eye, the brain will receive a message from the other, and so the object will be seen.

You can observe the existence of the blind spot in each eye by viewing figure 2-6 (page 24). Hold the page at arm's length, cover your right eye, and then with your left eye focus on the aeroplane on the right. It will be clearly recognisable as a biplane because it will be focused on your fovea (cone vision). You would also be able to detect the colour of this aircraft.

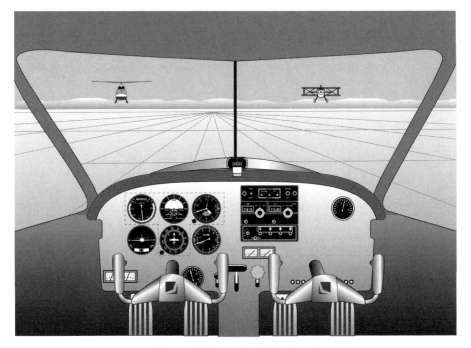

Figure 2-6 **Example of blind spot**

The helicopter will be visible in your peripheral vision, but it may not be defined clearly enough for you to recognise it as a helicopter, nor will you see its colour. Now move the page closer to your open left eye, continuing to focus on the aeroplane (right windscreen). At some point, the helicopter will disappear from your peripheral vision, and then come back into view as you bring the page even closer. The time when the image is not seen is when it falls on the blind spot on your retina. The lack of rods or cones here means that the image is not detected at all. The left windscreen at this time appears empty. Repeat the experiment by concentrating your right eye on the helicopter, in which case the biplane will disappear from view when its image falls on the blind spot of your right eye.

Now repeat the experiment again with both eyes open. Both aircraft should remain in view at all times, because the image from a particular object cannot fall on the blind spots of both eyes simultaneously. This is another advantage of binocular vision. Be careful when you are scanning the sky that another aircraft is not blocked from view by the magnetic compass or some part of the windscreen structure. If it is blocked from the view of both eyes, you will not see it at all; if it is blocked from the view of only one eye, you will lose the protection provided by binocular vision.

## Normal Functions of the Eye

### Visual Acuity – The Clarity of What We See

Visual acuity is the ability of the eye to see clearly and sharply. Perfect visual acuity (focus) means that the eye sees the object exactly as it is, clearly and without distortion, no matter how distant the object is. The degree of visual acuity varies between different people and also between the two eyes of any one person, as well as for the single eye at different times. This depends upon whether the person is fatigued, suffering hypoxia (lack of oxygen), or under the influence of alcohol or some other drug.

To describe differences in visual acuity, a standard is established being what a 'normal' eye is considered capable of seeing clearly at a particular distance. The eye test chart usually has lines of letters readable for a normal eye from 36, 24, 18, 12, 9, 6 and 5 metres respectively. (The large letter at the top of eye charts is the size at which a person with normal sight can read that letter from a distance of 60 metres.) The standard testing distance between the eye and the eye chart is 6 metres; the normal eye is capable of clearly seeing letters of a certain size at this distance. If another eye at 6 metres cannot read the 6-metre line clearly, and can only identify letters on the chart that a normal eye can see clearly at 9 metres, then the 'abnormal' eye is said to have 6/9 vision. This is compared with the 6/6 vision of the so-called normal eye. As a rule of thumb, pilots should be able to read a car number plate at a distance of approximately 40 metres.

 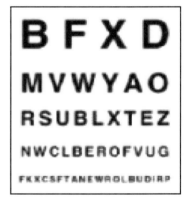

Figure 2-7 **An eye chart seen with 6/6 vision (left) and 6/9 vision (right)**

Perfect visual acuity within the individual eye occurs when the image is focused sharply by a high-quality cornea and lens onto the central foveal region of a healthy retina, where the cone receptors predominate. The cone receptors are very sensitive to small details and send very sharp, colourful images to the brain.

Light rays that are focused on the retina away from the central foveal region in areas where there are not so many cone receptors, but more rod receptors, will not be seen as clearly, nor will they be in colour. Visual acuity will therefore be less for these images.

To illustrate the difference between central and peripheral vision, look at the words on this page. You must move your eyes so that the image of the word that you want to read falls on the central foveal region. Whilst you can clearly read the word you are looking at right now, you will not be able to read words some distance away from it – up, down, or sideways from it – unless you move your eyeball so that the image of that word falls on the central highly visual acuity area of the retina.

### Vision Limitations

Rods and cones are the endings of the optic nerve. As an extension of the brain, they will be affected by anything that affects the brain. With a shortage of oxygen (hypoxia), or an excess of alcohol, medication or other drugs, sight is one of the first senses to suffer. High positive *g*-loadings, as in strenuous aerobatic manoeuvres, forces the blood into the lower regions of the body and temporarily starves the brain and eyes of blood, leading to a greyout (black-and-white tunnel vision) or unconsciousness (blackout).

## Colour Vision

Colours are detected in the central foveal region of the retina by the cone receptors, which are only active in fairly bright light. By differentiating between the various wavelengths of light in the visible spectrum (red light with its longer wavelength, through to violet light with its shorter wavelength), the average eye can distinguish over one hundred hues (single wavelength colours) and one thousand shades.

There are some eyes that cannot distinguish any colours at all, even in bright light, but total colour blindness is very rare. Males are more susceptible to colour blindness, with about 1 in 12 caucasian males having some colour blindness (better called *defective colour vision*), compared with only about 1 in 200 for females. Defective colour vision shows up as difficulty in distinguishing between red and green. The degree of visual confusion can vary enormously and there are various tests for colour vision standards. Loss of colour vision is not a prohibitive condition as far as flying is concerned. Modern radios are the prime means of communication and most aircraft carry two radios. The reliance on flares, coloured lights and signal panels is almost non-existent. Design efforts are now focusing on the sensible use of coloured symbols for head-up displays and *electronic flight instrumentation systems* (EFIS).

## Visual Scanning

### By Day

The central (foveal) region of the retina provides the best vision, and in full colour, but only during reasonable daylight. Objects are best seen by day if you can focus their image on the foveal region, and you do this by looking directly at them. The most effective method of scanning for other aircraft during daylight hours is to use a series of short, regularly spaced eye movements to search each 10° sector of the sky.

Systematically focusing on different segments of the sky for short intervals is a better technique than continuously sweeping the sky. This is sometimes called the *saccade/fixation cycle* where the saccade, or movement, takes about one-third of a second.

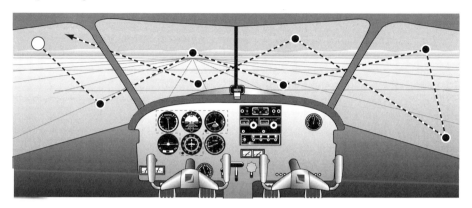

Figure 2-8 **Methodical scan**

If there is no apparent relative motion between you and the other aircraft, you are on a collision course, especially if the other aircraft appears to be stationary and simply becoming bigger and bigger in the windscreen. Because of the lack of movement across your windscreen, an aircraft on a collision course with you will be more difficult to spot than one that is not on a collision course.

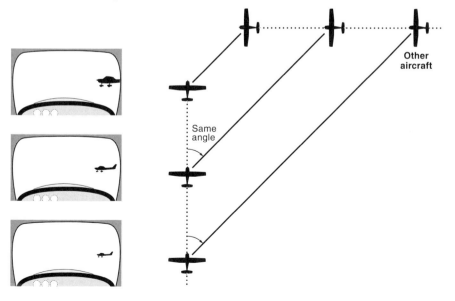

Figure 2-9 **Constant relative position**

Any relative movement of an object makes it easier to detect. The time available to avoid a collision may be quite brief. If you are flying at 100 knots and it is flying at 500 knots in the opposite direction, the rate of closure is 600 knots, i.e. 10 nautical miles per minute. If you spot the other aircraft at a distance of 1 nm, you only have ⅒ of a minute, i.e. 6 seconds, to act. If you spot it at 3 nautical miles (nm), you have 18 seconds. In hazy or low-visibility conditions, your ability to see other aircraft and objects whose edges might be blurred will be diminished and, if you can see them, they may appear to be further away than their actual distance, i.e. you might be closer than you think.

Unless you have a distant object in view, your eyes will tend to focus at a point about one to two metres ahead of you, especially if you are an older person with 'tired eyes', and you may miss sighting distant objects. This *empty field myopia* or *night myopia* (short-sightedness) can be compensated for by searching for distant objects and by focusing briefly on them.

To avoid empty-field myopia, you should focus on any available distant object, such as a cloud or a landmark, to lengthen your focus. If the sky is empty of clouds or other objects, then focus briefly on a relatively distant part of the aeroplane like a wingtip as a means of lengthening your focus.

## Specks

A small, dark image formed on the retina could be a distant but rapidly approaching aircraft, or it could be a speck of dirt or dust, or an insect spot, on the windscreen. Specks or sometimes a dust particle, a scratch, or an insect on the windscreen might be mistaken for a distant aeroplane. Simply moving your head will allow you to discriminate between marks on the windscreen and distant objects by any relative motion.

Figure 2-10 **Specks?**

## By Night

The central (foveal) region of the retina containing mainly cones is not as effective at night, causing an area of reduced visual sensitivity in your central vision. Peripheral vision off-centre, provided by the rods in the outer band of the retina, is more effective – albeit 'colour blind'. An object at night is more readily visible when you are looking to the side of it by ten or twenty degrees, rather than directly at it. Colour is not perceived by the rods, and so your night vision will be in shades of grey. Objects will not be as sharply defined (focused) as in daytime foveal vision. The most effective way to use your eyes during night flight is to scan small sectors of sky more *slowly* than in daylight, to permit off-centre viewing of objects in your *peripheral vision* and to deliberately focus your perception (mind) a few degrees from your visual centre of attention (i.e. *look at* a point but *look for* objects around it).

Because you may not be able to see the aircraft shape at night, you will have to determine its direction of travel by making use of its visible lighting:

- the flashing red beacon;
- the red navigation light on the left wingtip;
- the green navigation light on the right wingtip; and
- a steady white light on the tail.

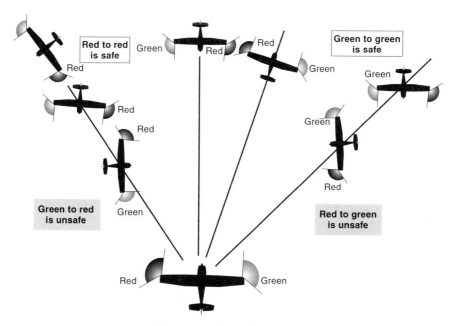

Figure 2-11 **Risk of collision**

# Night Vision

## Adaptation of the Eyes to Darkness

At night, there are some special considerations regarding vision. Your attention during night flying will be both inside and outside the cockpit. It takes the eyes some minutes to adapt to a dark environment, as most of us have experienced when walking into a darkened cinema and stumbling over other patrons in an attempt to find an empty seat. As mentioned, night vision is susceptible to hypoxia. It is affected by cabin altitudes above 4,000 ft.

The time it takes for the eyes to adapt depends, to a large extent, on the contrast between the brightness of light previously experienced and the degree of darkness of the new environment. Conversely, when the lights are turned on at the end of a movie the opposite effect takes place. Whereas the cones, concentrated in the central region of the retina, adjust quickly to variations in light intensity (about seven minutes to return to normal), the rods (which are most important for night vision) take some 30 minutes to adapt fully to darkness. In dim light the cones become less effective, or even totally ineffective, and there is a chemical change in the rods to increase their sensitivity. Thus we adapt more quickly to brightening lights rather than dimming light.

## Protecting Night Vision

It is a common misconception that, at night, we are using our night vision in the cockpit or looking at the runway. When we look at something that is well illuminated, then we are using normal vision. The night-fighter pilots of WWII sat in a darkened room, blindfolded, and used red cockpit lighting (and ate carrots) so that they could look for other aircraft or ground features that were not illuminated – there was a blackout. The only equivalent for us is when we are looking for ground features such as a lake or coastline or the shadow of hills on a moonlit night. Otherwise, we use normal vision. The disadvantage of red lighting is that red lines or tints on a map do not show.

Certainly we should keep the internal lighting to an acceptably low level to minimise reflections and to allow best transmission of light through the transparencies. It's the same as other natural processes; the transmission depends on the energy difference – outside to in. More light outside and less light inside provides the best transmission of light through the windows. Even wear a dark coloured shirt for night flying as the traditional white pilot's shirt adds considerably to the reflections off the face of the instrument glass.

We should avoid brilliant lights as they temporarily reduce the sensitivity of the eyes to less well lit objects. Be especially careful of viewing sunsets and then trying to see down-sun at the darkened earth. Exposure to glare and bright sunlight should be avoided before night flights – wear sunglasses. Vision is affected by reduced oxygen levels, and so, at night in an unpressurised aircraft, avoid smoking and use supplemental oxygen (recommended above 4,000 feet).

## Vision on Approach

There are three main visual tasks when landing without the assistance of aids:
- initial estimation and establishment of the approach path;
- maintaining the approach path; and
- judging ground proximity to initiate and conduct the flare.

Vision and visual estimation during the visual approach relates to the assessment of angles, distances, relative motion and closing speed. Let's look briefly at a typical visual circuit and landing. We may begin by positioning the aircraft at a set distance from the runway on downwind and at a set height above the runway. This then establishes two dimensions. The third is the position judged by the angle from the runway centreline at the threshold – the base turn position. If the aircraft is then configured in a standard way, at a set speed and thrust setting, it will enter the descent path from a known point. All the pilot then has to judge is the progress of the approach and the effect of wind. The progress is judged by the position of the chosen aim point below the horizon and any relative movement of the aim point. On final, a fixed (stationary) aim point is the prime cue to the approach.

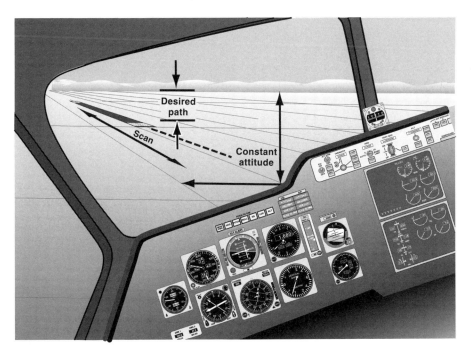

Figure 2-12 **Final turn**

## Estimation and Establishment of the Approach Path

The approach path angle is established by knowing where to fix your aim point with respect to the horizon.
By day:

Figure 2-13 **Final approach**

or night:

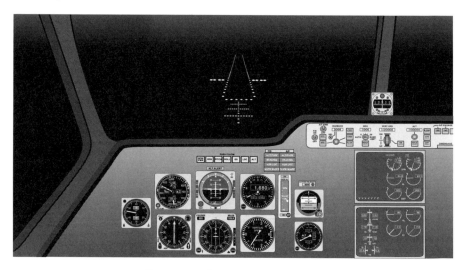

Figure 2-14 **Visual approach at night**

## Maintaining the Approach Path

The second task is achieved by simply keeping the aim point in a constant position. In a stabilised approach, constant airspeed and set configuration, the attitude is constant. Therefore, the aim point remains at a set position in the windscreen.

**Note:** With fewer visual references, and no visible horizon, it will take more concentration to check the runway position relative to the windscreen frame – but this is important confirmation of rate of descent and glideslope management. During the day the whole of the ground plane – i.e. to the horizon – is available to assess your approach path, whereas at night you may only have the runway itself as your guide.

## Judging Ground Proximity

Ground proximity is learnt from relative sizes and flow of visual texture away from the aim point. However, illusions may interfere with this behaviour pattern.

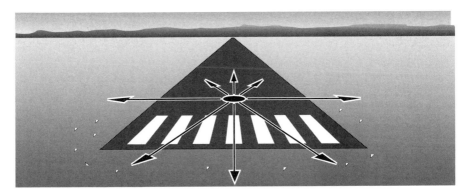

Figure 2-15 **Centre of radiating texture**

Texture assists in depth perception: the more defined the texture, the closer the object appears to be. On final approach as you near the aim point, the surface texture will appear to flow outwards in all directions from the point on which you are focused. This is one means by which you can visually maintain the flightpath to the aim point – adjusting attitude and heading, so that the point from which the texture appears to be moving outwards remains the desired aim point. Texture is also used for the estimation of height; for instance, as you approach flare height for a landing, the actual texture of the runway or the grass passing by the cockpit becomes increasingly noticeable.

Relative motion also aids in depth perception. Near objects generally appear to pass by the windscreen faster than more distant objects. This helps a visual pilot estimate height above the runway before and during the flare – the closer the aeroplane is to the runway, the faster the runway surface and the surrounding environment appears to pass by. Depth perception can also be difficult in hazy or misty conditions, where edges are blurred, colours are muted, and light rays may be refracted unusually. This gives the impression of greater distance, an impression reinforced by the fact that we often have to look at distant objects through a smoggy or hazy atmosphere. This illusion is referred to as *environmental perspective*. In hazy conditions, the object might be closer than it seems. In very clear conditions, the object might be further away than it seems. On hazy days, you might touch down earlier than expected. On very clear nights, you might flare a little too soon.

## Visual Illusions

Sometimes what we perceive in our brain (what we think we see) is not what the eyes see, because images sent from the eyes can be misinterpreted by the brain – deliberately, unconsciously or expectantly.

### Relative Movement
Movement of an adjacent vehicle causes the occupants of a stationary one to think that they are moving. An aircraft moving slowly into an air bridge may feel that they have speeded up if an adjacent aircraft is pushed back.

### Autokinesis
The visual illusion of *autokinesis* (self-motion) can occur at night if you are looking at a single light against a generally dark background. It will appear to move, perhaps in an oscillating fashion, after only a few seconds of staring at it, even though in fact it is stationary (it is the basis for many UFO reports). You could lose spatial orientation if you use it as your single point of reference. The more you try to concentrate on it, the more it may appear to accelerate.

You can guard against autokinesis at night by maintaining movement of your eyes in normal scanning, and by monitoring the flight instruments frequently to ensure correct attitude.

Autokinesis is normally associated with a single light source against a black background. However, at night in remote areas, an isolated, lit runway can be processed by your brain as a single light, i.e. a clump of lights will be treated as if it is a single light source, and subject to autokinetic 'movement'.

### False Expectations
We expect that a man will be taller than a motorcycle, so when we see the reverse, we assume that the man is further away. This is usually the case, but need not be, e.g. if the motorcycle is a toy and is close to the eye.

# Assessing Images

### Environmental Perspective

From birth, we develop the mental concept that objects we see as indistinct are far away, and anything we see as clear is closer. This diffusion is not always so, as atmospheric conditions alter visibility. This can cause us to incorrectly judge distances, especially from natural features and terrain. In hazy conditions, you may be closer to the runway than you appear to be, an illusion that may lead to a late flare.

### Judgement of Distance and Angles

The brain often has to make sense of a pattern of lines, and the interpretation may not always be correct, as can be seen from some of the figures which follow. Does a stick bend upwards as it is put into a bucket of water? No, it does not, but it certainly looks that way because of refraction.

An aeroplane on approach through heavy rain can sometimes experience quite a build-up of water on the windscreen that refracts the light rays on their way to the pilot's eyes, perhaps causing an illusion like the 'bent stick'.

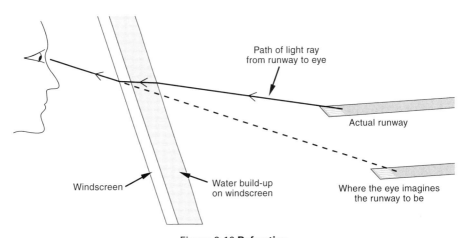

Figure 2-16 **Refraction**

## False Horizons

Sloping layers of cloud by day, angled lines on the ground, or areas of lights by night can sometimes present a pilot with a false horizon, and this can be very misleading. This is not uncommon with a ragged, lowering cloudbase, and associated drizzle or rain obscuring the horizon.

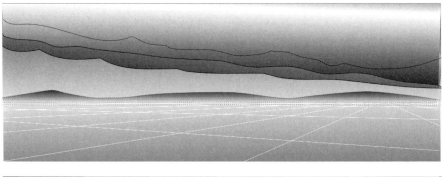

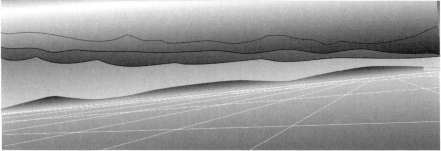

Figure 2-17 **False horizon**

Figure 2-18 **False level**

Figure 2-19 **False lateral level**

## Visual Illusions in the Circuit

The horizon, real or imagined, is very important.

### Visual Estimation of Height Versus Distance

We judge angles. Under certain circumstances, a pilot flying a right-hand circuit may get the impression that the aircraft is higher than normal. This illusion could occur to a pilot who has developed the habit of visually judging circuit height and position by relating the position of the runway lights to some feature of the aircraft, such as a particular position of a wingtip. Such a rule of thumb, which worked satisfactorily for the more common left circuits, could lead a pilot to descend lower to achieve the same picture when making right circuits. Like most habits, such a practice happens unconsciously unless we consciously monitor, question and confirm what we think we see (figure 2-20, page 38).

The first impression one gains is that of being too close or too high. There is a temptation to turn away or to descend. It becomes a matter of disciplined flying to ignore these influences and to maintain the horizon-to-runway depression angle and height above terrain (altimeter) as the prime cues. There is also another natural tendency to want to keep the runway in full view. This can result in a tendency to lower the wing and thus end up too close. This conflicts with the turn-away tendency and so self-cancels to some extent. However, it still confuses the mental processor. The other tendency is to keep the runway in view by descending. This is reinforced by the too-high cue. Thus the greatest danger and strongest tendency is an unconscious control input – by the automatic subconscious pilot flying the aircraft – to descend.

At night, the same situation becomes positively dangerous (figure 2-21, page 39). The need to keep sight of the runway, perhaps the only visual cue, is even more powerful. If the conscious mind does not maintain a disciplined scan of the flight instruments, and a double-check of what the subconscious pilot is doing, then there is serious risk of controlled flight into terrain (CFIT). The need for an active instrument scan during a visual night circuit, especially at an unfamiliar airfield, is paramount.

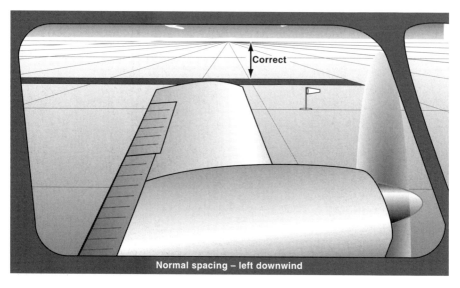

Normal spacing – left downwind

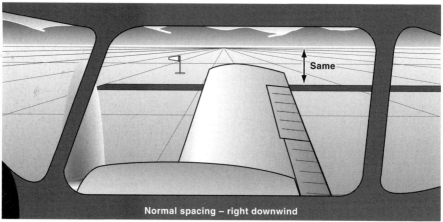

Normal spacing – right downwind

Figure 2-20 **Downwind spacing – day**

The pilot is particularly vulnerable if the conscious mind is diverted to other tasks, such as looking for other traffic, talking on the radio, briefing passengers or carrying out prelanding checks. Given these circumstances, we need a plan that allows the downwind and base legs to be flown without distraction. Other tasks must be carried out well before downwind, so that the conscious scan and visual positioning can be the primary task.

Be wary of unconfirmed feelings of being too high, too low, too close or too far.

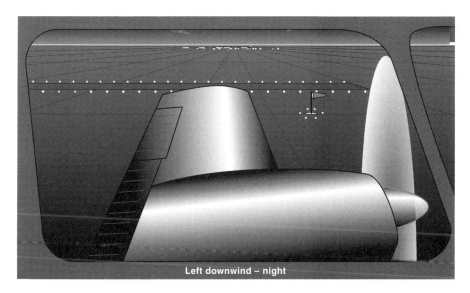

Left downwind – night

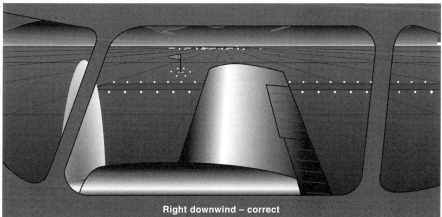

Right downwind – correct

Figure 2-21 **Downwind spacing – night**

You can observe this effect quite easily. Stand as close to a window as you usually are to the cockpit side transparency, and look at a point outside, below your height, to a level at about where the runway would be in a normal (left) circuit. Move back from the window and note the apparent change in height. If you perform this experiment with an open mind, you will feel that you are higher than normal – and experience the corresponding urge to descend to correct the error. This is the same feeling, producing an urge to correct, as when you are looking across the cockpit.

Remember these visual illusions, and, if prevailing visibility is going to have an effect on either distance or angular assessment, use active scanning, seek other information or abort the approach and start again.

## Focal Point

The most common visual illusion is not so much an illusion as distorted judgement. It is based on a familiar phenomenon known as the *inappropriate habit*. Let's say you routinely fly into a given airfield and you assess that you have reached the base turn position on the basis of a *that-looks-about-right* distance assessment. The distance that looks about right in CAVOK conditions will be greatly different from the distance that looks about right under heavy overcast, or through light rain, or at night. The basis of your distance judgement is stored knowledge, accumulated over the number of approaches you have made along that same track to that same runway. Habits are formed through repetition of experience. The vast majority of your flights through these points will have been made in good weather – clear skies and in bright sunlight, great visibility, not gloom or darkness.

Your habitual distance reading will most likely be wrong in any other conditions of visibility. If you know how and why, you can make corrections to your perceptions. As the judgement for that runway at that airport is based on past experience with a clear image, the tendency will be for you to fly closer to the runway, instinctively seeking a reference image of the same contrast or intensity. You will need to use discipline, and other reference features, to get the right distance.

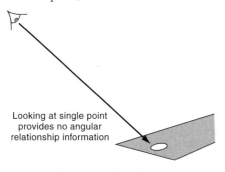

Looking at single point provides no angular relationship information

Figure 2-22 **Focal point**

The problem is compounded when you assess when to turn final. In good weather, you know the picture. Now that the visibility is limited, you concentrate on the runway – the threshold, where else? This is the *focal point* problem. Your cue, turn to final, is activated by your judgement of an angular relationship with the runway. But the human mind cannot determine an angular value – a number of degrees – between a line (track) and a point (where you are looking). Angles are formed between lines, i.e. your flightpath and the extended centreline. However, if you are focusing solely on the one point, in poor visibility, then you simply can't establish the right lead angle at which to commence the final turn. You need to force yourself to scan, looking at each end of the runway in turn.

The *single point lock-on* problem, and related difficulty in lining up on finals, is often seen at Lord Howe Island, when the approach is flown from a right-hand circuit on Runway 28. On late downwind, a range of hills blocks the view of all of the runway but for the threshold. Judging the base leg is difficult as there is only that single point of reference.

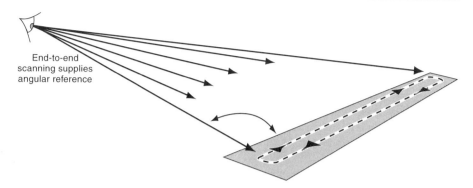

Figure 2-23 **Focal scan**

At night the problem is worse, and the need for a formal scan is greater. There is a similar problem in looking at the runway on approach. Focusing unconsciously, or otherwise, on one point denies you glideslope information. You will only get that through a conscious scan.

Figure 2-24 **Focal point (reduced visibility)**

*An aircraft stalled in a steeply banked turn onto final. The pilot (who survived, though some passengers did not) had been observed to fly a closer-in downwind than normal, though he did not appear to know that. There was low cloud and poor visibility (it was nearly last light). Without realising it, the pilot had left his turn onto finals too late. He progressively increased the bank angle until the aircraft stalled.*

## Focal Trap

There is an illusion called the *Mandelbaum effect,* or *focal trap.* It occurs when a textured surface (such as flyscreen or scratched perspex) screens vision at a distance approximately equal to the resting focal length of the observer's eye. Although resting focus varies between individuals, a typical distance would be between 50 and 100 cm. A textured surface appearing at this distance will tend to draw in the focus of the eye, making it very difficult to focus on distant objects. Again, move your head.

The accurate judgement of depth and distance to far objects is made difficult when the eyes are focused on closer objects. A pilot in the left-hand seat would be more likely to suffer a focal trap effect when looking out of the right-hand window than when looking out of the left-hand window. This is because the left window is considered to be too close to the eyes to act as an effective focal trap, whereas the right window would be at the right distance to induce a focal trap in many observers.

The focal trap effect would be even more pronounced when the window is textured, perhaps with dirt or rain streaking, or illuminated by low-level interior lighting. It has been suggested that an inappropriate focal distance can cause a misperception of runway height, and may account in part for the black hole illusion in which pilots descend too low on approach to a brightly lit runway over dark terrain.

## Visual Illusions on Approach

### Runway Slope

Most runways are of standard width and on flat ground. On every approach, you should try to achieve the same flightpath angle to the horizontal, and your eyes will become accustomed to this, allowing you to make consistently good approaches along an acceptable approach slope merely by keeping your view of the runway through the windscreen in a standard perspective. When approaching a sloping runway, however, the perspective will be different. A runway that slopes upwards will look longer, and you will feel that you are high on slope, when in fact you are right on slope. The tendency will be for you to go lower or make a shallower approach.

A runway that slopes downwards will look shorter, and you will feel that you are low when in fact you are on the correct path. The tendency will be for you to go higher and make a steeper approach.

A runway that slopes downwards will look shorter, and you will feel that you are low when in fact you are on the correct path. The tendency will be for you to go higher and make a steeper approach.

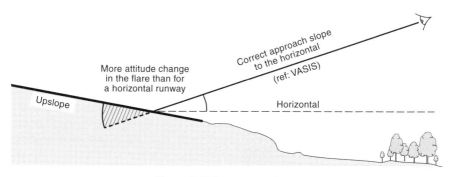

Figure 2-25 **Runway upslope**

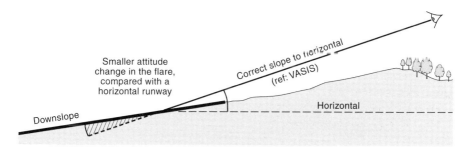

Figure 2-26 **Runway downslope**

If you know the runway slope, you can allow for it in your visual estimation of whether you are high or low on approach.

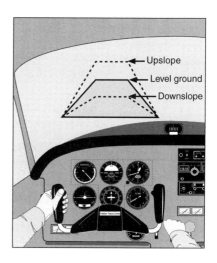

Figure 2-27 **Runway aspect**

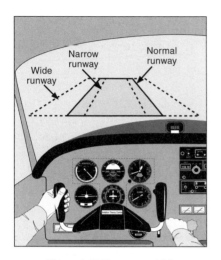

Figure 2-28 **Runway width**

## Runway Size

A runway that is wider than usual will appear to be closer than it really is. Conversely, a runway that is narrower than usual will appear to be further away than it really is. A wide runway, because of the angle at which you view it peripherally in the final stages of the approach and landing, will also cause an illusion of being too low, and you may flare and hold-off too high as a result. This may lead to 'dropping-in' for a heavy landing. Conversely, a narrow runway will cause an illusion of being too high, and you may delay the flare and make contact with the runway earlier (and harder) than expected. If you know that the runway is wider or narrower than your regular airfield, then you can allow for this in your visual judgement of flare height.

## Night Approach

A powered approach is preferred. Power gives the pilot more precise control, a lower rate of descent and a shallower approach path. The approach to the aim point should be stabilised as early as possible (constant airspeed, path, attitude, thrust and configuration). Use all the available aids, such as the runway lighting and a VASIS (visual approach slope indicator system). If the runway edge lighting is the only one, correct tracking and slope is achieved when the runway perspective is the same as in daylight. On centreline, the runway will appear symmetrical. Guidance on achieving the correct approach slope is obtained from the apparent spacing between the runway edge lights and the distance of aim point below the horizon.

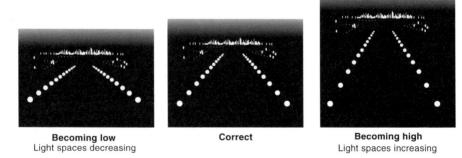

| Becoming low | Correct | Becoming high |
| Light spaces decreasing | | Light spaces increasing |

Figure 2-29 **Night runway aspect**

If the aircraft is low, the runway lights will appear to be closer together or closing. If above slope, the runway lights will appear to be further apart and separating. VASIS will provide correct indications, but the perspective provided by runway edge lighting may be misleading due to runway slope or width.

### Black-Hole Approach

Flying an approach to a runway with no other visible references can often be difficult. This can occur when approaching a runway on a dark night where the only lights visible are the runway edge lights, with no town lights or street lights to be seen, and no indication of the nature of the surrounding terrain. This is what is known as a *black-hole* approach. Alternatively, there could be city lights in the area beyond the airfield but no visual cues near the threshold.

Black-hole approach                          Approach with good
                                             ground reference

Figure 2-30 **Black-hole approach**

Black hole approaches occur on tropical atolls, at remote desert airfields, or on approaches to runways that are surrounded by water.

The tendency is to think that you are higher than in fact you are, resulting in an urge to fly down, and to fly a shallower approach – to sink into the abyss, the black hole.

The worst black hole problem of all is to be found in remote airfields, on a dark night (say, under cloud), and where there is no other light source nor any ground texture, and, as discussed earlier in the chapter, autokinesis might generate an impression of movement when there is none. Rely on the instruments, not your eyes, to maintain horizontal and vertical navigation plots.

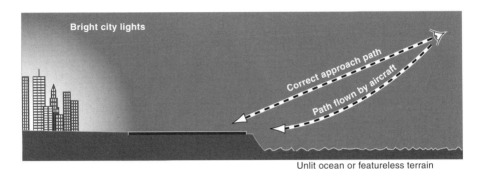

Unlit ocean or featureless terrain

Figure 2-31 **Black-hole – high contrast illumination**

If VASIS is not available, crosscheck the *vertical speed indicator* (VSI) to ensure that the rate of descent is proportional to the approach speed ($V_{REF}$). As a guide, the rate of descent should be close to 5 times the ground speed for a 3° approach.

Similar situations to a black hole approach arise in conditions where the ground is covered with snow, making it featureless. The lack of an horizon and details around the runway threshold make depth and slope perception much more difficult.

Obscured approach                                    Normal perspective

Figure 2-32 **Reduced visibility**

A variety of atmospheric and terrain conditions can produce visual illusions.

| Situation | Illusion | Result | |
|---|---|---|---|
| Upslope rwy or terrain | Greater height | Lower approaches | Shallower |
| Narrower-than-usual rwy | Greater height | Lower approaches | |
| Featureless terrain | Greater height | Lower approaches | |
| Rain or the windscreen | Greater height | Lower approaches | |
| Haze | Greater height | Lower approaches | |
| Downslope rwy or terrain | Less height | Higher approaches | Steeper |
| Wider-than-usual rwy | Less height | Higher approaches | |
| Bright rwy and approach lights | Less distance | Higher approaches | |

Figure 2-33 **Visual illusions – approach**

## Vision Defects

With normal vision, the lens focuses an inverted image of the object on the rear of the eyeball (the retina). The shape of the lens changes to adjust for the distance of the object from the lens to ensure the visual data is focused on the retina. Inability to focus may result naturally from a lens that has become less flexible with age, or it may result from a lens that is not shaped correctly. In almost all cases, artificial lenses in the form of spectacles or contact lenses can be made to correct the specific deficiency and restore sharp vision, just like the focus of a camera.

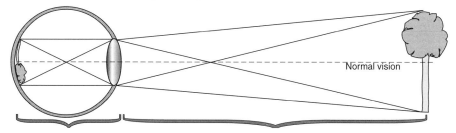

Figure 2-34 **Normal vision (focus)**

### Short-Sightedness (Myopia)

Short-sightedness is a common problem. It occurs when the eye is relaxed and the cornea and lens focus the rays from a distant object, not on the retina, but in front of it. By the time the light rays reach the retina they have moved apart and are no longer concentrated at a point. The resultant image formed on the retina is therefore out of focus. A short-sighted person might see near objects clearly, but distant objects (which require less focusing) might be blurred.

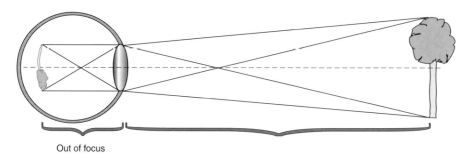

Out of focus

Figure 2-35 **Short-sightedness**

Poor distant vision caused by short–sightedness can be corrected by using an artificial concave lens to reduce the overall refraction of the light rays. The light rays will then focus at a greater distance behind the lens, which ideally will be on the retina.

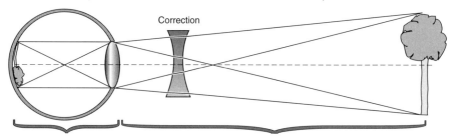

Correction

Figure 2-36 **Corrected vision**

## Long-Sightedness (Hyperopia or Hypermetropia)

Long–sightedness occurs when the eye is relaxed and the cornea and lens do not focus the rays from an object before they reach the retina. The resulting image formed on the retina will therefore not be in focus. The point of focus for the rays is beyond the retina. A long-sighted person might see distant objects clearly, but near objects that need more focusing might be blurred.

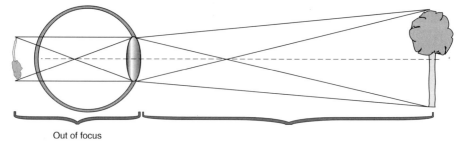

Out of focus

Figure 2-37 **Long-sightedness**

Long-sightedness (hyperopia) can be corrected by a conscious effort to focus the image, or by using an artificial convex lens to increase the overall refraction of the light rays so that they focus earlier, ideally on the retina.

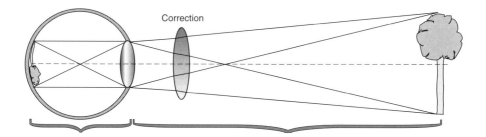

Figure 2-38 **Corrected vision**

A form of long-sightedness that occurs quite naturally in people in their forties or older is *presbyopia*. It is caused by the lens material losing some of its flexibility and so the muscles are less able to increase its curvature. Rays, especially from near objects, will not be focused by the time they reach the retina, i.e. the eyes have lost some of their ability to accommodate for near vision. This is when people say that their arms are not long enough, i.e. not long enough to hold a book or newspaper at a distance where their eyes are capable of focusing the words.

Presbyopic people, with diminished near-vision, may have distant vision that requires no correction. The solution for them, to improve reading vision without affecting distant vision, is to use look-over half-glasses with a half-moon convex lens in the lower half to increase the refraction, and nothing in the upper half. However, the overhead cockpit panel can be a problem.

## Astigmatism

*Astigmatism* occurs when the curvature of the cornea, and less commonly the curvature of the lens, is not perfectly round, i.e. may be ellipsoid rather than spheroid. This causes uneven refraction of the various light rays passing through the lens, and the formation of distorted images. It can be corrected by a lens which has varying curvature over its surface.

## Cataracts

In the aging pilot, eyesight can be affected by *cataracts*. A cataract is the progressive clouding  of the lens of the eye. The clouding affects the transmission of light through the lens and so ultimately degrades the clarity of vision. It may affect only one eye but, more generally, will affect both. One eye will deteriorate before the other. In many cases the condition does not become severe and the treatment by laser is routine.

## Glaucoma

Glaucoma is the build-up of pressure within the eyeball. This pressure damages sensitive structures and nerve endings in the eye. It can start without symptoms followed by progressive deterioration from peripheral to central vision, or can occur suddenly, accompanied by severe pain. Untreated, it can lead to permanent and total loss of vision. Treatment varies from medication to surgery. Pilots over 40 years of age should be tested regularly.

# Eye Protection

### Glare

When flying at high altitudes, especially above cloud layers or flying into a rising or setting sun, the pilot is exposed to light of very high intensity, possibly coming from all angles. While the eyes are protected from light coming from above by the forehead, eyebrows, eyelashes, and strong upper eyelid, they are not so well protected from light coming from below. Bright sunlight reflected from cloud tops, for instance, can be particularly bothersome because of this lack of natural protection. In conditions of glare, it is advisable to protect your eyes by using high-quality sunglasses that reduce glare but not your visual acuity.

The contrast between the glare of a very bright outside environment and the darker cockpit interior may also make it difficult for the eyes to adjust quickly enough to read instruments and charts inside the cockpit. Sunglasses:
- should be impact resistant – have thin metal frames;
- transmit 10 to 15% of the light;
- filter out damaging ultraviolet rays; and
- should not be worn in decreased light.

(Polarised sunglasses may produce some areas with total loss of vision.)

When landing towards the sun, 100% of your vision is lost at the moment of flare. Even when the sun is 40° to the side, vision is reduced by 42%.

### Dry Eyes

The pressurisation system removes moisture from the cabin air, and this causes other discomforts, such as dry eyes and skin. The system does include cabin humidifiers but the air remains relatively dry. As a result, your lungs, eyes, throat and skin may feel it. If your eyes are dry and irritated, use eye drops or even moisten your finger with saliva and wet the corners of your eyes. It all helps.

### Sport/Hobbies

Vision is by far the most important sense. Yet, it is amazing how frequently, and unnecessarily, eye injuries occur from sport, hobbies and especially using power tools without safety glasses. Also be careful when using aerosol sprays or garden chemicals. Don't rub your eyes – bathe them.

Our eyes are our most important asset.

Chapter 3

# Hearing and Balance

Although sight is the most important sense for flying, visual messages to the brain are reinforced, or at times contradicted, by messages from other sensory organs, especially the balance mechanisms in the inner ear *(vestibular* inputs), as well as skin and muscular feeling from all over the body (seat-of-the-pants or tactile inputs, known *somatosensory* inputs).

## Ears

The ear provides two senses: hearing and balance. Hearing allows us to perceive sounds and to interpret them; the sense of balance lets us know which way is up and whether we are upright and steady.

Sound is energy that we can detect with our ears. It may be pleasant, as with voice messages and music, but excessive sound may be annoying and fatiguing and can even lead to damage within the ear. Unwanted, unpleasant, disturbing or excessive sound is noise. Sound signals are caused by pressure variations travelling through the air as pressure waves, and these cause sensitive membranes like the eardrum to vibrate. The inner ear translates these pressure vibrations into electrical signals that are sent via the auditory nerve to the brain, where they are interpreted.

### Structure of the Ear
The ear is divided into three areas: the outer, middle and inner ear.

#### Outer Ear
The outer ear includes:
- the external ear (known medically as the *pinna* or *auricle*), which is used to gather the sound signals;
- the outer canal through which the pressure waves pass; and
- the eardrum, which is caused to vibrate in harmony with the pressure waves.

Any obstruction to the outer canal, such as earplugs or an excess of wax, can reduce the sound pressure waves reaching the eardrum. Similarly a padded cover over the external ear will reduce the sound waves entering the ear, unless the cover is a headset that blocks external noise, but has a small speaker for radio and interphone messages.

#### Middle Ear
The middle ear is an air-filled cavity containing three small bones, known as ossicles, that are forced to move by the vibrating membrane of the eardrum, converting the pressure wave energy into mechanical energy. The ossicles are arranged like a series of

levers to amplify the initial movement. Together with the eardrum they constitute the conductive tissue. This energy then passes on to the cochlea in the inner ear.

The air in the middle ear is maintained at ambient pressure via the *Eustachian tube* that connects the interior of the middle ear to the nasal passages. There is (or should be) no leakage of air across the eardrum, and there should be easy passage of air through the Eustachian tube when needed to equalise pressures – when climbing or descending. This is sometimes hindered by swelling and inflammation, e.g. when a person has a cold, and can have serious consequences.

Interference to the movement of the ossicles or their joints will reduce or distort the sound signal. This can be caused by middle–ear infections, damage to the bones or joints, or a blocked tube with air trapped inside the middle ear *(barotitis)*.

The middle ear provides sensations of movement and balance and, for this reason, middle ear infections affect the sense of balance. Further, disturbed signals from these sensors lead to nausea. In extreme cases, vertigo – total loss of balance, massive and disturbing disorientation – results.

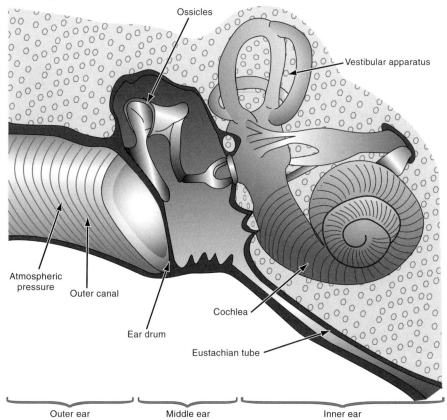

Figure 3-1 **Internal ear**

**Inner Ear**

The inner ear contains three very important pieces of apparatus:

- The *cochlea* for hearing – it converts the mechanical energy from the ossicles into electrical signals that then travel via the auditory nerve to the brain for interpretation.
- The *vestibular apparatus,* which consists of three fluid-filled *semicircular canals,* used for sensing balance. Each canal has a cluster of small hairs at their base. As we shall see, interaction between the fluid in the canals and the hairs provides sensations of movement – in the three axes of flight – and resulting electrical signals are sent to the brain as orientation information. The sensing hairs sit at the base of each semicircular canal in a chamber known as the *cupula.*
- In the same region is the *otolithic organ* (also called the *utricle*), a device that detects and 'reports' linear acceleration or deceleration and verticality. It is co-located with, but separate from, the vestibular apparatus.

Fluid in the cochlea is moved by the mechanical energy from the ossicles, and this causes a wavy movement of small hairs protruding into the fluid. The movement is converted to electrical signals at the bottom of each hair, and these signals are sent along the *auditory nerve* to the brain. Excessive noise can lead to damage of the hairs in the cochlea, and infection or injury can damage the auditory nerve, possibly causing ringing in the ears *(tinnitus).*

# Hearing

The ear is never switched off, and loud or particular noises, to which we have a conditioned response, can stir us from the deepest sleep. It is interesting to note how you can extract messages important for you out of a noisy background – for instance, a radio message directed at you, the sound of your own child on a crowded beach, or your own name mentioned in a distant conversation – known as the cocktail party effect.

## What Is Sound?

Sound is a pressure wave, and each sound has:

- *Frequency* or *pitch:* the number of pressure waves per second (or hertz, Hz) that the sound source produces. Perfect human hearing is in the range of 20 Hz to 20,000 Hz, and voices use the frequency range 500 Hz to 3,000 Hz.
- *Loudness* or *intensity:* the strength or amplitude of the pressure waves, measured in decibels (dB), a logarithmic scale where an increase of 20 dB signifies an increase in intensity of 10 times (20 dB is 10 times as loud as 0 dB, which is the threshold of hearing; 40 dB is 10 times louder again, i.e. 100 times as loud as 0 dB; 60 dB is 1,000 times as loud as 0 dB and 100 times as loud as 20 dB; an increase from 80 dB to 100 dB is an increase in loudness by a factor of 10).
- *Duration:* how long the sound lasts.

## Fatigue and Damage From Noise

Noise can be mentally fatiguing through its effect on our ears, but it also affects the rest of our body, especially if it is associated with vibration. Noise can interfere with communications, and with our concentration. It also increases stress.

| Level | Sound |
|-------|-------|
| 130 dB | Standing near a jet aircraft (noise becoming painful). |
| 120 dB | Standing near a piston-engined aircraft (noise becoming uncomfortable). Several hours per day for 3 months could lead to deafness. |
| 110 dB | Maximum recommended for up to 30 minutes exposure. |
| 100 dB | Maximum recommended for 2 hours exposure. |
| 90 dB | Maximum recommended for 8 hours exposure (a working day). |
| 80 dB | Standing near heavy machinery. Above 80 dB for long periods can lead to temporary or permanent hearing loss. |
| 60 dB | Loud street noise, trucks, etc. |
| 50 dB | Conversation in a noisy factory. |
| 40 dB | Office noise. |
| 30 dB | Quiet conversation. |
| 20 dB | Whispering. |
| 0 dB | The threshold of hearing. |

Figure 3-2 **Noise levels of typical sounds**

Extreme noise levels can also do permanent damage to our ears, with duration of exposure being as important as loudness. Indicative cockpit noise levels (no headset) are as follows:

| Aircraft Type | Take-Off | Cruise | Landing |
|---------------|----------|--------|---------|
| Aero Commander 680 | 102 dB | 92 dB | 83 dB |
| Beechcraft A 36 | 97 dB | 86 dB | 75 dB |
| Cessna 172 | 94 dB | 89 dB | 75 dB |
| Piper Pawnee | 103 dB | 102 dB | 98 dB |
| Bell 206 | 91 dB | 92 dB | 89 dB |

Figure 3-3 **Ambient cockpit levels**

## Loss of Hearing

A person can experience a temporary hearing loss after exposure to noise. The noise of an engine, for instance, may no longer be heard after a while even though the engine noise is still there. Some factory workers lose the ability to hear frequencies to which they are subjected all day long. A temporary hearing loss may disappear after a few hours or after a few days.

Exposure to high noise levels greater than 80 dB for long periods can lead to a permanent hearing loss, especially in the high-frequency range. Very, very gradually, and imperceptibly, a person can lose the ability to hear certain sounds clearly, speech becomes more difficult to comprehend, and radio communications become more difficult.

Sudden, unexpected loud noises greater than about 130 dB, such as an explosion or the sound of an impact, can cause damage to hearing, possibly even physical damage to the eardrum or to the small and delicate ossicles behind the eardrum.

Hearing loss can also result from:

- problems in the conduction of the sound, due to a blocked outer canal (ear wax), fluid or pressure problems in the middle ear (barotrauma caused by a cold, for instance), or faulty ossicle bones and joints – this is known as *conductive* hearing loss;
- loss of sensitivity of the hair cells in the cochlea, by exposure to noise, infection, or age – this is known as a *sensory* or *noise-induced* hearing loss;
- *presbycusis*, a natural loss of hearing ability with increasing age, especially in the higher frequencies (down about 5% by age 60 and 10% by age 70); and
- alcoholism, or excessive use of medications.

### Precautions for Minimising Hearing Loss

A noise-induced hearing loss may develop gradually over a period of years without the person noticing. This is something which cannot be reversed, hence the need for prevention rather than cure. Try to wear hearing protection when in noisy areas. A good noise-cancelling headset is highly recommended for the cockpit, and earplugs or earmuffs for when you are moving around the tarmac. Earplugs can reduce noise by about 20 dB, and good earmuffs by about 40 dB. The squelch control on the radio will reduce background hash, and you should keep the volume turned down as much as possible. Exposure to jet-engine noise can also be hazardous to the balance mechanism in the ears.

## Balance

The sense of balance makes it possible for us to remain upright. The most powerful stabilisation information, by far, comes from the visual channel. If you can see, you can tell directly if you are vertical (if there is a vertical or horizontal reference). If you close your eyes, things are not so easy. You can confirm this by standing on one leg and closing your eyes. Even if you only lose sight in one eye, things still become difficult.

The secondary sensing mechanisms (other than vision) are those devices through which your brain might be sent orientation messages. These secondary signals are very feeble indeed, compared to those generated by visual cues. They really only supplement visual perception. In other words, they can only make sense in partnership with the vastly more powerful visual picture.

These sensory mechanisms were certainly not designed with three-dimensional orientation in mind, and certainly not as a guide to movement in three dimensions. On the other hand, when you are denied sight, or if you have no visual horizon, these other sensors will supply fall-back information. In the absence of the powerful sight messages, their apparent strength will be significantly promoted, to 'fill the void'. Nature abhors a vacuum.

In the absence of a powerful visual cue, your system will crave orientation signals and accord them equal weight. They will be sensed as very strong indeed. And they will always be misleading. You cannot rely on any. Not a single one. You must never use them to judge your flightpath. You can only guard against that by knowing – intimately – what they will try to tell you, and by gaining, through careful experimentation, real familiarity with their signals.

It a classic illustration of the skills/knowledge dichotomy. You cannot learn skills by simply reading about them. There must be practical exercise, sufficient for the experience to be 'deeply imprinted' into memory, and the familiarity thus gained must be maintained through regular exposure to experience. Most pilots would prefer not to subject themselves to the levels of discomfort inevitably involved. However, the true professional knows that these are essential references that must be in the 'library'. To be confident/competent in cloud requires training, experience and recency in cloud or in a motion simulator.

> *The pilot of a cattle-mustering helicopter had taught himself to fly at night. However, the aircraft had no primary flight instruments. As it was not intended for night flight, it also had no provision to dim the low-fuel warning light. Shifting jobs, the pilot encountered a chief pilot who, on learning of this illegal night flying, forbade any more of it. Nevertheless, this night, he set off for an outstation, to position for the next day's work. He made a radio call to the homestead at one point, saying he was cruising at three thousand feet, then was not heard from. It was later calculated that the trip to the planned destination would have exceeded the fuel available. Although it was a dark night, under high overcast, it was surmised that he had been able to maintain a semblance of orientation with a faint horizon, until the fuel warning light came on. That would have dazzled his dark-adapted eyes. The aircraft broke up in flight, in a manner consistent with loss of control.*

### Human Balance Mechanism

The balance mechanism is designed to keep us upright – i.e. vertical and not falling. In the absence of visual references, the inner ear can sense what it believes is vertical by two means:

• sensing tilt (angle); and
• sensing tilting (motion – backwards/forwards or left/right).

The tilt is sensed by the equivalent of a pendulous mass (which senses gravity) and the tilting by the fluid-filled semicircular canals.

## Sensing Gravity (Verticality)

Gravity is detected by sensory hairs in a sac filled with gelatinous material, commonly known as the *otolithic organ* or *utricle*. The sac's outer membrane is studded with small crystals of calcium carbonate. These are called *otoliths* and give the organ its name.

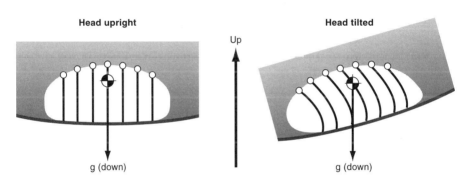

Figure 3-4 **Sensing vertical**

Figure 3-5 **Pendulous effect**

The otolithic organ has a resting position when the head is upright. The brain interprets the message sent from the small hairs at this time as 'up', i.e. the sac is affected by a 1$g$ force directly downwards. If the head is tilted to one side, or forwards or backwards, then the otoliths act as weights to move the sac under the force of gravity to take up a new position, bending the hairs, which then send a different signal to the brain.

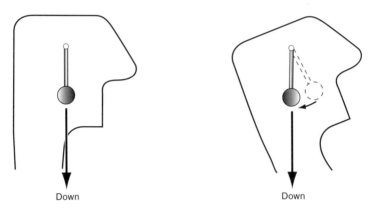

Down                                    Down

Figure 3-6 **Fore and aft (pitch)**

The otolithic organ detects the direction of $g$-forces, but cannot distinguish their origin – the force of gravity, or a centripetal force pulling you into a coordinated turn. We must remember that the body was designed for fairly slow motion on the face of the earth, with a consistent 1$g$ force of gravity exerted on it, and not for the three-dimensional forces we experience in flight (or zero $g$ for that matter). In a turn it will recognise a false vertical.

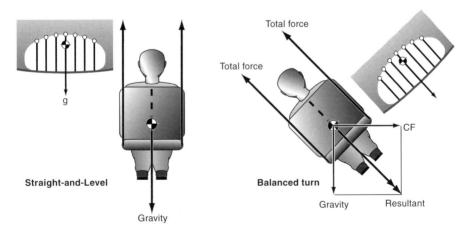

Figure 3-7 **Balanced turn**

## Sensing Angular Movement

You have been introduced to the three semicircular canals – the vestibular apparatus. The canals contain fluid. The three semicircular canals are at right angles to each other (they are orthogonal) like the pitch, roll and yaw planes of an aeroplane, and can detect angular accelerations (change in motion) in pitch, roll and yaw.

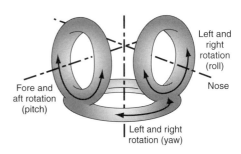

Figure 3-8 **Semicircular canals**

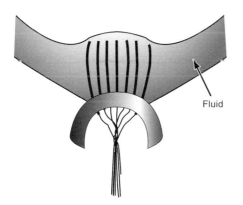

Figure 3-9 **Cupula**

The *cupula* is a saddle-shaped chamber at the base of each canal as depicted in the diagram opposite. It has a cluster of fine hairs that protrudes into the fluid. Movement in the fluid is sensed by these hairs. Nerve endings at their base send corresponding signals to the brain for interpretation (perception).

The semicircular canals are designed not to detect linear motion or linear acceleration (figure 3-10).

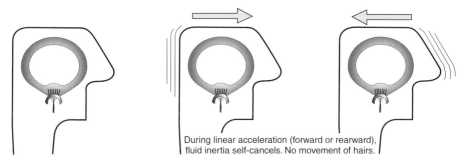

Figure 3-10 **Linear acceleration**

As is the case with any stimulus or sensation, there is a threshold below which movement will not be detected. For example, you will sense a smart roll rate, but not a gentle one. The semicircular canals do not sense linear motion or linear acceleration because the upper and lower volumes of fluid will be self-cancelling. Thus, you will detect the entry to the roll, but not its continuing steady state. Similarly, you will sense the opposite acceleration as you stop the roll at the required bank angle.

In flight, the sensory mechanisms are suppliers only of crude and potentially deceptive messages (compared to the direct orientation images flowing through the sight channel). In reality, when you detect the angular acceleration that commences the roll, you will feel that as a rolling sensation. Similarly, you may sense the roll acceleration that stops the roll at the selected bank angle. However, you may also sense rolling signals from adjustments to the control input while adjusting either roll rate or angle of bank. More importantly, in many flight regimes, your control inputs will be so gentle that you will not detect any rolling sensation at all. The potential for confusion is serious. During angular acceleration, the relevant semicircular canal moves around the mass of fluid that lags. This lag in the fluid bends the sensory hairs, sending a signal to the brain that the head is rolling.

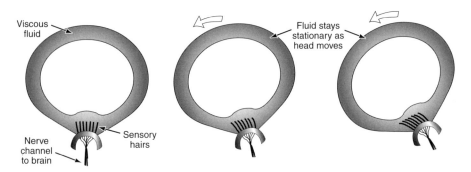

Figure 3-11 **Rolling**

## Normal Sensations Associated with a Level Turn

This phenomenon is best seen in the act of commencing a turn to change heading. The roll needed to enter the turn is angular acceleration. Its counterpart – angular deceleration – occurs when you stop the roll at the desired bank angle. The roll onset (build-up) period lasts very briefly – from the time you move the controls until the roll is under way – a fraction of a second. The stop-the-roll period is also brief. None the less, it is these accelerate–decelerate stages that may or may not be sensed by your semicircular canals because they have a minimum threshold of detection. Very low rates will not be noticed; however, you will sense sharp roll commencement and cessation. In the instance illustrated below, the aircraft is rolling into a right turn.

Note that the sensation of rolling is induced by the controls having moved the aircraft structure to commence the roll. The pilot's head also rolls. Immediately, the little sensing hairs are bent by the fluid lagging in the canal. It flows relative to the canal, but it is actually the canal (your head) that is moving around the fluid. Owing to inertia, the fluid temporarily lags – attempting to maintain its original velocity before the turn – until friction with the walls of the canal brings it 'up-to-speed'.

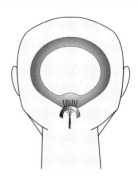

Figure 3-12 **Erect**

Tilting or rolling
(lagging fluid
tilts hair)

Figure 3-13 **Rolling**

The hesitant fluid in the canal bends the hairs. Electrical signals go to the brain, *'We are rolling to the right'*.

Once a steady roll is under way, the fluid will catch up and the hairs will return to their normal erect position. The sensation of rolling thus dissipates, though the roll could be continuing. However, as most roll movements are brief, the dissipation of the roll sensation is not significant. The roll will be stopped before the hairs are neutralised.

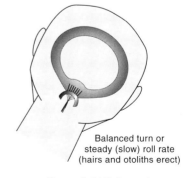

Balanced turn or
steady (slow) roll rate
(hairs and otoliths erect)

Figure 3-14 **Balanced**

In a sustained turn, there is no rolling motion. The bank angle is constant. Further, the resultant of the force of gravity and centrifugal force aligns the otholithic organ to a false vertical. In a perfectly coordinated 60° banked turn, you will experience a 2*g* force exerted by the seat on your body at an angle of 60° to the vertical.

With no visual reference, you will feel that you are still sitting upright with respect to the external forces. You cannot know if you are level or in a banked turn, hence the need for visual cues to confirm your actual attitude.

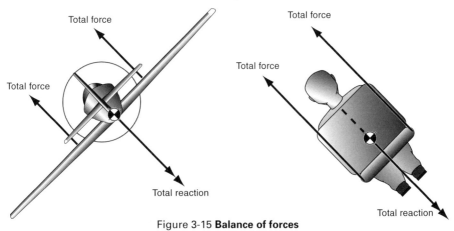

Figure 3-15 **Balance of forces**

## Disorientation and Illusions

### Linear Acceleration Versus Tilt

The otolith detects linear accelerations. During a linear acceleration, the body accelerates away from the otolith and the cupula is temporarily 'left behind', causing the hairs to bend and send a new signal to the brain. The hairs will return to their normal position once the body is no longer accelerating and is moving at a steady speed.

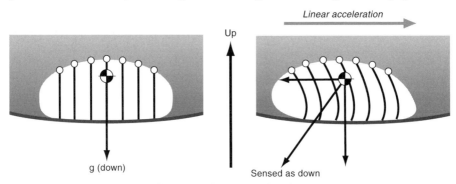

Figure 3-16 **Linear acceleration**

You will notice that the relative position of the otolith during a linear acceleration is the same as that when the head is tilted back; this can lead to an illusion of the nose rising, when in fact you are accelerating. In the case of deceleration, the reverse is true.

## Nose-Up Pitch Illusion of Linear Acceleration

The otoliths are tiny 'weights' on the membrane enclosing the utricle sac and its sensing hairs. When you tilt your head back, or lean backwards, the weights cause the sac to slump that way. The corresponding sensor-hair movement tells your brain that your vertical axis is now inclined rearwards.

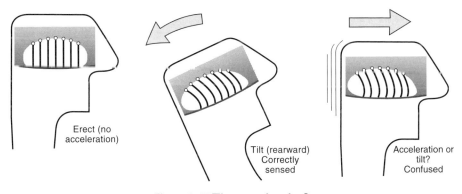

Figure 3-17 **Tilt or acceleration?**

The same movement of the otolithic sac – and thus the same sensation – is caused by linear acceleration. That is, under acceleration, the sac lags behind, causing the sensor-hairs to send a message of tilting backwards. This sensation of the nose rising as you accelerate is known as the *somatogravic illusion* (*somato* meaning originating in the body, and *gravic* meaning sense of gravity).

The greater the acceleration, the stronger the feeling. Obviously it is not a problem when there are clear visual cues, but it can have very serious consequences when there are few, or none, like on a dark night. The forward acceleration through take-off and then to climb speed will be sensed as backwards tilt, that is, a higher nose-attitude and pitch-up than actually exists.

*A Beechcraft Queen Air was flown by an experienced pilot known to be both competent and meticulous in every way. However, it crashed after take-off on a dark, moonless, night. The aircraft, which hit the ground shortly after take-off, was found to have been in good order and fully serviceable. The BASI report concluded that the accident was caused by the pilot's feeling the somatogravic effect as excessive pitch-up, and reacting by lowering or not raising the nose.*

## Nose-Down Pitch Illusion of Linear Deceleration

There is a converse to the somatogravic illusion, but not as serious, as it is less likely to happen near the ground. Deceleration in flight is sensed as tilting forwards. It is particularly noticeable in higher-performance aircraft when reducing thrust and extending the speed brakes. If the aircraft is already descending, the deceleration will be sensed as a steepening descent.

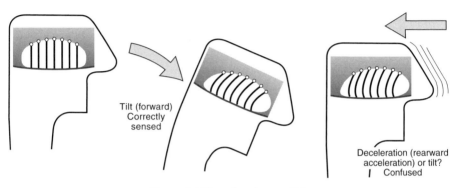

Tilt (forward)
Correctly
sensed

Deceleration (rearward
acceleration) or tilt?
 Confused

Figure 3-18 **Deceleration or tilt?**

As a general rule, aeroplanes in flight decelerate at a gentler rate than the acceleration through take-off to climb speed. Again, if there is clear visual reference, the sensation is hardly noticeable. If the horizon is less clear, then they are more powerful. Fly attitude.

## Spatial Orientation

Orientation is the ability to determine your position in space. It is usually achieved by a combination of three senses:
• vision being the most powerful sense of all;
• the vestibular sense of balance (gravity, acceleration and angular acceleration); and
• seat-of-the-pants (bodily feel or the *proprioceptive* sense).

The brain uses all information that it has available to assemble a picture. If there are conflicting signals, vision is given first priority. In most situations, each of the three senses reinforces the others, but in flight this is not always the case. Each of these senses can sometimes have its messages misinterpreted by the brain. Not knowing your attitude in relation to the horizon (i.e. which way is up) is called *spatial disorientation*. When you are denied external vision, and flying is solely by reference to the instruments, a range of false sensations can be perceived. Hence the need to rely totally on your flight instruments (provided that they agree with each other).

## Impression of Climbing when in a Turn

In a turn, the body experiences a force through the seat-of-the-pants greater than the normal $1g$ in straight and level flight. It is the same feeling as if the aeroplane were being pulled up from straight and level into a climb.

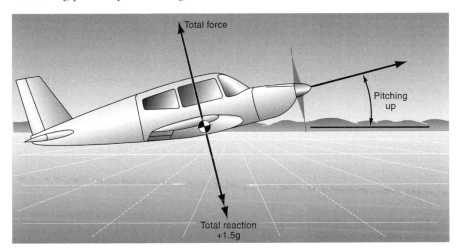

Figure 3-19 **Pulling up**

The fluid in the semicircular canal may have stabilised and stopped indicating a roll, so you will not be getting any sense of a turn from the vestibular apparatus.

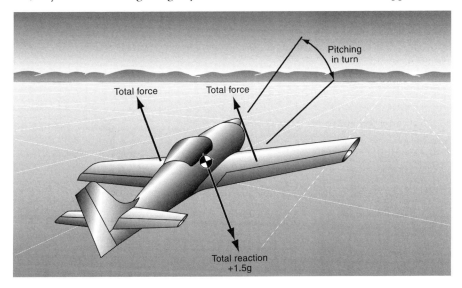

Figure 3-20 **Pitch in level turn**

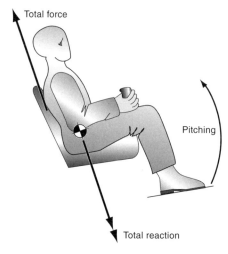

Total force

Pitching

Total reaction

Figure 3-21 **Pitching in turn**

In the turn, we must override the tendency to push the control column forward to stop the imagined climb or else it will cause a descending turn.

## Impression of Descending after Being in a Turn

After being in a steady turn for some time, the body gradually acclimatises to the slightly increased $g$-forces. Immediately after rolling back to wings-level, and reducing the $g$-forces to $+1g$, the body momentarily feels this reduced $g$-force as less than $1g$, inducing the same sensation as pushing the nose over into a descent.

## False Sensations of Motion and Bank Angle

As noted earlier, rolling movement will only be detected at the onset of a moderate rate of roll, either to enter a turn, or to establish a desired bank angle by smartly stopping the roll rate (or the cycle in reverse when rolling wings level). Our senses are limited in sensing low rates of angular acceleration and are tricked into giving a false attitude. The sequence of turn entry is:

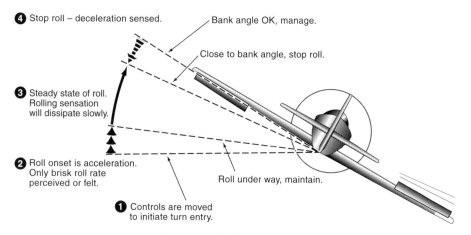

❹ Stop roll – deceleration sensed.

Bank angle OK, manage.

Close to bank angle, stop roll.

❸ Steady state of roll. Rolling sensation will dissipate slowly.

Roll under way, maintain.

❷ Roll onset is acceleration. Only brisk roll rate perceived or felt.

❶ Controls are moved to initiate turn entry.

Figure 3-22 **Rolling into a turn**

Say, for example, you have entered a right turn smartly, and the roll onset is detected. The signal goes to the brain, which perceives *'rolling right'*. The sensation of rolling will dissipate during the steady state phase, but very slowly. As you get close to the desired bank angle, you lead a little, and briskly apply control to cease the roll – that is, to stabilise the turn at the required bank angle. Just as roll onset involved a brief period of roll acceleration, cessation of the rolling movement is effected by roll deceleration. If that is detected as an equal and opposite effect, it will cancel it out. Your perception will thus be of being in straight and level flight even though you are in a turn.

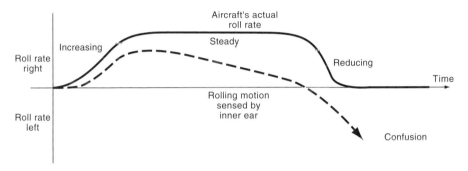

Figure 3-23 **Real and sensed roll rate**

This is a highly simplified view of the perceived rolling sensations, ignoring many factors such as:
• turbulence;
• the fact that some roll movements will be detected, but not all;
• adjustments to roll rate while 'hunting' for the desired bank angle;
• bank adjustments in the turn; and
• the reality that you have a great deal more on your mind than just this particular turn.

It is, however, vital to understand the sources and nature of blind sensations as they can mislead you. When you start believing what you feel and react accordingly, there is a danger. If you know why, for example, you just picked up a very strong dose of *leans* and can control the reaction, you will be better able to override it. Before getting to that, there is one more basic issue to ensure you have understood this essential message: that is, while you are in a turn you will sense that you are in straight and level flight.

## Sensations in Turning Flight

In a balanced turn, a full glass of water on the instrument shroud will remain unspilled (level with respect to the glass). It is as if the weight of the fluid is acting through the aircraft's vertical axis. (It is. The apparent weight is the result of gravity and centrifugal reaction.)

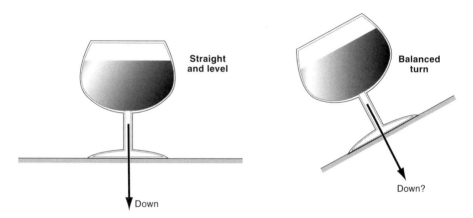

Figure 3-24 **Apparent vertical**

Your body will sense up and down as acting in the same axis. In the above example, you sensed the start roll and stop roll movements (in the diagram), and the latter cancelled out the residue of the former. There is no longer any rolling sensation, nor is there any other sensation source other than seat-of-the-pants. In other words, once you are established in a turn, you will feel that you are in straight and level flight. And that feeling will be the same regardless of bank angle, except that the load factor is increased.

When you bring together this feeling of certainty of where 'down' is, and the sensation of rolling, things can become very confusing – a condition generally known as the *leans*. The leans can profoundly interfere with your mental equilibrium, but only if you let them.

## The Leans

Shown previously was a situation in which the roll acceleration was sufficiently positive to be sensed, and the stop roll deceleration produced an opposite sensation.

Let's look at another situation – say the turn entry was very gentle, not sensed by the semicircular canals, but that the stop roll deceleration is detected.

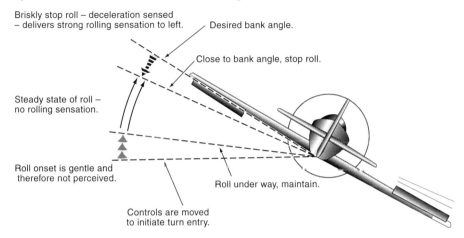

Briskly stop roll – deceleration sensed – delivers strong rolling sensation to left.

Desired bank angle.

Close to bank angle, stop roll.

Steady state of roll – no rolling sensation.

Roll onset is gentle and therefore not perceived.

Roll under way, maintain.

Controls are moved to initiate turn entry.

Figure 3-25 **Roll entry**

The end result is quite discomforting:
- the gentle onset of roll into the turn was not perceived;
- next, no sensation was available during the steady state roll;
- but, when the stop roll control movements are made briskly, the angular deceleration that stops the roll and establishes the bank angle is felt – strongly;
- however, it will be felt as a roll to the left; and
- as there is no cancelling sensation available, the sensation of rolling – continuous rolling – will persist, though it will slowly dissipate as the fluid stops moving and the hairs of the cupula begin to stand up straight again.

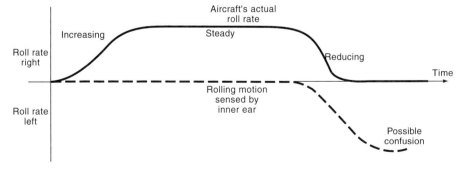

Aircraft's actual roll rate

Increasing

Steady

Roll rate right

Reducing

Time

Rolling motion sensed by inner ear

Roll rate left

Possible confusion

Figure 3-26 **Roll entry and false sensations**

Here's another way of looking at how this particular case of the leans was acquired. In entering this turn, the only sensation perceived was the *stop roll* angular deceleration. The signal sent to your brain is read as roll to the left. With no corresponding 'cancelling' sensation, it will be a sensation of continuously rolling. When you then roll out of the turn, and the roll out is briskly commenced (enough to be detected), you will then experience the sensation that the *left roll* movement has become faster.

Perception of rapid roll rates can quickly produce strong sensations of disorientation. You can get the leans from turn entry or exit. That is:

• you might be wings level, and absolutely convinced you are rolling into or established in a turn; or equally
• you can be in the turn, and certain that your wings are level.

We have seen that slow rates of roll (or movement around the other two axes) will not be detected. Brisk control inputs will induce sensations, and the brisker, the stronger. A common leans scenario is where:

• you slowly let a wing drop then suddenly notice the wing low condition;
• you spontaneously – and rapidly – roll to wings level (and perhaps be looking down at a map or over your shoulder for the runway after a night take-off); and
• you get a strong rolling sensation.

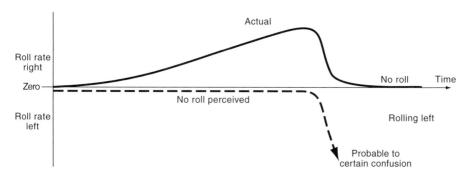

Figure 3-27 **Reversed roll sensation**

So far, your getting the leans has only been attributed to deliberate movement. Turbulence and your own random variation of control pressures will also contribute their share of movement pulses likely to trigger an unwanted sensation – the quicker the movement, the stronger the discomforting perception.

These feelings can become very powerful. To counter them, you need to have available tools that are even more powerful. The best of all is real confidence in your ability to manage flight by reference to the instruments, especially to do that so smoothly as to avoid the leans altogether. It can be done. As a skill, it needs hard work to develop and serious practice to maintain. Every pilot should have a flight simulator program on the home computer and use it regularly. Another aid is a strong sense of situational awareness. If you have planned the flight in detail, and kept ahead of all demands and needs, then you will be operating at well below the saturation or mental overload threshold.

When you are feeling *on top of the game*, you are more relaxed and less likely to make the jerky control movements certain to introduce unwanted sensations. Perceptual control means overriding any messages from balance mechanisms. Treat them – always – as wrong, dangerously misleadingly wrong. They may not be, but you should never even let that thought enter your head.

*A debate raged in the 1970s as to the value of motion-in-flight simulators. Most people will have seen – or seen a picture of – these devices of the front of an aircraft mounted on spiders' legs of hydraulic jacks. They have the freedom to move in all three axes and in three directions (called six degrees of freedom). The role of artificial motion is fiendishly subversive: it acts so as to fool the human inside the cockpit. Say you are the pilot on this flight. Flying along, you roll into a turn. The simulator's motion computer delivers, through the hydraulic legs, a tiny impulse of roll – a minor tilt of the cockpit, but smartly done. Then real motion stops. Inside, your vestibular apparatus has detected the angular acceleration and the rolling left signal is processed. Though the simulator is now stationary, you sense a continuing roll – until you get to the desired bank angle and introduce stop roll control deflections. Another sharp tilt sends the cancelling sensation through your vestibular receptors. As far as you are concerned, the aircraft is in a 30-degree banked turn to the left. The simulator deck is dead level. (It could hardly be any other way. Imagine rolling to 90 degrees of bank. If the machine simply replicated the instruments in the cockpit everyone would hang out of their chairs, there being no g-force to keep people pinned in.)*

*The motion systems similarly employ these slight-but-sharp pulses of movement to fool you in other ways as well – accelerate/decelerate, nose up/down. (Adding to the realism of their effect, of course, is noise – engines wind up and down, speed brakes, etc., and the visual images and instruments.) The accumulation of a series of small tilts can build up to a major lean or droop on the part of the cockpit. To prevent this, the motion system at all times slowly – so slowly as to be undetectable – resets itself to a level platform. None the less, after some busy periods of activity, quite large unusual attitudes can develop. Crews are never allowed to unbuckle their restraint harness until the all-clear from the outside instructor saying the deck is level. At the same time motion for simulators was being perfected, so too were their visual systems. High-definition TV screens were placed at the cockpit windows. Computer-generated imagery has got to the point where the aircraft represented by the simulator can be flown entirely by visual reference to the countryside outside. Even though several discrete TV sets are projected – there's one at each window – you can, from within the cockpit, scan the entire visible outside view with perfect consistency and powerful real-life fidelity. It has been said several times now that your visual channel provides the most powerful orientation cues. Modern visual systems are so realistic that, even in simulators with no motion, flight crews have been rendered terribly airsick by violent manoeuvres.*

*The argument then developed: If the visuals were so good, what was the point of motion? After all, a simulator that had visuals-only was going to be quite a few million dollars cheaper than one on those spider's legs. Support grew for the visuals-only design strategy, and not just on the grounds of cost. It was found that we all possess different levels of perception of movement. Some people are more sensitive than others, with lower perceptual thresholds. (Several experienced IFR pilots have claimed that they never experienced the leans.) Indeed, it soon became clear that the motion systems were detectable by the majority of pilots in such a way that, in their simulator rides, they could tell it was the sim, not the plane. That is, the artificial motion did not supply an accurate replication of the aircraft. The whole reason for motion was realism. Pilots' flight management and decision-making was to be tested as if they felt they were in an aircraft. If they felt it was the sim, their, for example, anxiety levels in an emergency would be less, and the test would not be a true appraisal of performance capacity. On the other hand, simulators with high-fidelity visual systems, but without motion, were found to convince most pilots that it was the real plane they were flying, not a nice, safe, ground-based box. However, what every pilot can take from this experience is that PC-based flight simulator programs can supply extremely valuable training.*

While the study of the human sensory limitations may seem academic, it is highly relevant. You need to know about the sensations you will get from abrupt rates of roll (with pitch and yaw changes it is less likely that acceleration rates will be detectable, though they may be). If things get rough, you will be processing belts of rolling messages at random, from your control inputs as well as from the plane's responses to turbulence. Even when it is not rough, your vestibular apparatus can get you to perceive all sorts of feelings that will make flight on instruments very difficult. Time management, strong perceptual control, and instrument flight so well learned and practised as to be instinctive become survival skills.

## Head Position and Movement

We have examined in detail all aspects related to movement detectors located in your head and body that send out messages about balance and motion. The movement was of course generated by the plane through control inputs or turbulence. The assumption was that your head would remain stationary relative to the cockpit/plane. Things could obviously get much more complicated if, as well as sensing motion induced by the plane, you started moving your head around as well. Involuntary head movement has the potential to aggravate – grossly aggravate and totally confuse – any ambient tendency to disorientation.

Autonomous head movement is common but incorrect. Next time you follow a motorcyclist through a corner, note the rider's head position. It will nearly always be vertical – or nearly vertical. Your natural instinct is to keep your head oriented up-down, to enable other sensations – such as vision, forward acceleration – to make sense, all being based on a common axis – the vertical. In the aircraft, as long as your turn entries are gentle, your natural tendency to align your head with the vertical will not be strong. Use the cockpit coaming as your head reference. However, the tendency will be there, and it will be strongest when you are least relaxed.

Head movement can be a serious problem. The previous section dealt with the semicircular canals, and their function of sensing aircraft acceleration in the roll axis. In a classic illustration of how the human body was not built for flight, the brain can only make sense of a signal from one channel at a time. This is an important feature of your balance mechanisms. This means that they can only cope with a signal from one axis at a time. Motion in two axes simultaneously is virtually impossible in nature. Or it was, until aeroplanes came along.

Two very dangerous situations are common:

- turning crosswind after a night take-off, rolling into the turn and looking over your shoulder for the runway as you do so; and
- rolling into a turn and then looking/reaching down for the hand-held mike or something on the cockpit floor.

The effect of the combined motion can be alarming and, if it is experienced, concentration is needed to retain control. It is called the *Coriolis effect*.

## Coriolis Effect

If you simultaneously induce motion in two semicircular canals, e.g. by moving your head in pitch while the aircraft is rolling (turn after night take-off), you will spontaneously trigger a process known as the *Coriolis effect*, and your brain will react violently and reflexively (i.e. uncontrollably). The result can cause total disorientation – vertigo. Let's say that you are about to roll smartly into a turn to the right, and having just dropped your map, you have bent over to retrieve it. Were you to execute the roll at the same time as raising your head to the upright position, you would induce motion in two semicircular canals and become closely acquainted with the Coriolis effect. Clearly, this is too dangerous to attempt to check out in the air. You can, however, familiarise yourself with the effect in a kiddies' playground that has one of those 'rotating disc' devices with holding rails. Start it rotating (if the kids don't mind your joining them) hold a rail firmly, and gently lower your head to your chest. Then, a little less gently – but not rapidly – raise it. There will be wild reflex muscular spasms accompanied by powerful nausea. If you know how it is induced, then you should be able to ensure that you never do it. With quite modest amounts of movement, you can thus visit the threshold of what can be a terrifying and debilitating syndrome – vertigo. I do recommend you try this exercise. Holding on firmly is essential as the reflex spasms can literally throw you to one side. Head movements in the air must always be very gentle, deliberate and controlled. Be careful if you raise your head quickly.

The two hazardous situations are:

- looking over your shoulder for the runway as you turn after a night take-off; and
- rolling into the base/final turn.

*The early-model F-104 Starfighter suffered some unusual and unexplained accidents early in its service life. The aircraft would enter the continuous base turn, then plummet into the ground. It transpires that the undercarriage down indicator – the three greens – was mounted on the right-hand side of the cockpit. If the pilot was in a steady-state turn when looking to check 'undercarriage down', everything was OK. However, if the pilot made that head movement while rolling, Coriolis would strike with instant vertigo. There would be an instinctive reaction to pull back on the stick, with a consequent departure and incipient spin. Later in this manual is a section on cockpit design. It's sobering to reflect on the hard way in which many of those lessons were learned.*

## Vertigo

Vertigo can also be brought on by a flashing light, such as strobe, or flickering sunlight or shadow from a propeller on the rotor blades of a helicopter. This is known as *flicker vertigo,* and is mostly noticeable when the frequency − i.e. pulses or reflections per second − is close to your pulse rate (60 to 90 beats a second). In a process similar to *sympathetic resonance* − e.g. the opera singer who can shatter a glass with a high note − your *system* amplifies the pulses as they come close to coinciding with the heart beat. That is, one builds on the other. The maximum effect will be a crescendo as synchronicity is achieved. This is obviously something to avoid − and averting the eyes will generally do the trick. It is a particular concern for helicopter pilots as rotors may 'chop' sunlight coming into the cockpit, or cause reflections into the pilot's eyes that will prove hard to avoid. Susceptibility varies with individuals. Epileptics can be affected significantly. You may become mesmerised (hypnotised), known as flicker unconsciousness. Truck drivers can be mesmerised by the passage of dashes of the white centre line.

Strobe lights often feature at discos and the like, being used for entertainment value. A lesser-known application of the technique is in torture. Few people can withstand strobe flicker for long before becoming pliant and cooperative. Another form of vertigo known as *pressure vertigo* can result from the effect on the balance apparatus following collapse of the eardrums due to blocked Eustachian tubes. This could occur, in an extreme case, if flying with a cold or other similar infection.

## Motion Sickness

Motion sickness is usually caused by the balance mechanisms of the inner ear continually being overstimulated by motion. This can be caused by turbulence, or manoeuvres such as steep turns or spins, in which forces other than the normal will be experienced. A hot, smelly cockpit does not help, especially if there is no clear horizon.

Psychological aspects can also play a role in the onset of motion sickness − for instance, a fear of flying or apprehension at seeing the horizon at different angles or not seeing the horizon at all. Anxiety, in particular, will make the condition worse by causing the sufferer to lose control over where he or she looks and focuses attention. Visual scanning is likely to become purposeless and random.

The visual channel is, by far, the most powerful spatial reference. If the messages coming in through non-visual channels − the balance organs − are accorded priority, the sensory confusion causing airsickness will predominate. If the airsick person focuses the gaze on a spot on the horizon, the visual messages will be given a chance to assert their authority, and to 'tone down' the strength of the signals coming from other sources. This phenomenon can work both ways. Motion sickness can also be caused by a mismatching of balance signals from the ears and visual signals from the eyes. For example, an experienced pilot practising instrument flying in a fixed-base (non-moving) simulator may experience motion sickness because the visual sense (what is seen on the flight instruments, which may be a steep bank) is different from the vestibular signals being received from the ears ($1g$ straight and level). In this case it is termed *simulator sickness*.

Many pilots have experienced airsickness, especially early in their training when stress levels are higher, and slightly unusual attitudes and $g$-forces are encountered perhaps for the first time, so do not be discouraged if you experience it occasionally.

To avoid airsickness:
- anticipate turbulence by checking weather forecast, or from your own knowledge of local effects (e.g. side of hills) (if not a local, seek the views of someone who is);
- eat lightly before flight;
- fly the aeroplane smoothly, gently and maintain trim and balance;
- focus on the horizon as much as you can;
- avoid manoeuvres involving unusual $g$-forces;
- avoid areas of turbulence if possible; and
- ventilate the cabin with a good supply of fresh air.

If turbulence is encountered:
- fly at optimum speed;
- relax, don't fight it;
- involve a potentially airsick passenger in the operation of the flight, especially if this involves looking outside the aeroplane and into the distance (e.g. helping to identify ground references) or at the horizon;
- comfort the passengers and provide a bag;
- as a last resort, recline the airsick passenger's seat to reduce the effect of the vertical accelerations; and
- land as soon as is reasonably possible.

## Load Factor

Speed has relatively little effect on the human body, whereas acceleration or deceleration may produce pronounced effects ranging from the fatiguing characteristics of flight to a complete collapse of the cardiovascular system. In aviation, acceleration is usually expressed in multiples of the acceleration due to gravity of 9.81 metres/sec$^2$ (32.2 fps$^2$) and is represented by the symbols $g$ or $Gz$.

The brain and eyes need a continuous supply of oxygen. They have little storage capacity, so strong or prolonged $g$-forces, which reduce the supply, lead to reduced visual acuity, loss of colour vision, loss of sight and even unconsciousness. When the acceleration is centripetal, as in turn or pitching manoeuvres, it is felt by the pilot as an increase in weight. In a 60-degree banked level turn, you will experience +2*g*, or feel you are twice as heavy.

All parts of the body are affected by *g*. The blood, for example, also gets heavier. It therefore is harder to pump and circulate, and tends to pool in the legs and lower abdomen. At higher load factors, say, +3.5*g* and upwards, this can produce physiological symptoms.

Reduced blood circulation results in less blood supply and reduces local blood pressure. Specifically, it diminishes the transport of oxygen and sugar to the head. As there is very little stored oxygen and sugar in the head (as opposed to muscles, which have some storage capacity), the reduced blood supply can cause an immediate effect.

The first to notice anything is the eyes. As the eyeballs must remain balls – as opposed to being squashed by surrounding tissue – they are inflated to positive internal pressure (they feel hard to the touch.) A side-effect of this necessary condition is that blood flow to the eyes – and the oxygen and sugar supply it carries – is inhibited. It's an 'uphill slope'.

If *g*-force is reducing the blood pressure in the head, then the eyes will be affected first because of this pressure gradient. The supply of oxygen and sugar is necessary to process sight signals. As the *g* increases, sight becomes affected, with colour vision the first to go. If you are not used to high load factors, this stage of the phenomenon might occur at 3.5 to 4.5*g*. It is called *greyout*. All images are seen as shades of grey and white.

If the *g* keeps building, the field of view will begin to shrink, starting from the sides. This limiting vision effect is called *tunnel vision*. Still increasing *g*-forces will lead to total loss of vision, or *blackout*. At this point, the pilot is temporarily blind, though still conscious. Further *g* increase will inevitably lead to insufficient oxygen and sugar supply to keep the brain functioning, resulting in loss of consciousness.

So far, we have only talked about positive *g* – the plane is the right way up. If the aircraft is inverted, the effect of negative *g* is not only uncomfortable, it is potentially dangerous. It's one thing for large amounts of blood under higher pressure to be accumulating in the legs and lower abdomen, surrounded by tough and flexible muscle. To have that happening in the head around all that delicate machinery is another thing altogether.

Most pilots, once they have accommodated to aerobatic manoeuvring, can withstand up to negative 2.5*g*. If, however, you push beyond that, you will encounter the phenomenon called *redout*. When you red out, the impression is of total loss of sight, because a 'red veil' is in the way. The reason for it is that your lower eyelid muscles have evolved to match the human bodies needs. As we mostly stand erect, blinking requires the lower eyelid to move only upwards. Gravity will organise the return journey. There is no corresponding muscle group to 'unblink' the lower eyelid. So if you are inverted, and push to a certain negative *g* limit, the lower eyelid will drop, covering the pupil, and you cannot get it out of the way.

Many pilots will never experience any of these *g*-related phenomena. However, some will go on to learn aerobatic manoeuvres, or to fly military jets capable of high *g*-forces in turns and manoeuvring. For those who do, there is an especially insidious potential trap: *g-induced loss of consciousness,* or *g-loc.*

We saw earlier how positive *g*-force brings on a sequence of sight-related changes before getting to the point of unconsciousness – greyout, tunnel vision, blackout. As all of these occur while conscious, they can be controlled and relieved. Relaxing the back pressure on the controls will bring nearly-instantaneous relief from the degraded sight condition. Indeed, in the case of blackout, the reaction to diminish the *g*-force by easing the control forces is nearly reflexive. However, *g*-loc occurs with high rates of onset of *g* where the warning symptoms are overruled.

*There have been several fatal accidents attributed to g-loc in recent years. Both involved aerobatics or display flying.*

As this diagram shows, the greyout to blackout phenomena act as a threshold or warning of unconsciousness. They enable forewarning, and the chance to reduce the control pressure. That is what happens at the normal rate of *g* onset. However, there is appreciable lag before the effects are felt. There's some time taken to return to normal.

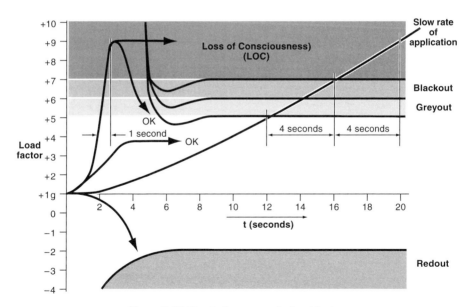

Figure 3-28 **Physical response to load factor**

If, however, the rate of onset of *g* is rapid, the warning signals of degraded sight will be bypassed. The pilot will become instantly unconscious. If you blackout, you will intuitively relax the control pressure to reduce the *g*, and immediately regain full sight and you remain conscious throughout. However, if you lose consciousness, it takes at least 15 seconds to recover. Loss of consciousness is a debilitating experience. Think of the last time you saw someone faint – recall how disoriented and incapable they were during the ensuing period.

Loss of consciousness in an aircraft can never be safe. Being out of control for 15 seconds will often prove fatal. However, only aerobatic aircraft have the structure and control power capable of causing *g*-loc.

## Coping with *g*

Your personal resistance to *g*-forces is highest if you are not only physically fit, but also toughened – hardened by regular exposure. Serious exercise is a good idea for all pilots, but it is especially so for those who want to be good at aerobatics. On the other hand, no matter how fit you are, there will be times in your life (or day) when your resistance levels are down – recovering from illness, tired after a long day, domestic stress or work problems.

## A-loc

Another term that has been recently coined is *a-loc*. A-loc is *almost* loss of consciousness due to *g*. The reason for the differentiation is that, even if the pilot does not lose consciousness, there is a temporary period of confusion and even euphoria, where the pilot either does not recognise, or does not care about, the seriousness of the situation. It is momentary but it is believed to have caused some otherwise unexplained pilot lack-of-response and delayed or inconsistent recovery from high-*g* manoeuvres.

## Chapter 4

# Health, Fitness and Well-Being

## General Health

### What Is Average?

The previous description of the effects of flight on the human body and mind is representative of an average human in good health. Obviously, ill health adversely affects all of our functions, capabilities, capacities, stamina, concentration, memory, and tolerances to the stresses of flight.

Medical checks keep us under periodic scrutiny, but the annual medical can, in itself, be routine or stressful. For professional pilots, the medical should be as if almost irrelevant – a mere confirmation of our constant state of good health.

### Health Indicators

We are the result of two primary influences:
- heredity or parentage (*nature*); and
- environment (*nurture*).

One of the most reliable indicators of general health is the parentage from which we are born. If our parents were healthy and lived long lives then all we need to worry about are the environmental factors. We are born with these characteristics and traits.

Environmental factors include our relatives and friends, schooling, education, religion, culture, training and examples set by elders or respected colleagues, whether in or out of the aviation environment. We observe, we learn and we are moulded into attitudes and patterns of behaviour. Our personal hygiene, eating habits, lifestyle, exercise, sports, interests and hobbies are significantly influenced by these environmental factors.

### Blood Relations

Blood is the fluid of life. It carries the oxygen and nutrients to the cells for the production of energy and it removes waste. Blood includes red cells, part of which carry oxygen (*haemoglobin*). The difference in colour of arterial and venous blood (red versus blue) is due to the oxygen in the haemoglobin of the arterial blood. Blood also contains white cells which are the body's defence mechanism against disease (the *auto-immune* system). The fluid base contains clotting agents (*platelets*) to stop the loss of blood from wounds. About 90% of blood is water (*plasma* or *serum*).

**Blood Donations.** It is recommended that pilots not fly for at least 24 hours after donating blood.

**Blood Pressure.** There are two levels of blood pressure:
- *systolic* being when the heart pumps (should be around 120); over
- *diastolic* being when it pauses (should be around 80).

The resting (diastolic) blood pressure is a good indicator of potential problems. High blood pressure can pertain with no apparent, underlying cause. It can be controlled by drugs. If identifiable, the cause of the high blood pressure (*hypertension*) should also be addressed – whether it be physical or psychological.

## Cholesterol

Cholesterol is formed by the body in response to dietary intake. There are two levels of cholesterol in the blood:
- LDL, which is related to animal fats; and
- HDL, which is related to exercise.

The former is not good and should be controlled by diet and exercise.

## Obesity

The piloting profession is vulnerable to obesity. The Western lifestyle compounded by good food, good hotels, alcohol and a sedentary lifestyle leads to a high likelihood of obesity. We will have to actively fight against it in later years – especially if we didn't in earlier years.

**Related Diseases.** Diseases that have been directly related to obesity include osteoarthritis, hypertension (high blood pressure), diabetes, various cancers and coronary heart disease.

**Body Mass Index (BMI).** As flight crew, we should maintain a reasonable degree of physical fitness. It allows better physical and mental performance during flight and, in the long term and quite apart from flying, improves our chances of a long and healthy life. Physical fitness helps us to cope better with stress, tiredness, fatigue and the reduced availability of oxygen at higher altitudes. Medical examiners calculating your body mass index use the formula:

$$\text{BMI} = \frac{\text{weight in kg}}{(\text{height in m})^2}$$

A body mass index of 19 to 25 is considered normal. Above 30 is considered obese. For example: weight = 80 kg and height = 1.8 metres:

$$\text{BMI} = \frac{80}{1.8^2} = \frac{80}{3.24} = 24.7 = \text{OK (just)}$$

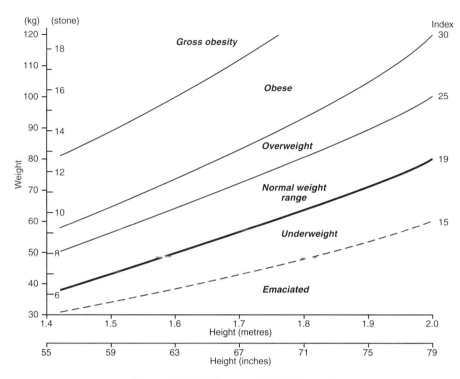

Figure 4-1 **Weight verses height (stature)**

## Medical Fitness

### General
As flight crew we all undergo an annual inspection. As we age, the checks become more comprehensive and more frequent – as they should be. Our medical health, especially in later years, depends on our physical and physiological health over the previous years. It's like superannuation – if we invest now we will enjoy the rewards later in our lives. The more we invest, the greater the return.

### ECG
The normal electrocardiogram, or resting ECG, is a sensor that measures the heart-beat from 12 locations. It is carried out while the body is resting to check whether there is a deficiency in the action of the heart muscle. It shows the heartbeat on a paper trace. It is a here-and-now indicator that shows congenital or pre-existing defects but it cannot predict future problems.

## Stress ECG

If there are symptoms such as shortness of breath, lethargy, or palpitations there is a more strenuous, but not totally reliable, test known as the *stress ECG* where the same sensors are applied and the body is simultaneously placed under physical stress on a treadmill. It will show heart defects and partial blockages that otherwise would not be evident at rest. It shows if the heart is not able to meet the demand. However, in the absence of other symptoms, the test can give false indications for healthy individuals and must usually be supported by additional testing such as an angiogram – not a simple procedure. It can also give false negatives (saying there's no problem when one exists).

## Pregnancy/Motherhood

Pregnancy is such a special condition. Our response is personal and individual. It affects our body, attitudes, personality, mood, outlook, attention and motivation – for better or for worse. In some cases it is almost a routine affair. In others it is a major life drama. In all cases there is a need for specialist advice. The first three months carry the greatest susceptibility to miscarriage and to morning sickness. The middle three months are relatively stable and the last three are a little unpredictable. Physical size also may become a constraint. For pilots, flying after six months is not generally recommended. Pregnancy requires permission of a DAME to continue flying.

Pilots are assessed on an individual basis for safe operation of the aircraft as well as the safety and health of the mother and child. Passengers require specific approval from their doctor to travel by air within four weeks of the expected birth date. However, seat harnesses may become ineffective before this time.

## Menstruation

A woman's body and psyche responds to her cycles in a very individual way. For a member of a flight crew, it is strongly suggested that you seek expert advice on nutrition, especially if you are involved in long-haul operations.

## Physical Fitness

### Exercise

Commercial air transport flying is a sedentary occupation. We spend most of the time sitting down, yet some of that time we are highly stressed where the heart rate is high and we are sweating profusely. It is good for neither the body nor the mind. There is little opportunity to exercise in flight and there is little physical demand on the human body. The body needs exercise and physical demand – in balance – to relieve stress. Leo Tolstoy would work the fields with the peasant farmers to clear his mind. He believed that working his body would divert the mental focus, clear his soul and relieve the stress. He was right. For the average commercial pilot refuelling and loading bags may actually be a positive aspect of the daily work routine. Keeping fit takes some effort and this effort must be continuous for fitness to be retained; but it can also be good fun and very recreational. Walking, jogging, digging the garden, dancing, sailing, cycling, swimming, in fact anything that steadily raises your pulse rate and maintains it at a raised level for at least 30 minutes, will greatly improve your fitness. Give up smoking (if you haven't already).

If you are grossly unfit or obese, then allow yourself several diet-conscious months with moderate exercise that is gradually increased, and consider medical supervision. It might seem like a long haul, but the quality of life and your self-esteem will improve along with your fitness. Physical activity also promotes a hunger for healthy foods as well as encouraging good sleeping patterns. Exercise improves fitness and mental performance. To be effective exercise must be regular with a minimum of 20 minutes at least three times weekly. Is is even far better to have some form of exercise in every day's itinerary in the form of at least 30 minutes of moderate physical activity, say, brisk walking, dancing, gymnastics, cycling, sailing or gym (yes, every day). Try to have some variety. Schedule something every day so that, if you miss the occasional day, it won't be too deleterious.

Exercise should be sufficiently demanding to get the heart pumping, the skin sweating and the breathing rate up. As you become fitter you will need to work harder to achieve this. An exercise programme should consist of mobility, muscle strengthening and heart/lung exercises (*aerobic*) – move, lift, stretch, puff, pant, groan and glow.

Before starting an exercise programme you should record your resting pulse rate. Then, by checking your heart rate during exercise and how long it takes to return to normal after exercise, you can check the effectiveness of your exercise programme and guard against over-exertion. The time taken to return to your resting rate is a good indicator of fitness. *Always discuss your fitness with a doctor before starting an exercise programme.*

## Lifestyle

The lifestyle of flight crew consists of disrupted sleep patterns, late nights, time-zone changes, long periods of duty, unsuitable rest periods or facilities, stress and separation from family, none of which are conducive to a normal healthy body. Most hotels now have a gymnasium, spa or pool. Rest days are wasted if they are spent in the bar. Fresh air, golf, swimming or walking refresh the body and mind and are stress relievers (depending on the golf score). Fatigue, tiredness and sleep deprivation can lower a pilot's mental and physical capacity quite dramatically. The nature of flying is such that moderate levels of these symptoms are involved. As a pilot, you must train yourself to cope with them, and to recognise when your personal limits are being approached.

Take cat-naps if you can. Don't fly if you are deeply tired or fatigued. Fatigue can ultimately become deep-seated and chronic. If personal, psychological or emotional problems are not resolved, they prevent deep rest and good sleep – perhaps over a prolonged period. The condition becomes chronic and will only be cured when the problems are resolved, or at least are being addressed, and the person can relax and unstress. Short-term fatigue can be caused by overwork, mental stress, an uncomfortable position, recent lack of sleep, raging a little too much, a lack of oxygen or lack of food.

## Stress

Stress is part of our lifestyle. It is inevitable but manageable. Management of stress is relatively easy – once learnt. But we each have to learn a way that best suits us. We need to find the particular technique that tickles our own fancy. The objective is not to confront stress head on. Like a kite it will climb against the wind and become even more challenging. The idea is to defuse it – to divide it into bite-size chunks – and remind yourself that it is temporary. It will pass and there is a future. Alcohol doesn't defuse stress, it defers it and then it is added to the next day's lot. Coping/defusing techniques include:

- *Exercise/sports.* Physical demand takes your mind of mental problems – and is good for you. Physical demand that also demands mental concentration is even better – i.e. golf, or sailing, is more diverting than jogging.
- *Fresh air.* The wide world around us keeps everything in perspective and reinforces our hope and realisation that we are both small, and large in the scheme of things;
- *Diversions/hobbies.* Mental and manipulative occupation is a marvellous relaxant – something that requires total concentration.
- *Relaxation therapy and meditation.* These use the same technique of mental occupation and diversion so that the build-up of stress is deflated by inattention. It is not the same as lying in the sun and snoozing as the brain dwells on the problem. They are effective and easy-to-learn techniques for focusing the single-channel processor of the conscious mind on a trivial routine symbol.
- *Sex.* Good for the soul, the mind and the body and. . .

# Diet and Nutrition

We are what we eat. Diet concerns what we eat, how much and in what proportions. It receives much attention in the media these days because in Western society our dietary intake is poorly managed: too much animal fat, too much processed sugar, too few vegetables, cereals and fruit. In all, too much quantity and too little activity.

## Eating Habits/Patterns

We are habitual eaters. The suggested eating pattern is to have small, varied serves often rather than sporadic large serves. Snacks, such as fruit, yoghurt, muesli bars and cereals keep the hunger at bay and avoid the temptation to eat a large meal too quickly. Eating slowly allows the digestive system to process the food and to feel satisfied with a lesser quantity.

## Culture

We are heavily influenced by the diet of our culture and our forebears. Some are very favourable. Some are damaging. Our cuisine, style of cooking and the frequency and size of meals are related to our upbringing. All affect our health, energy and well-being. The mediterranean cuisine is currently assessed as best: seafoods, salads, olive oil, fruit and time spent enjoying it.

# Nutrition

Nutrition is fuel for the body and mind. We have discussed the importance of oxygen for generation of energy, and there is a need for fuel in the form of nutrients, which the body converts from the food we eat, and roughage, which is important for internal hygiene.

## Glycaemic Index (GI)

There is much discussion regarding the natural sugar content of foods. A rating called the *glycaemic index* (GI) has been adopted and may appear on the packaging of foods in future, similar to the fat and cholesterol content.

High GI foods give a quick but short-lived boost followed by a depressed level of energy and focus. OK for sprint athletes - not so good for long-haul flight crew.

## Elements of Our Diet

### Fats

Intake of animal fat, in any form, should be carefully controlled. Meat does not necessarily mean fat, nor does milk. There are lean choices for both.

### Meat

Choose lean lamb, beef and chicken – no skin on the chicken. Keep fatty bacon to a minimum. Do not be too heavy on the sauces. Minimise preserved or processed meats, such as sausages and hams. Women don't eat enough meat. Lean meat is the best source of protein and iron.

### Fish

Oily fish/bluefish, sardines, kippers, herrings, salmon and tuna are marvellous. All grilled, steamed or poached fish is great. Avoid fried, battered or crumbed as the coating collects the fats and the calories.

### Oils

Vegetable and fish oils are good. Olive oil is best but don't overheat when cooking. Limit coconut and palm oils.

### Legumes

Peas, and all types of beans, are good for you (pulsars). The cowboys' staple diet of baked beans has much to be commended for it. Lentils are a good source of protein.

### Salad

Any salad is wonderful if raw, fresh and clean. If you are sure of the source, eat lots. Watch the dressings though. Light oil and vinegar is good. Mayonnaise not so. Moderate the additives such as cheese, bacon, potatoes and eggs. Salad, fruit and vegetables protect against cancers and heart disease.

## Vegetables

Vegetables should be undercooked and undressed, and steamed or stir-fried rather than boiled to death – crunchy is good. Eat lots of them. Go overboard. Spinach or silver beet is a good source of iron. Have many different-coloured vegetables on your plate. Brighter-coloured vegetables contain greater levels of anti-oxidants. These neutralise free radicals, the ageing and health-threatening agents that encourage cancers and heart disease. Soups are a wonderful way to serve fresh vegetables as the juices remain in the serve. Don't add too much salt. Potatoes boost energy but only in the short term (that GI again). Rice has the same effect. Avoid bulk quantities of either.

## Fruit

Eat unlimited amounts, if fresh. Fruit is the best source of vitamins, energy and water and also acts as anti-oxidants, especially red fruits, strawberries, and tomatoes. However, tropical fruits increase blood supply quickly (GI) and lead to an immediate uplift that is short-lived. It is followed by a loss of energy and concentration. They provide short-lived energy.

## Nuts

Nuts should be eaten sparingly – watch the oil and salt.

## Carbohydrates – Fibre/Cereals/Grains/Rice

Bread is the staff of life. Granular and unprocessed is best with oil rather than butter. Rice and potatoes are good – steamed or boiled rather than fried. However, large amounts of rice or potatoes act to rapidly build the glycaemic level (blood sugar), but there follows a sudden let-down. Ever feel hungry and weak not long after a rice meal? It is doubly negative when it happens half way into a long flight sector. Additionally, watch the sauce, cheese and butter.

## Milk and Dairy Products

Choose the low-fat/high-calcium versions. Restrict intake to small amounts of good cheese. Use vegetable oil or margarine in preference to butter. Low-salt, low-fat versions should be selected.

## Yoghurt

Yoghurt is excellent. Natural unsweetened varieties are best. Acidophilus is an important element in the functioning of the bowel. Some yoghurts culture forms of this essential bacterium (e.g. *lactobacillus*).

## Eggs

Cholesterol is high in egg yolk so keep to only two or three eggs a week. Poached or boiled is better than fried. Omelettes and custards can be high in egg content. Nevertheless, eggs are good food.

## Desserts, Cakes, Sweets, Chocolates

Fruits are better than sweet snacks but avoid adding sugar and serve the fruit with yoghurt rather than cream or ice cream. Biscuits, cakes, puddings, sauces, custards and chocolates should be a special (rare) treat.

## Snacks

Fresh fruit is best, or vegetables (celery, carrots, etc.), yoghurt, dry biscuits, or small amounts of nuts or seeds. Health bars are okay. No chips, hot or cold, in any guise.

## Undercooking versus Overcooking

Always steam or poach rather than boil, and grill rather than fry. Undercooked is better for most foods, but some personal taste must be allowed, and also the source of the food. In some areas, well-cooked food, stewed or curried, is safest – provided it is not reheated, nor presented in full public view to customers and to flies.

## Minerals, Vitamins and Nutrients

Previously, we could assume that a daily intake of calories, in the form of a varied diet, would automatically ensure that we had sufficient vitamins and minerals. Later research is suggesting that, in modern society, the food value and eating habits are not the same as they were and that supplementary vitamins and minerals may be essential. The body does not store all vitamins and so a daily need has to met by a daily supply. The general recommendation is that we take supplementary multi-vitamins. We are also only beginning to understand the roles of various elements, minerals and anti-oxidants.

## Salt (Sodium Chloride)

We no longer need to preserve meat or fish in salt and so our taste must change to value food without salt. We have grown accustomed to salt in and on our meals but our diet contains too much. It does take time to lower the salt level as meals initially taste less flavoured. It's like giving up sugar or stopping smoking: our taste buds adjust and we eventually appreciate the taste of the actual ingredients. There is enough salt naturally in all food. If there is a need for supplementary salt to replace that lost by perspiration – for example, in the tropics or when exercising severely – then the doctor will prescribe it.

## Minerals and Mineral Salts

Calcium, iron, magnesium and other elements are essential in our diet. They are inherent in a balanced diet. Iron deficiency is common in women and specific advice should be sought for your individual cycles. New dairy products include high-calcium, low-fat alternatives.

## Sugar

Minimise your intake of unprocessed sugar – preferably none. Eat sweet fruit rather than chocolate. Bananas are great.

## Fast Foods/Take-Away

*So much to eat – so little time.*
- Chinese and Thai – yes but choose those with no MSG and avoid deep fried meals. Steamed rice rather than fried or noodles - in small quantities.
- Indian – okay if high turnover and not reheated - but watch out for the fat in curries.
- Western – burgers are not so good on a regular basis but quite okay occasionally. Have lots of salad or coleslaw and less of the bread, butter and fries. Tomato sauce is good. Have chicken without the skin. Sandwiches are good if you choose the right contents. Grainy bread and no butter is ideal.
- Seafood plus salad – good.
- Fish and chips – not so good. Crumbed, or grilled, fish and chips cooked in vegetable oil – much better. Potato cakes, dim-sims and pluto-pops – not so good.
- Chicken – better without skin and with salad, or coleslaw, rather than mashed potato and gravy.

## Drinking Habits

### Fruit and Vegetable Juices and Water

Good, good, good. Water is best. Drink lots of it. Don't wait until you feel thirsty. Drink regularly. The colour of your urine should be light straw or paler. Any darker means potential dehydration. Too much fruit juice can cause bowel problems and also adds calories.

### Soft Drinks

The mineral-enriched health drinks are for athletes. Use them for severe exercise; otherwise, drink straight mineral water. Avoid sweet, sticky, sugary soft drinks. They make you even thirstier.

### Tea and Coffee

Caffeine is a drug and a stimulant. Coffee has most – especially expresso. Excess caffeine increases pulse rate, prevents sleep, increases urination and therefore fluid loss (it is a *diuretic*), causes headaches and increases the level of stress. It may wake you up but it won't let you rest. Keep caffeine to a minimum (one or two cups a day) and drink plenty of water.

### Dehydration

Without realising, many pilots fly partially incapacitated by *dehydration* or *hypoglycaemia* (low blood sugar). Sixty per cent of body weight is water and a serious loss is incapacitating. We lose, on average, one litre per day and up to five litres a day in hot weather. In temperatures greater than 30 °C we should drink 250 ml of water every 30 minutes to prevent dehydration. Always carry bottled water in the cockpit and sip regularly. As mentioned, caffeine is a diuretic and causes a lowering of the water content of the body, thus it is a negative health influence. Drink extra water when you are having coffee. A party night is severely dehydrating due to alcohol and dancing. Drink plenty of water in parallel with party activities.

The best indicator of dehydration is the amount and colour of your urine. If you do not go as often as usual, and the urine is a darker yellow, then you need to increase your water intake. Have at least eight large glasses of fresh clean water daily plus one per cup of coffee or glass of alcohol, plus more if you are exercising or perspiring.

## Dependencies

### Alcohol

Even small quantities of alcohol in the blood can impair one's performance, with the added danger of relieving anxiety so that the person thinks he is performing marvellously. Alcohol severely affects a person's judgment and abilities; high altitudes, where there is less oxygen, worsens the effect.

Alcohol is a depressant. It lowers the body's natural sensitivities, cautions and fears (showing as over-confidence) and, at the same time, it lowers capabilities – a deadly combination as we know by the road accident statistics. It also represses social mores and allows emotions, that would otherwise be controlled, to run free. Hence loudness, aggression, anger, passion, violence, showing-off and risk-taking. In some personalities it actually causes depression and low self-esteem. The World Health Organisation defines an alcoholic as someone whose excessive drinking repeatedly damages their physical, mental or social life. (I would add their professional life also.)

It takes time for the body to remove alcohol. As a general rule, a pilot must not fly for at least 8 hours after drinking small quantities of alcohol, and increase this time if greater quantities are consumed. After heavy drinking, alcohol may still be in the blood 24 hours later. Sleep will not speed up the removal process; in fact it slows the body processes down and the elimination of alcohol may take even longer. Exercise is better. Having coffee, soup or water between drinks only helps if they are taken *instead* of an alcoholic beverage. Otherwise, the body receives the same total amount of alcohol in the same time – it takes the same time for it to be discarded and for its effects to be removed. Also of concern are the long-term effects of alcohol consumption, such as dependency and damage to kidneys, liver and brain.

Studies suggest that females who drink 14–21 standard drinks per week, or less, and males who drink 21–28 per week, or less, should not suffer long-term problems. A standard drink contains 10 grams of alcohol.

### Non-Prescribed Drugs

Don't touch them.

### Tobacco

Nothing good can be said about smoking. Smoking is detrimental to good health, both in the short term and in the long term. Smoking also significantly decreases a pilot's capacity to perform by reducing the amount of oxygen carried in the blood, replacing it with the useless and potentially poisonous by-products of cigarette smoke. A pilot does not have to be the active smoker to suffer the effects; smoke from any person in the cockpit (or anywhere in the aircraft, if it is small) will affect everyone.

Carbon monoxide, which is present in cigarette smoke, is absorbed into the blood in preference to oxygen. The maximum blood oxygen concentration for a smoker is 90 per cent of that for a non-smoker. This means that, at sea level, a smoker is already as hypoxic as a non-smoker at an altitude of about eight thousand feet. A smoker's night vision is affected by hypoxia – even at sea level. Any oxygen deficiency reduces the body's ability to produce energy (and it affects brain functions).

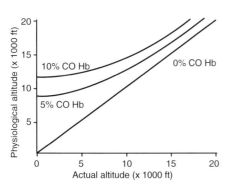

Figure 4-2 **Carboxyhaemoglobin**

The level of carbon monoxide in the blood is measured by the *carboxyhaemo-globin* level (COHb). Smokers with a COHb of 5% are already equivalent to an altitude of 8,000 feet and, at an actual cabin altitude of 5,000 feet, are at a personal altitude of 10,000 feet. (They should already be on oxygen.)

An average smoker will have a COHb level of 4–10%. A passive smoker may be as high as 5%. It is now recognised that cigarette smoking plays a significant role in cardiovascular (heart) diseases, cancer and other mental and physical diseases.

Most doctors will now tell you that whatever else you do for your health do not smoke. Besides, it is unfair to threaten the health of those who choose not to. If you must smoke, smoke alone.

## Medication

All drugs affect the body (as well as the disease they are taken to combat). They may be incompatible with flying. Sedatives, and their side effects, are a prime example of this, also anti-histamines. Some drugs may have long *half-lives*, that is their concentration stays too high for too long, e.g. certain sleeping pills.

Other drugs, called potentiating agents, change or exaggerate the effect of other drugs taken in combination with them, especially alcohol. Until cleared by a doctor, it is safest to assume that *any* drug or medication will temporarily ground you. Common medications considered incompatible with flying include:

- *antibiotics* (e.g. penicillin) used to combat infection – it is the disease rather than the medication that may cause the problems;
- *tranquillisers,* i.e. anti-depressants and sedatives;
- *stimulants* (caffeine, amphetamines) used to maintain wakefulness or suppress appetite;
- *anti-histamines,* often used to combat colds and hay fever;
- drugs for the relief of high blood pressure (when commenced or when the dosage or the drug is altered);

- *analgesics* to relieve pain; and
- *anaesthetics,* with a local, including dental purposes, usually require about 24 hours before returning to flight duties, and, for general anaesthetics, at least 72 hours are required.

## Toxic Substances

Some pilots will come in contact with toxic substances – i.e. fuel additives, cleaning agents, aerial agriculture sprays and powders, defoliants, compressed gases and extinguishants. Don't ever take short-cuts. Observe the special precautions and protections required for each. If in doubt, don't.

# Hygiene/Protection

## Precautions/Protections/Habits

### Exposure to Radiation

There are primarily two kinds of radiation (*electromagnetic radiation*) that pilots need to think about:
- *ionising radiation,* which is nuclear radiation (atomic energy), including alpha, beta, gamma and X-rays, all of which relate to the radiation of ions (ionised atoms); and
- *non-ionising radiation,* which are light rays, including the visible spectrum, infrared, ultraviolet, lasers, radar and microwaves.

Our common exposure is to radiation in the *ultraviolet* spectrum. It causes damage to the eyes and to the skin. Most ultraviolet radiation from the sun is filtered by the ozone layer and the upper levels of the atmosphere. However, pilots are more exposed than most especially at higher altitudes. Eye protection is readily available and the skin should be covered.

Sunburn or prolonged exposure can lead to skin cancer. Sun screen creams are effective. The heat is doubly damaging, causing:
- skin damage (sunburn and possible cancer); and
- dehydration.

Always cover your body with shirts, creams and hats. The degree of cosmic nuclear radiation varies with altitude, season, latitude and duration of exposure. Protection is provided by the atmosphere. However, research is being conducted as there is some fear that pilots who fly regularly at high altitudes could be exposed to risk.

### Drinking Water

The most important advice for maintaining a healthy body is to control what goes into it – food, drink and other substances – and how they are administered. Water is fundamental. Don't drink water from the tap and don't accept water, cordials or ice in your drink unless you know it is suitable for drinking.

## Food

Only eat freshly prepared, and freshly cooked, food. In some areas, meals that have been on open display, or have been reheated, are high-risk substances. Avoid dairy products of unknown origin and soups or stews unless you know they are freshly prepared from new ingredients. Fresh stir-fried meat, seafood and vegetables are safer. Overcooked is safer than that which is undercooked. Eat foods that are locally produced or canned. Pick meals that have a high turnover.

## Sharing

Mucus membranes are those areas of coated, thin, skin, which are particularly sensitive to bleeding, vulnerable to damage and can be a receiving ground for transmitted diseases. They include the mouth, nose, genitalia and anus. The mucus can receive disease and any tear will allow ingestion of bacteria or viruses via mucus, blood and saliva. Don't share lovers, toothbrushes, razors, drinking containers nor eating utensils.

## Bugs

The greatest risks are flies on food and mosquitoes on you. Air-conditioned hotels are relatively safe. In rural areas take precautions such as netting and sprays. Ticks and leeches are a tropical problem. If you are trekking seek expert advice on protection and removal.

# Hygiene

## External

**Washing/Showering.** Regular baths or showers are routine and necessary – but not always available. Aussie ingenuity has developed some marvellous devices in the field.

**Digital Hygiene.** Wash, wash, wash your hands. They are in contact with chemicals, fuel, oil, diseases, other bodies, our own bodies, and then we put them in our eyes, face, nose, ears and mouth. Get into the habit of using gloves.

**Oils.** Dry climates and dry cockpit air can affect sensitive skin and lips. Moisturising creams and oils are very effective.

**Dry Eyes.** Our pressurised, air-conditioned cockpit is dry. Moisten irritated eyes with a water spray, drops or even saliva.

**Cuts and Abrasions.** Always clean and sterilise the cut – lick it, if necessary – remove any visible dirt, apply some form of antiseptic cream and protect the cut with a sterile cover. If there is a foreign object, think carefully before removing it in case the removal will do further damage – e.g. fish-hook, splinter or serrated or rusted metal.

## Internal

**Inoculation and Vaccination.** The greatest protection from disease is inoculation. It prepares the body's defence mechanism for the disease and, consequently, antibodies are built up. Check with your company doctor or travellers' centre for advice on which precautions are advisable for which areas and when. Some vaccinations require a course of injections over several weeks or months, so take advice early. Flu vaccination has its pros and cons.

**Condoms.** Unless you are in a permanent, and trustworthy, relationship, use a condom.

**Roughage.** An important part of our diet is fibre. It is vital for regular cleansing of the intestines and bowel. It is available in natural foods (cereals, etc.) or in supplementary capsules.

**Worms.** These include tapeworm, roundworm, tropical hookworms, and flatworms (*bilharzia*). Some are found in uncooked, or partly cooked, meat. Others are found in contaminated water. They may damage the liver, bladder, and intestines. If you have been based in the Third World for any length of time it would be worthwhile having tests.

### Oral/Dental
**Regular Checks/Repair.** Dental checks should be as frequent as medicals – and corrective treatment is most effective, and much cheaper, if done early.

**Regular Cleaning/Flossing.** Diet affects the need for cleaning. If we live on fruits, cereals and grasses there is less need for mechanical cleaning. However, for our average Western diet, cleaning after each meal would be ideal – every night is a minimum. Take the time to do it thoroughly. Flossing is as important as brushing. We may not be paying due attention to our gums. Ask your dental hygienist about the correct methods for brushing. The electric toothbrush is a major advance.

## Illness and Disease

### Natural Defences
The body and mind are exposed to disease on a daily basis. We have an automatic defence mechanism for most dangers – our immune system.

### Colds/Flu/Middle Ear Infections
Each eardrum has ambient pressure, from the atmosphere or cabin, on one side, and air pressure in the middle ear on the other side – the middle ear being connected indirectly to ambient air via the Eustachian tube. During a climb, atmospheric pressure decreases. The differential pressure across the eardrum forces out the eardrum and also causes air to flow from the middle ear through the Eustachian tubes into the throat. Thus the pressure differential is equalised. Any blockage to this equalisation process is hazardous because of the pain and the potential to perforate the membrane of the eardrum.

Most pressurised aircraft have a low rate of climb (500 ft/min or less), for the cabin and cockpit, allowing adequate time for pressure equalisation to occur through the Eustachian tubes. This means that ear problems during the climb are generally not serious. During descent, however, difficulties with the ears may be more serious due to high rates of descent and problems with pressure equalisation within the middle ear (the air finds it easier to escape through the collapsed tubes during the climb but cannot pass through the collapsed tube during the descent). Further, the greatest proportional pressure differential occurs at lower altitudes, and so the first few thousand feet, on the way up, and the last few, on the way down, are the difficult ones.

Although the cockpit may be kept at 5,000 feet the pressure change is very significant. Moreover, a depressurisation with blocked Eustachian tubes could be mind-blowing. High rates of descent worsen the situation:
- pain in the ears can be debilitating;
- there is a danger of the eardrums collapsing inwards as the external pressure builds up, giving rise to a loss of hearing which may be permanent; and
- in extreme cases, the balance mechanisms could be affected – a situation known as *pressure vertigo*.

Blocked ears can sometimes be cleared by holding the nose and blowing hard (a technique known as the *Valsalva* manoeuvre), by chewing, swallowing or yawning. It is best not to risk flying with a head cold if you have difficulty clearing your ears. Problems can also arise in the sinuses, the cavities in the skull connected by narrow tubes to the nasal/throat passages. Blockages can cause severe pain, equivalent to the most severe headache, such that you cannot concentrate on flying.

## Malaria

Malaria kills more than any other disease. It is a fever caused by parasites in the blood. It is carried by mosquitoes. Prevention is better than the cure, so that mosquito nets, spray, and avoiding areas where you may be bitten are effective.

## Yellow Fever

Yellow fever is another mosquito-borne infection where vaccination is effective.

## Polio

Polio is an acute infection of the central nervous system. In Australia, most children are protected by vaccination.

## Typhoid and Cholera

These could be called the diseases of disaster. The breakdown of sanitation that accompanies natural and unnatural disasters, such as flood, volcanic eruption, earthquake and war, assist in the spread of the diseases. Symptoms of both are similar. Some protection is provided by vaccination but strict attention to hygiene is essential. Clean drinking water is paramount but not always guaranteed. If in doubt, drink bottled or canned drinks.

# Hepatitis

Hepatitis is an inflammation of the liver caused by a virus. There are three commonly identified types:

- Type A is conveyed by drinking water that is contaminated by sewage. It is not so serious as B and most infected people survive without problems.
- Type B is passed by infected blood, saliva and mucus. Type B can be serious and may be life-shortening. However, it generally clears without long-term effects. It is being contained by protective measures. Blood donors are screened.
- Type C is passed by blood, saliva and mucus. It is common among drug users (via sharing needles) but can be managed – if the lifestyle can be changed. It is life-shortening.

# Rabies

Rabies is spread by the bite of an infected animal. The virus moves to the brain and is usually fatal. Inoculation can prevent the illness. It is not present in Australia.

# Sexually Transmitted Diseases

Prevention of sexually transmitted diseases relies on using physical protection and by avoiding promiscuous relationships (multiple partners and one-night stands). HIV/AIDS attacks the immune system and has reached epidemic proportions in some countries. It is also passed by sexual contact and by infected blood and blood carriers such as toothbrushes, razors and needles. It can be passed to unborn children. The risks from blood donations and dental treatments are carefully managed in Western clinics.

# Tetanus

Tetanus occurs when soil bacteria enter a puncture-type wound (generally a deeper wound, such as caused by standing on a rusty nail). It affects the nervous system and, if untreated, results in convulsions and death. Immunisation is very effective and all pilots should make sure they are vaccinated. The booster shot is only required every five or ten years.

# Cancer

In Australia, the greatest risk to an otherwise healthy individual is skin cancer. Smoking has a direct relationship with lung and throat cancer. Older men should be checked regularly for prostate cancer and females for breast and cervical cancers. Most cancers are now preventable or respond to treatment – if detected early.

# Cardiovascular Diseases

Diseases affecting the heart and circulatory system include:

- *Thrombosis.* Coronary thrombosis is caused by blood clots (*embolisms*) obstructing the flow of blood to the heart. The heart cavities may go into irregular spasms (*fibrillation*).
- *Myocardial infarction.* Otherwise know as a heart attack, the death of heart tissue as a result of sudden blockage.

- *Angina.* Any reduction in blood flow deprives part of the heart of oxygen when demand is increased. It is felt as pain in the chest, neck, shoulders and arm, especially the left, that comes and goes with exercise (stress ECG). If untreated, angina causes heart inefficiency and gradual or sudden heart failure.
- *Arteriosclerosis.* The blocking of the arteries by fats is the result of high cholesterol due to poor diet and lack of exercise.
- *Aneurism.* The bursting of an artery, generally in the brain.
- *Stroke.* An interruption to the blood flow in part of the brain can leave loss of sensation or paralysis in almost any part of the body, but commonly on one side of the face.

Cardiovascular risk factors, in order of priority, appear to be:
- family history of heart disease;
- smoking;
- high blood pressure;
- high cholesterol;
- obesity;
- lack of exercise;
- diabetes; and
- stress.

Excessive alcohol consumption may also be an influence, but moderate consumption may actually be beneficial in controlling stress and cholesterol. All of the above factors relate to inheritance or lifestyle, and as pilots, we particularly need to manage the latter.

## Deep Vein Thrombosis (DVT)

DVT sometimes called the *economy class syndrome* has received recent attention in the media. The condition has been known for some years and is not restricted to airline travel. Any prolonged period of inactivity, especially accompanied by dehydration and other risk factors, can lead to the formation of large blood clots, especially in the lower leg/calf area. It can occur on buses, trains or sitting at a desk. However, in a large long-haul aircraft, especially in cramped economy class cabins, and where movement around the cabin is discouraged, the risk is increased.

The clot forms and, when activity is resumed, it can then move to an area of the heart or lungs that may then lead to serious, even fatal, consequences.

### Risk Factors

The risk of clotting is enhanced by inactivity (reduced blood circulation), dehydration (reduced circulation and thickening of the blood), smoking, kidney disease, oral contraceptive pill, later stages of pregnancy (in some women) and recent surgery.

### Prevention

The vital rule is to mobilise the lower leg, ankle and toes. Even twiddling toes and rotating the feet helps. Walk around occasionally if possible. Stretch and tense muscles.

Drink water regularly and avoid drinks that are diuretic: coffee, tea and alcohol dehydrate the body. Don't bomb out by taking large amounts of alcohol or sleeping pills in order to sleep through the long-haul flights. This technique is fraught with danger as the circulation is reduced to dangerous levels. Your doctor may prescribe small doses of aspirin to thin the blood and improve circulation.

Check before flight if you are in any of the above risk categories. Plan long flights in short sectors if possible. If you have a choice of leaving the aircraft while at a transit stop do so – go to the terminal and walk around.

### Symptoms

In flight, or shortly after, any swelling or pain in the calf/lower leg that does not dissipate – especially if the pain is in one leg and not the other. Any breathlessness, palpitations or chest pain should be investigated. The clot can be detected by ultrasound and can be removed before causing catastrophic symptoms.

### Migraine and Headaches

Headaches can be compromising due to stress, pain, distraction and reduced attention. Migraine headaches are due to the constriction of the arteries in a particular part of the brain. They can be totally incapacitating if accompanied by vision impairment, nausea, vomiting, severe pain and over-sensitivity to light and sound. Some, rare, migraine attacks are accompanied by temporary, partial paralysis (one arm or one side of the body). Migraine headaches seem to be triggered by allergic reactions to certain foods such as cheese or chocolate, by stress or by the removal of stress or by the menstrual cycle. Many are short lived and may be related to temporary circumstances – but seek medical advice. There are treatments that are sometimes, but not always, effective. Heredity seems to be a significant factor in our susceptibility to migraine attack.

### Epilepsy

Epilepsy is an electrical disturbance within the brain. It can cause visible reactions such as fits or loss of consciousness.

### Diabetes

Diabetes is a condition where the body cannot produce sufficient insulin. Insulin is needed for the metabolism of glucose and thus the production of energy. Absence of insulin leads to an excess of unprocessed glucose – a serious situation. It is controlled by diet, oral medication or by self-administered injections.

### Ageing

**Alzheimer's Disease**

Recent reports suggest that folic acid may be a stabilising influence that may deter the conditions that are conducive to Alzheimer's disease. Folic acid is available in the *folates* – from food such as tomatoes and in tablet form. Above all, stay mentally active. The brain, like a muscle, needs regular and demanding exercise. Be careful of approaching retirement – plan ahead.

## Memory Loss – Short-Term Memory

It is usual to notice a loss of short-term memory with ageing. Write everything down.

## Sight and Hearing

A form of long-sightedness *(presbyopia)* and loss of hearing are normal after forty. Cataracts are the clouding over of the soft jelly of the lens of the eye. Laser treatment is simple and effective.

## Gout

Gout is the result of an excess of uric acid in the blood that crystallises in the joints – especially worn or damaged joints of the toes, feet, ankles and fingers. It is exceedingly painful and can prevent work and sleep. There are effective preventative treatments. The pain can be controlled by anti-inflammatory tablets, but these may cause internal bleeding in some patients. The symptoms of gout can be confused with arthritis.

## Lower Back Pain

An inherent part of the pilot's career is the prospect of lower back pain due to poor posture, high *g*, pushing aircraft, lifting baggage or rolling fuel drums. Take care of your back. The pain is best eased by gentle exercise rather than bed. Sometimes the pain is caused by worn discs in between the vertebra allowing the spinal nerves to be pinched. This causes a particular muscle to go into *spasm* (total contraction). Massage, acupuncture and anti-inflammatories may help. Seek expert guidance but be cautious about undergoing surgery.

## Varicose Veins

Varicose veins are enlarged, twisted and protruding veins, usually in the lower legs in the rear, inside calf area. They are generally only a nuisance because of their appearance. If there is discomfort, tingling or loss of sensation there could be a constriction that should be treated. They can be removed. They seem to be hereditary.

## Piles

The pilot's, and the pregnant woman's, disease. Haemorrhoids are anal varicose veins. They are caused by prolonged sitting, constipation and consequent, forced defecation. They are indicated by pain or slight bleeding. They are fairly common. They are not serious and are uncomfortable rather than painful. They can be prevented, and the disturbance minimised, by proper diet and exercise.

# Incapacitation

## Recognition, Prevention and Remedy

### Loss of Consciousness

Any loss of consciousness is a cause of concern. Generally, it will be either a fit or a faint. A faint is a change in consciousness caused by disturbance to blood flow to the brain due to loss of blood, shock, standing quickly after sitting (especially when hot or dehydrated), lack of food or lack of fluids. A fit or a seizure usually is a symptom of epilepsy that involves electrical disturbances of the brain, even though it can occur without any previous history. However, a fit, or loss of consciousness, can result from head injury from some years previously.

## Gastroenteritis

Gastrointestinal disorders are *the* most common cause of in-flight incapacitation. They may result from an improperly prepared meal (food poisoning), impure drinking water or infection. Onset may be almost immediate following consumption of the food or drink, or it may not become evident for some hours. Even then, onset may be very sudden. The stomach pains, nausea, diarrhoea and vomiting that accompany food poisoning can make it physically impossible to perform pilot duties. Some of the reflexes are uncontrollable (projectile vomiting and diarrhoea – sometimes simultaneously). A wise precaution is never to have the same meal as your crew. For the day prior to flight, avoid foods that are associated with food poisoning, including shellfish, fish, mayonnaise, creams, overripe and thin-skinned fruits, uncooked foods such as salads and raw foods, and old, tired, food (e.g. food that has been cooked, stored or reheated for some time or several times). If you suspect that some symptoms of food poisoning are present or forthcoming, do not take the chance – don't fly. After the event you will be dehydrated and weak – very weak. You should not fly for at least 72 hours after the last symptoms of even a mild case of food poisoning. Gastroenteritis, flu, food poisoning, and dysentery can leave you sitting on the toilet and vomiting simultaneously. You cannot possibly fly with those symptoms. You are literally and totally incapacitated.

## Heart Attack or Stroke

Generally presented by severe incapacitation due to pain or collapse. However, report any severe chest pain, shortness of breath or palpitations to your other crew member. Delegate pilot-flying duties and try to relax.

## Pain and Pain Management

It is not macho to tolerate pain. Any lingering pain, sharp pain or severe pain at least deserves some investigation. Stress can cause tightening and pain in the chest or abdomen which may be interpreted as ulcers or heart problems. They are probably not serious – but have them checked anyway. Similarly, head and neck pain. Back pain is a condition that pilots are liable to feel, but it can be debilitating and prevent concentration on the flight.

## Severe Headache/Migraine

A blinding headache can be so distracting as to prevent a pilot from operating. Mostly there are warnings and there is time to hand over. If vision is becoming affected hand over control of the aircraft.

## Recognition of Incapacitation

Incapacitation can be represented by total collapse, spasms, fits, irrational behaviour, unconsciousness and obvious symptoms of pain or distress, It can also be very subtle and only be noticed by irrational decisions, confusion, changed speech, lapses in memory, incoherence and vague loss of awareness. It is difficult to judge. Like the *Mutiny On The Bounty*, you must act in accordance with your judgement and your conscience and be prepared to justify your actions later. There is only one rule. If you think that the safety of the aircraft could be prejudiced, act. You can begin, quite effectively and reasonably, by suggesting that you fly the aircraft and that the suspect crew member takes a rest. You can ask the purser to visit the flight deck and give the crew member a glass of water. Check his or her eyes and coherence. Suggest that he or she may have eaten something unfavourable or be dehydrated. Suggest a rest in the cabin and that you will give notification when about to land. Have a crew member stay with any other sick crew members.

## Coping Strategies for Crew Incapacitation

There are fairly obvious steps in immediate response to a fellow pilot who appears to have suffered sudden incapacitation:

- isolation from the controls;
- ensure the flightpath of the aircraft is under control;
- alert the cabin crew and ask for assistance; and
- provide the affected member with appropriate attention.

In general:

- placement in the spare crew seat or on the floor;
- removal of any constrictive clothing such as ties and belt;
- ensure airways are clear;
- check pulse and breathing;
- fit a crew oxygen mask if appropriate;
- apply a cold, wet, towel to the forehead;
- consider diverting to a nearer airfield with ambulance/hospital availability; and
- declare an emergency.

Ask the cabin crew to check if there is a doctor is on board.

## Chapter 5

# Stress, Arousal, Fatigue and Sleep

## Stress

### Stress and Distress

Stress is normal. Stress is healthy. Unresolved stress is not. Stress is the result of our body and mind preparing to deal with a crisis. It is when the crisis remains unresolved that damage can occur. Stress results from situations in which we are placed requiring us to make conscious decisions so as to be able to proceed. The risk associated with the decision and our confidence in coping with the outcome determines the level of stress. Training and preparation for the situation helps considerably to reduce the associated stress. If we defer the decision, or are unable to resolve the situation, then unhealthy stress results.

For example, consider engine failure. We are stressed but we have to make an immediate decision about where to land. If the decision is made, the stress disappears even before we have landed; we fall back on our training. A contrary case exists when, for example, a personal relationship is breaking down. We are stressed but we don't seem to be able to solve the communication problem. We remain stressed and yet have to go about our daily lives, including flying. There is a constant tension that adds a burden and distraction to everything we do. Everything is just that much more difficult. If the combined situation and personal stress accumulates, then we can be over-stressed – distressed. We can manage stress by resolving the *loose end,* by avoiding additional stress until the situation is resolved or seeking help to resolve the situation. There is no discredit in seeking expert advice. It is not giving in. It is professional, and personal, common sense.

The cause of the stress is called a stressor. Exposure to constant stress can bring about changes in the balance of hormones in the body, which threatens health. Also, exposure to one form of stress tends to diminish the resistance to other forms. A potential stressor can be *acute* in the sense that it is immediate and disappears after a short time; another can be *chronic,* long lasting and fatiguing. It is important for general health, and for longevity, that all stress and demand is managed so as not to be stressful for us, as much as is possible.

### Responding to Demands and Stimuli

Every person operates under some degree of stress, which serves as a stimulus to act. The person responds to demands. For a pilot, demands are many and varied. The maintenance will include feedback on the desired flightpath and airspeed, cockpit procedures, navigation requirements, radio procedures, etc., often happening almost simultaneously. But the pilot is a human and so the flight stresses are

added to the stress of daily life. How well a person copes with these demands varies with the person's make-up, and this may depend on:
* general health;
* personality, and how at ease the person feels;
* having a happy and organised personal life;
* sufficient rest having been taken;
* the degree of preparation for the task; and
* the person's intelligence and aptitude for the activity.

A particular situation can cause differing degrees of difficulty for different people, and in the same person under different circumstances. The situation can be a stressor for one person and routine for another. For instance, a strong crosswind on final approach will be more demanding for a trainee pilot than for an experienced and in-current-practice one.

However, if the experienced pilot were tired or fatigued, concerned about family life, and trying to cope with an emergency, then his/her stress level might be equally high during the crosswind approach.

## Coping with Stress

Some stress is necessary. The risk is not the stress itself, but an overload of it and an inability to cope.

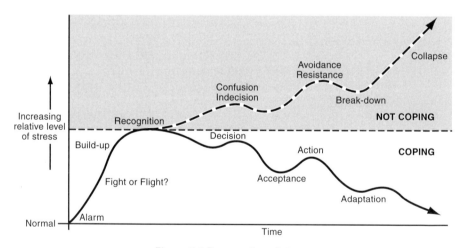

Figure 5-1 **Progression of stress**

In the case of demands on your brain's computing capacity – cognitive load and overload – things are very different. For a start, while the 'upslope' of the stimulus response curve is much the same – as the demand increases, your performance improves to cope – the breakdown divergence is dramatically and dangerously different, as shown here, and may lead to total collapse.

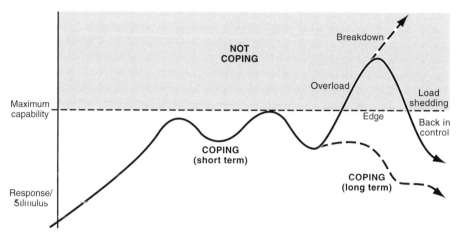

Figure 5-2 **Overload**

The cognitive effects of increasing stress are losing the plot, forgetting, inability to concentrate and difficulty in making decisions. Eventually, it reaches overload. The cognitive overload phenomenon is discussed later. It is worth stating – often – that there is a huge difference in the physical and cognitive responses to peaks of load.

However, as you know, pilots can and do become overloaded, having to process a multitude of information sources and channels, including uncertainty and anxiety. If you have experienced utter confusion – i.e. you have gone over the edge – you know that the only way to recover the perspective (control + priority) is through massive load-shedding, by reverting to the basics. (The case exists, of course, powerfully, for load-shedding before you go over the edge, and thus keeping things under control.) You can sense the presence of adrenalin in many ways. For example:

- a feeling of 'flushing' or warmth from the heightened blood flow, through the muscles (and the corresponding tendency to 'clench'); or
- sensations of prickly skin or scalp due to altered blood movement arrangements, etc.

The overall sense of alertness – *we are ready!!!* – can also be detected. In cognitive terms, it can be 'read' as 'standby to receive information'. All of these sensations and impressions go back to the brain via the feedback mechanism to confirm that adrenalin is running, doing its thing, and either in need of, or not in need of, adjustment – 'send more', 'send less'. You can use feedback to your advantage. The signal to issue adrenalin is activated through an autonomic process not subject to conscious control – and thus it can easily be fooled. Say you are flying at cruise height from Rome to London. It's going to be 4 hours before descent point and the most exciting thing you will do for most of that time is turn through maybe 20 degrees. This is a classic case of absence of stimulus over time. You progressively become very under-aroused, nearly asleep.

Advice is to take active control over your mental attention. Consciously force the pace and adopt an entirely artificial but very high rate of searching out information. Focus on mental problems – the traffic over Paris, the weather at Heathrow, alternatives in the event of decompression, etc. The brain then sees a need to process information – i.e. it receives a stimulus – and activates the adrenalin pump. If you actively maintain your state of artificial arousal, you will continue to receive the adrenalin 'boost'. Having said all that, it is very difficult. However, it can be done. (Long-haul pilots use the technique extensively.) As with any skill, you'll get better with practice. And you don't need to be in an aircraft. You can practise in the car, or just walking around. It is a very handy skill both in the air and in other circumstances. So don't wait till you need it. If you've practised, and become familiar with it, you'll know it is there and effective when you need it.

Tolerance to stress is increased by physical and psychological fitness. Being healthy, well rested, on top of your job, on top of your life, and ready to face challenges allows you to cope. Reduce the level of stress by tying up loose ends if you can, giving you a greater capacity to handle new situations that might arise. Resolve emotional problems to a point where they do not interfere with your work. Knowledge is also important, such as knowing the emergency procedures for your aeroplane so that you can confidently cope with basic emergencies. Manage time efficiently so that you are never rushed. Running late or running out of time is a major stressor in all facets of our lives. Stress can also be reduced if you control your environment as much as possible, keeping unwanted noise and vibration to a minimum, for instance, and maintaining a comfortable ambient temperature.

### Physical Preparation

- Be fit and well exercised – eat sensibly and eat regularly.
- Sleep well and go flying with plenty of sleep-hours in credit.
- Take time out to relax – learn some relaxation techniques.
- Manage your time so that you do not have to rush.
- Control your physical environment (noise, temperature, humidity).
- Manage your finances – a major stressor.

### Psychological Preparation

- Be well prepared regarding knowledge, skills, and standard operating procedures.
- Have well-placed confidence in your ability (practise regularly).
- Leave your domestic and financial worries at home – preferably arrange your life so that you have these matters well under control – have a well-rounded social and/or family life (strive for it).
- Do not allow yourself to procrastinate – tackle your problems and solve them, or at least have a timetable for attempting to solve them. Seek help. Seek advice.
- Don't be afraid to discuss concerns. Share your problems.
- Try not to allow yourself to become over-excited about non-events (mountains out of mole-hills), or to become resigned and pessimistic unnecessarily – control your psychological environment.

You will be equipped to manage the normal demands of life, as suggested above, by the way you think and behave (cognitive/behavioural techniques), relaxation, and by managing your time. But sometimes you find yourself in one of those situations that arise where, even though you are generally in control of your life, the current situation seems about to get out of hand. You need to recognise this, and take appropriate action.

## Overload

If the demands become too much, the person is overloaded, and performance drops dramatically. Different people can cope with different levels of stress. Each one of us, though, has probably been overloaded at one time or another. It is important then that we develop a strategy to prevent overloads, or to cope with them if they occur. Family and social life should be under control. If not, this can cause a high level of stress. Generally good health and fitness is also important. Always be well rested and well prepared, so that you can approach the task in a responsible, but natural and easy manner. Knowledge, experience and flight proficiency will keep stress levels manageable.

## General Adaptation Syndrome

This syndrome postulates that there are three stages in the progress of one's adaptation to stress:

* alarm;
* resistance; and
* collapse.

People generally learn to adjust their behaviour to a new challenge quite quickly before moving on to the resistance stage, where they appear to be coping well. But there comes the time when coping abilities are exhausted, and 'something has to give'. Note that we are not saying that stress must be avoided – on the contrary. Most of us get pleasure from doing some task well, especially if it challenges our capabilities.

## Perceived Stressors

Stress is the degree of tension or strain resulting from a demanding situation, environment or relationship. It can be positive or negative. When we react to perceived pressures, a response is usually demanded from the brain. These perceived pressures may not, in fact, be real pressures – something which is very important for us to appreciate when we find ourselves having to deal with a potential overload.

### Imagination

The highly intelligent, imaginative brain is prone to higher levels of stress as the perceived problems and outcomes are more complex and potentially more damaging, hence the unfortunate dependence on alcohol and drugs in professional people. Their perceived stress is added to the high levels of actual stress. The total stress can be intolerable. Problems don't go away by themselves. People who dwell on potential problems can *worry themselves to death*. If the problem can't be solved, a solution is to fill the brain with other tasks that prevent dwelling on the particular stressor. That is why golf, painting, dancing and sailing are so successful. The required concentration removes any capacity to worry about other things. In some people meditation works successfully – others cannot remove the distraction of the problem and therefore cannot relax. It depends on our personal make-up. We each need to find our personal stress distractor.

*The first question to ask, once you decide that you want to reduce the level of stress, is: 'Does the stressor – the item causing the stress – really exist? Or am I exaggerating its importance, risk or outcomes (a mountain out of a mole-hill)?'*

## Physical Threat – Fright, Fight or Flight?

A sudden fright, like the perception of physical danger, causes your brain to rapidly prepare for action. The sympathetic nervous system responds by triggering the adrenal gland. The body prepares for action. The adrenal gland sends out the hormone *adrenalin* that stimulates your body physically and psychologically to meet the threat – to fight or to flee. You have no doubt experienced the sudden rush of adrenalin on occasions. The heart rate increases quickly, certain blood vessels constrict to divert blood to where it is most needed for physical action, and many other changes occur in the body.

Your performance will be enhanced, within the limits of your experience and training. Your responses may be quick and exact – the well-practised ones may even be automatic – and you will be very sensitive to your surroundings. In cases like this, the stimuli can enhance the level at which you function. Whether you fight or flee depends on many things, including personality and aptitude (or suitability) for the job, and the level of perceived danger. It is when you do nothing, and feel trapped, that stress becomes a negative factor. The preparation of the body and mind to fight or flee is a normal response, but it should be followed by action. Stress becomes debilitating where there is no action. There is no release. In the modern work and home environments, there are many such unresolved situations:

- an unfriendly or unrewarding work environment that must be tolerated because of financial commitments;
- excess financial commitments or debts demanding excessive work; and
- an unpleasant domestic environment (e.g. accepted 'for the sake of the children' or due to inability to get out).

In these, and other similar situations, the individual is under an inappropriate level of continuous stress. Any additional demand can take a person over their personal limit.

## Non-Physical Threat

Some stressful situations arise, not from a perceived physical threat, but from intellectual, psychological and emotional causes. These could be the pressure of time (too much to do in too little time), difficult decisions to be made (to continue into deteriorating weather ahead or to divert to an alternate aerodrome), a lack of self-confidence, a strained personal relationship, or an emotional overload. Consider the golfer facing a 2-metre putt. In a social game, the stress level is low. In a competition where the successful putt could win the million-dollar tournament, the stress level is high. The amateur player will also be more stressed than the confident, experienced professional. The level of stress is a function of the difficulty of the task, the probability of success or risk of failure, and the reward for success versus the consequences of failure. Training and practice for equivalent scenarios are the means to contain our personal stress.

Some psychological or emotional demands, such as a failing personal relationship, can be debilitating on a long-term or chronic basis, whereas some intellectual pressure can prepare you for quick mental activity. Some stimuli can be performance-enhancing; other types can be inhibiting. In all cases, some action must be taken. Prolonged stress affects your physical health.

### Psychological and Emotional Stress

Psychological and emotional stress can be caused by problems at home. Domestic-related stress can be very damaging to a pilot. If distracted by emotional problems during highly charged periods such as following the death of a spouse or child (considered the most stressful life experience), a divorce, or when experiencing severe financial difficulties, responsible pilots should consider grounding themselves. Domestic-related problems can lead to lack of sleep, chronic fatigue, emotional instability, and a dangerous flight operation.

## Environmental Stressors

If you are working in an environment that differs from the ideal environment for humans – for instance, in an environment which is excessively hot, cold, noisy, damp, dry, turbulent, vibrating, dark, light, smelly, or lacking in oxygen – you can become tired and stressed more quickly.

### Stress Caused by Heat (Hyperthermia) and Lack of Humidity

In very high environmental temperatures, say 35 °C and above, the body struggles to keep its internal temperature at just under 37 °C and so prevent itself from overheating *(hyperthermia)*. The perspiration rate, heart rate and blood pressure all increase. In a humid atmosphere, as opposed to a hot, dry atmosphere, your perspiration will tend not to evaporate, hence no latent heat is absorbed into the air from your skin, so there is a greater tendency for your body to overheat. Your attention becomes narrowed and restricted, affecting your decision-making. Try to take a drink before you actually become thirsty, since thirst is a symptom that you are already becoming dehydrated. In fact, you should drink 250 ml of water every 30 minutes to prevent dehydration when air temperatures are above 30 °C. Above 30 °, heart rate and blood pressure increase as a result.

To minimise heat stress you should try to control the environmental temperature, and, most importantly, drink enough fluids. Water is ideal. Remember that tasks outside the cockpit prior to flight, such as loading the aircraft or flight planning, or even just standing or sitting in high temperatures, may cause your body to overheat and/or dehydrate. Take appropriate measures by drinking fluids, staying under shade, and not rushing. Humidity levels also affect our stress levels. Humidity in a cockpit can fall as low as 5%. The human body's comfort range is within 40–60% relative humidity.

## Stress Caused by Cold (Hypothermia)

In a cold environment, the body automatically sends more blood to the body core, rather than to the extremities. This is an attempt to keep the internal temperature at about 37 °C by minimising heat loss from the skin. Heat loss can occur by:

- radiation from exposed areas of skin, especially from your head, which has many blood vessels near the surface of your scalp;
- conduction as wind flows across your skin and carries heat away, which is known as the wind-chill factor; and
- evaporation of perspiration or other moisture from your skin, which causes cooling by absorbing heat from the skin and underlying blood vessels, and using it to change the state of the moisture from liquid to vapour (latent evaporation).

In low temperatures, your toes and fingers may feel cold, your muscles might feel stiff and weak, you may feel tired and drowsy, and you might start to shiver – this is an attempt by your body to generate warmth by muscle activity. It is said that if your hands and feet feel comfortable, then 'all is well'. Most people normally clothed are comfortable around 20 °C.

## Stress Caused by Vibration

Vibrations transmitted to the body from the aircraft via the seat, seatbelts and the floor can make you feel uncomfortable, distract you from your main tasks, and lead to fatigue. A vibrating instrument panel may make the instruments difficult to read. Severe vibration may even cause your eyeballs to vibrate, making it almost impossible to read your flight instruments or your navigation charts, or to scan for other aircraft. Even though it might be impossible to reduce the vibration from the aircraft itself, the vibration reaching your body can be reduced by well-mounted and well-cushioned seats.

## Stress Caused by Turbulence

Turbulence causes irregular movements of the aircraft, varying from small movements associated with slight turbulence to very strong movements that may damage the aircraft associated with severe turbulence. Turbulence can cause discomfort to the pilot and passengers by shaking them around, exerting unusual *g*-forces on them, and perhaps causing motion sickness. It may cause the instrument panel to vibrate or the eyeballs to judder, making it difficult to read the instruments, and it may make the aircraft very difficult to control.

## Stress Caused by Noise

Excessive noise in the cockpit, especially if it is high pitched and loud, can cause stress and fatigue. An industry limit for continuous noise is 85 dB (decibels), with ear protection required above this level. Noise levels in a typical cockpit are in the range of 75–80 dB, but this is only background noise, and noise from radio messages will superimpose on it. Noise above about 90 dB will cause stress that raises your arousal into the poor performance area, making you irritable, and leading to fatigue. Inability to sleep due to environmental noise is called *situational insomnia*. Your attention span becomes narrowed and restricted. Above about 80 dB, you should wear protection to avoid stress damage to your ears. Stress can also be caused by having to strain to understand radio messages against a high background noise level. With your ears protected from background engine and air noise by a high-quality headset, you should be able to hear radio messages even when the volume is quite low.

## Stress Caused by Being Uncomfortable

The nature of our job as pilots is that we are confined to sitting in small cockpits for long periods of time. The stress of sitting in a noisy, vibrating aircraft for long periods, and having to cope with the usual problems of flight, such as turbulence, navigation, radio calls, and so on, can lead to an accumulation of stress and fatigue. The best means of combating this form of stress is to keep yourself fit, be well rested prior to flight, maintain a good posture (sit well back into the seat and ensure your lower back is well supported), and exercise periodically by wiggling your toes and feet and stretching your arms. It is also important to be appropriately dressed for the job. Wearing too much or too little clothing will make you uncomfortable, and this is distracting. You should also make sure that your clothes fit well. There are few things worse than a tight shirt collar, tight trousers, or tight shoes.

## Stress Caused by Feeling Unwell

If feeling unwell, you may be easily overloaded and prone to becoming fatigued. Your body will be using up energy to combat the illness, and so you will have less energy available for other tasks. Your general performance will be much lower than normal.

If you have a headache, an upper respiratory tract infection, a sporting or other injury, a stomach upset, hay fever or a sneezing attack, you should consider whether to commence your flight. If you feel unwell in flight, then you should consider landing immediately. Motion sickness (feeling airsick) can make a person feel very low and uninterested in events. It is not confined to new student pilots and passengers – on rare occasions even experienced pilots feel airsick. Their knowledge that it might cause them to feel apathetic, however, is some protection against lowered performance. A pilot will also be subject to unnecessary stress if not eating regularly or well, resulting in possibly being *hypoglycaemic*, a low blood sugar level. Its symptoms are headache, stomach pain, lack of energy, nervousness and shaking. Hypoglycaemia can be relieved in the short term by eating a snack, e.g. a banana or chocolate.

## Stress Caused by Eye Strain

Eye strain due to impaired vision or poor lighting can cause stress and fatigue. Impaired vision can be remedied with glasses or contact lenses. The solution to bad lighting is obvious. This need not mean that the whole cockpit should be brightly lit when all you need to see are the instruments and your charts – simply turn the instrument lights up and use a small spotlight or torch for your charts. If the main cabin lights are turned up too brightly, you may have to strain your eyes to scan outside for other aircraft and weather.

## Stress Caused by Flashing or Strobing Lights

A flashing light is designed to attract attention, usually to other vehicles or aircraft. Seeing a flashing light will raise your level of alertness. If, however, the warning does not apply to you, the flashing light may be very distracting and even fatiguing. For instance, a flashing amber light from a fuel truck parked right in front of your cockpit at night can be very distracting if you are trying to complete your flight preparation tasks.

Reflected light from your own strobe lights when flying in cloud or drizzle at night can be highly distracting, so turn the strobes off temporarily: other aircraft will not be able to see them while you are in cloud anyway.

## Stress Caused by Concentration

Skill stress that leads to fatigue can result if you have to maintain a high level of performance for an extended period; for instance, hand-flying on instruments in turbulent IFR conditions, or for a student pilot even straight and level visual flying.

## Stress Caused by Lack of Sleep

A lack of restful sleep leaves a pilot fatigued, and needing to struggle to stay awake to handle the demands of flying. The pilot has to fight off sleep, and really force concentration, leading to a high stress level and even deeper fatigue. It is a vicious circle. The solution to this is, of course, not to fly unless well rested.

## Psychological and Emotional Stressors

Psychological or emotional stress can arise from a number of sources and constitutes a major source of overload. It could be work related (a difficult flight about to begin, or a strained relationship with management or colleagues), or it could have a domestic cause (marital or financial problems).

The result of psychological stress is that a pilot may be over-aroused and move into the area of poor performance:

- concentrating on a single problem and not maintaining a complete overview of the flight;
- exhibiting poor judgement;
- becoming disoriented quite easily;

- being distracted from prime tasks;
- taking a resigned attitude to problems ('why does this always happen to me?'); and
- becoming fatigued (worn-out, burnt-out) at an early stage.

## Work-Related Psychological Stress (Workload)

Most pilots experience a certain amount of apprehension regarding a forthcoming flight, but this is quite normal and can raise the level of arousal into the optimum area for good performance. A pilot who is stressed and over-anxious, however, may be too highly aroused to perform well – a common situation with inexperienced student pilots, and in many experienced pilots who are facing a demanding flight. Actual workload in flight should be tailored, by the design of hardware and procedures, to remain within the capability of the human operators – with some reserves.

## Anxiety

Anxiety is the extreme worry that results when a person is overloaded, particularly for prolonged periods. It is a state of being uneasy, apprehensive or worried about what may happen, and experiencing a generalised, pervasive fear.

An anxious person will probably perform poorly – the condition is often apparent to a sensitive observer (such as a flying instructor or cockpit colleague) by signs of:
- physical discomfort, such as perspiring, nervous twitching, a dry mouth, breathing difficulties, panting, increased heart rate;
- inappropriate behaviour, such as laughing or singing at inappropriate times, painstaking self-control, extreme over-cooperation, rapid changes in emotion, impulsiveness or extreme passivity;
- unreliable behaviour – not showing up, not consistent, not ready, tending to avoid responsibility;
- mood changes, perhaps from extreme light-heartedness to depression;
- unreasonable behaviour, unnecessary anger, impatient/rude behaviour, self criticism;
- fatigue – the extreme and deep tiredness that can result from being under pressure for too long; and
- incorrect thought processes, poor concentration, or concentrating on one point to the exclusion of others, an inability to set reasonable priorities, forgetting important items such as the use of flaps for take-off or on final approach, or failing to read a checklist.

A person suffering from a chronic stress overload may show a personality change, behave poorly and erratically towards others, perform at a low level, become ill with stomach pains or headaches, drink, smoke or eat excessively, and may well become accident-prone.

Anxiety is a dangerous condition, and top priority should be given to reducing the anxiety level before making a flight. It is advisable to seek expert advice or counselling. Certainly remove the cause (if it can be identified) and have plenty of deep rest, exercise, and perhaps a holiday (but not if you have to return to the same unresolved situation).

## Symptoms of Stress

Symptoms of stress may be classified into three main classes: physiological, behavioural and mental.
- *Physiological symptoms* are those that affect the body, such as increased heartbeat, sweating and butterflies in the stomach.
- *Behavioural characteristics* include obvious activities, such as laughing, hand wringing, speech difficulties and increased frequency of urination.
- *Mental symptoms* can be divided into cognitive or thinking symptoms such as forgetfulness and lack of confidence, and subjective or emotional symptoms such as aggression and depression.

### Recognising a Potential Overload

The first step in coping with a potential overload is to recognise its presence. As we have seen, a certain amount of pressure is essential if we are to live a normal life and handle everyday problems, both at home and in our workplace, but an overload can drastically reduce our performance and our happiness. Remember that we respond to perceived pressures (rather than actual pressures), and to our perceived ability to handle these pressures (rather than our actual ability). After consideration, you might find that the excessive pressures are not there to begin with or, if they are, your ability is such that you can confidently handle them.

### Taking Action

Coping satisfactorily with stress usually involves taking action to:
- remove the cause (fight); or
- remove yourself (flight).

For instance, you can minimise the cause of noise stress by wearing a good headset. You can minimise the cause of domestic unhappiness by discussing matters openly with your partner. These actions will remove or reduce the cause of the stress. On the other hand, you can remove the stress caused from learning to fly aerobatics by giving up aerobatics and taking up something less demanding – in other words, by removing yourself from the scene. You can remove the stress of flying in severe turbulence near a thunderstorm by turning back or landing – you will not remove the turbulence, but you will take yourself away from its stressful effect. You can remove (or reduce) the stress caused by an unhappy relationship by moving out, physically and psychologically.

Acute stress is usually easily relieved. For instance, if you are under pressure of time to solve an undercarriage problem during an approach to land, make a missed approach and join a holding pattern. You can now take longer to resolve the problem, and the pressure of time is relieved. Chronic long-term stress is another matter, and resolving it may mean a change in lifestyle or activity. Consult your partner, your doctor, your adviser, your minister or priest, a friend, a counsellor, or some other appropriate person. Prolonged exposure to stress will accelerate the ageing process, unbalance the body chemistry, and lead to mental and physical illness – certainly no way to have a happy life.

## Unacceptable Means of Coping with Stress

There are some means of trying to cope with stress that are not really acceptable if you want to be a competent pilot, such as:

- closing your eyes to the problem and pretending it does not exist (*cognitive coping*); or
- taking medication, drugs or alcohol to relieve the symptoms of the stress, but not its cause (sometimes referred to as *symptom-directed coping*).

The body and mind have certain defence mechanisms that sometimes operate subconsciously to remove painful matters from our consciousness. Defence mechanisms remove the symptoms but not the cause, and this can be dangerous for a pilot. Common defence mechanisms include:

- lack of awareness whereby the brain subconsciously denies/represses the existence of the stressor;
- rationalisation through a subconscious attempt to justify actions that would otherwise be unacceptable, often indicated by a person substituting excuses for certain behaviour rather than logical reasons;
- phantom illness developed to avoid having to face up to reality;
- daydreaming by staring into space as a means of mentally escaping by creating a fantasy of being in more pleasant surroundings or circumstances;
- resignation by being mentally lost or bewildered, and ready to accept whatever comes, including defeat; and
- anger that may range from mild expressions of frustration, such as the use of bad language, to more violent expressions of physical behaviour, such as rough use of the flight controls.

None of these attempts to cope with stress will actually eliminate the problem. Instead, some realistic method of managing the load should be adopted.

## Avoiding Self-Imposed Stress

To some extent, the pilot has some control over the stress level, and can often defuse the situation.

Some ways in which this can be done are:

- Make early decisions – turn back or divert before flying into bad conditions, or land well before last light if necessary.
- Do not accept an air traffic control VFR clearance leading into clouds – keep clear of cloud and request a new clearance.
- Do not be distracted from checklists: request your passengers, flight instructor, or examiner not to interrupt.
- Do not interrupt or change your usual routines unnecessarily.
- Request ATC to stand by if you are busy coping with an emergency or having trouble handling the aeroplane – flightpath and airspeed always come first.
- Be prepared for delays – weather may force a delay, as can refuelling and aircraft unserviceabilities; always allow a time buffer, even for the drive to the airport.
- Do not press on regardless – many situations arise because of lack of decision.

## Arousal

How well you respond to a task also depends on your state of arousal. Many types of stimuli increase your arousal level – for instance, a fright – whereas other types of stimuli decrease your arousal level – such as fatigue. Arousal can be measured by the presence of adrenalin in the blood stream, causing high levels of alertness.

A low level of arousal is associated with deep sleep, fatigue, sleep deprivation, a lack of motivation, and low body temperature, which will occur naturally when internal body temperature is at a low point in its circadian rhythm. A high level of arousal is associated with fear, panic, under-confidence and narrowing of attention. Being under-aroused – for instance, over-confident, overly casual or apathetic – may lead to poor performance of a task; being over-aroused – for instance, highly keyed up and tense – will also lead to poor performance.

Between these two extremes, however, there is a region of optimum arousal leading to optimum performance of the task. Within this optimum range of arousal, it is obvious that complex tasks requiring a calm approach are best performed at a lower level of arousal, and simple more energetic tasks can be performed on the higher side. The measure of performance may be the speed with which you respond to the situation, the intensity and accuracy of your response, how well you are coordinated in your response, and how quickly you react in modifying your response as the situation changes. Your response to the situation will be best in the region of optimum arousal, between low and high arousal. Poor performance will be the result at both extremes of the arousal scale; good performance will be the result in the central region where arousal is optimum. This connection between state of arousal and level of performance can be shown graphically.

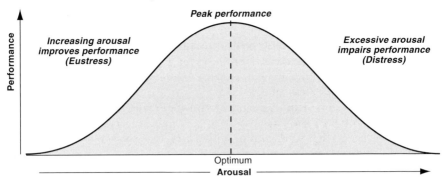

Figure 5-3 **Performance versus Arousal**

For peak performance during take-off, landing and emergencies, you should be in the intermediate area of arousal – aroused, but not over-aroused. For satisfactory performance in the relatively low workload period of a long-haul cruise, a moderate level of arousal is adequate (but not under-arousal where you might miss important things such as a reporting point and heading change, or a developing emergency).

## Active Management of Arousal

In the case of most human factors affecting flight, there are things you can do to make them work better for you, or interfere less. In other words, you can either let nature take its course, or intervene positively to manage your capabilities. One example is time-attention management. You can let your gaze drift where the need takes it, or you can make it scan rapidly and deliberately. It's a case of whether you are content to let the aeroplane fly you (i.e. let an automatic human factor do its own thing) or whether you are going to consciously fly the aircraft (take positive charge of human responses). The arousal state is a case in point, and it can be managed in conjunction with time-attention scan control.

*The cricketer comes to the crease, severely under-aroused (or over-confident) after hours of waiting, nearly asleep. (There's no doubt he senses the pressure and the adrenalin is running, but it all takes time to have effect.) The ball flashes in and rears up at him, he plays a terrible shot, but gets away with it. The crowd roars. The adrenalin pump is now at full stroke, so when he gets the 'hit' it's more of a 'jolt', and takes him right over the top and down into incompetence (in terms of the stimulus response diagram). Surviving a few more poor shots, he begins to settle down, and eventually achieves optimum performance. Every person who has played sport can relate to the experience – feeling terrible, jerky hand movements, poor control over where to look, etc.*

In the stimulus-response diagram above, you can see that arousal steadily increases (this is sometimes known as the *stimulus-response curve*) as the pressure comes on. The reason for the change is adrenalin. The 'fight or flight' mechanism has been activated, your heart rate is up, and larger amounts of oxygen are being carried around, and so on, as earlier described. You eventually reach a state of optimum arousal where the syndrome, working as designed, has you performing at peak proficiency. Then you can go too far – become over-aroused. From a level of proficiency, you slowly slide downhill into diminished capacity and incompetence. It is important – absolutely vital, in fact – that you note two things about the stimulus-response syndrome. Firstly, it is primarily a physical response. That is, it is your body that is becoming more competent. Your brain also becomes more capable – but not to the same extent.

The capability of a current and fit pilot during a normal flight is represented by the upper line in figure 5-4 (page 116). The demand (workload) is shown for the phases of the flight. High workloads generally occur during take-off, the approach and landing. They will also occur with an emergency or in poor weather. The ability of a pilot to cope with this demand is represented by the upper line, which can vary.

Good training, recency, being fit and well rested, raise the capability line, and increase the safety margin between capability and demand. Being fatigued, nervous, under-confident, uncurrent, and unwell will lower the capability line, diminishing the safety margin, and perhaps removing it altogether. Under normal conditions, you should be able to operate using only about 50% of your capability, with the other 50% in reserve to cope with unforeseen events and emergencies. During a long and tiring flight, you can expect your capability line to gradually lower.

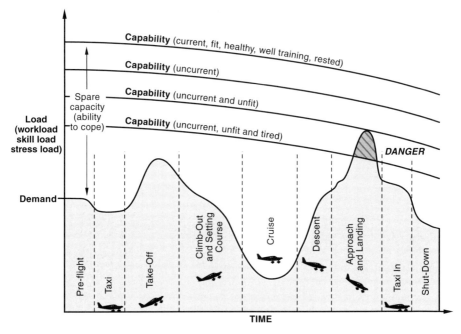

Figure 5-4 **Demand versus capacity**

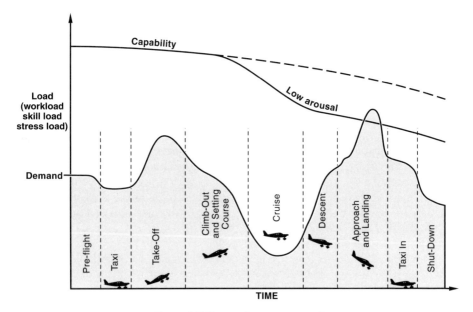

Figure 5-5 **Demand versus arousal**

Of course, low levels of arousal also affect the capability level. A routine flight to a regular destination in good weather can be a set-up for a landing accident. You can see that progressive deterioration of the state of alertness – and competence – is arrived at passively. That is, you allow it to happen. The situation on long flights can be quite different, much worse if something goes wrong. Note the steep response slope required after the low-demand, low-arousal state during the cruise.

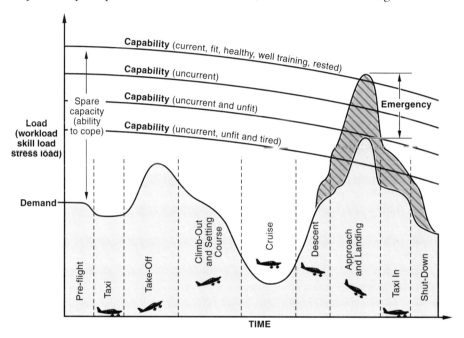

Figure 5-6 **Overload**

## Automation

Aircraft are becoming more automated. The routine tasks, including flying of the aircraft, are delegated to a machine. This is a deliberate progression. In the case of repetitive tasks, and closed-loop operations, the computer will perform more reliably, more consistently and more accurately. This automation can include autopilot functions. Computers can perform tasks that are beyond human capabilities: for instance, the routine rapid processing of massive amounts of data that would saturate our human mental processor. Future air traffic management will not be possible without this processing.

### Advantages

When considering automation, we must consider the things that computers do better than humans, such as long-term monitoring (the computer doesn't become fatigued or bored), repetitive routine tasks (the computer doesn't become distracted or bored), and detailed data storage (the computer classifies and stores information for rapid retrieval in an objective and repeatable way). Other advantages of computers are the reduced cockpit workload, a reduced crew and the fact that the computer is not subject to stress, moods, fear, fatigue and personality conflicts. The computer (automation) contributes greatly to the amount of information available to the crew for decision-making.

### Disadvantages

Disadvantages of automation include the potentially reduced level of situational awareness (the human switches off), the complacency and boredom, the unquestioning acceptance of computer-generated information (stronger even than the traditional printed word) and, to a certain extent, the deterioration of piloting skills. It is significant in long-haul operations that pilots may now be getting as few as one or two landings a week.

## Arousal on the Automated Flight Deck

To maintain an acceptable level of arousal one must be motivated. The enemies of arousal are complacency and laziness: if we can't be bothered checking, double-checking, or monitoring, then we are very vulnerable. The great danger with highly automated aircraft, such as the Airbus, is over-reliance on the automatics and an inadequate understanding of what they are doing and what they can do.

The introduction of the brilliant little GPS is a classic example. How many are caught, by not having a mental cross check or flight log, when the battery dies or when the data entry was one digit in error. We must mentally keep all of the electronic systems *honest*. Always do an approximation, a mental plot, to check the general orientation, order of magnitude or common sense of what the device is saying or doing. They are blind fools willing and ready to serve or to lead us astray – and they don't mind which.

By conscious management of our arousal we can learn to maintain higher states of alertness through artificially stimulating our arousal mechanism. But this takes self-discipline. The pilots and crew in the electronic aircraft must find ways to remain motivated and alert. The cabin crew have in-flight tasks that occupy them physically and mentally, and they have people to chat to. It is again the overnight long-haul flights, where the cabin is put to sleep, that they may become lethargic and drowsy. On the flight deck, the problem is more acute. There isn't a physical task and there is little mental demand. The conversation is restricted to two people who may or may not be communicative or share common interests. The reliability of automated systems, together with the decreased load-stimulus in the automatic cockpit, leads to boredom – and thus a low arousal state. There is now a critical vulnerability in terms of being able to cope with a serious, and unexpected challenge, such as an emergency.

Furthermore, excessive confidence in the systems brings about complacency. We believe the numbers and our natural laziness leads us to not bother keeping a mental check of calculations and a manual plot of the progress of the flight. Worse, not keeping a mental plot while the plane is navigating itself will result in total geographic disorientation.

## Sleep

### Purpose of Sleep

The purpose of sleep is to revitalise your mind and body in preparation for the activities of the following day. A typical person requires 8 hours of restful sleep in preparation for 16 hours of activity: in very approximate terms, one hour of sleep gives you an energy credit for two hours of activity.

### Strategies for Getting Good Sleep

There are some measures that you can take to assist you in sleeping well.

- Sleep in a comfortable bed in a dark and quiet room. Darkness and quietness encourage sleep, whereas bright light and noise have the opposite effect. Maintain a pleasant temperature, with fresh air available if possible.
- Try to maintain a regular sleep schedule. Going to bed at the same time each night, falling asleep, then waking up eight hours later feeling rejuvenated, will become a habit.
- Keep fit, eat well, and go to bed tired, but not overtired. A body that is healthy as a result of exercise and a good diet will not only perform better during the hours of wakefulness, it will also rest better during sleep. Being fit and healthy is natural and desirable. Exercising earlier during the day so that you go to bed 'tired' will encourage sleep, provided you have not had too many naps. A cup of warm milk or some form of carbohydrate before going to bed will also encourage sleep (but avoid stimulants like coffee or tea, and avoid alcohol, animal fats and high protein foods). Exercising or eating a big meal just before going to bed should be avoided.
- Try to turn off mentally. If possible, avoid excessive mental activity or thinking about emotionally stressful matters before turning in for what you want to be a good sleep. Relaxing with a good book or soft music can sometimes take your mind off the worries of the day.

### Stages of Sleep

The nature of sleep is not the same throughout the whole sleep period. As we all know from experience, being woken at an early stage when we are just drifting off to sleep is quite a different matter from being woken from a very deep sleep, when it may take some minutes to return to full consciousness. Also, just prior to waking, we often feel in a semi-conscious state, with thoughts running around in our head, and eyes darting around behind closed eyelids – quite different from when we are in a deep stage of sleep, with the body relaxed and mental activity slowed right down. The study of sleep is fascinating and far from complete (we seem to know more of what is going on in outer space than what is going on in our heads); however, we can say that there are four recognisable stages in terms of depth of sleep or unconsciousness.

After you drift from wakefulness into sleep, you go down through the four stages into ever-deeper sleep, where you stay for a while, and then rise through the stages, sometimes missing one or two, before sinking back into deep sleep. This occurs in a series of cycles that take about 90 minutes each. In a normal night, you may go through four or five cycles, each one perhaps a little different from the previous one, with some stages missing or lasting for shorter or longer periods. As can be seen in the diagram below, the very deep stage 4 sleep is commonly more predominant in the early cycles than in the later cycles.

Often, after you return to a lighter level of sleep and before you sink back down into a deeper stage (or continue rising into wakefulness), you experience a totally different type of sleep, known as *REM (rapid eye movement)* sleep. This is so different that sometimes the first four stages are known as non-REM sleep in contrast to it.

Stages 1–4 non-REM sleep has fairly low-frequency electrical waves in the brain and so is sometimes known as *slow-wave* sleep. Slow-wave sleep rests and repairs the body. Electrical waves in the brain during REM sleep are high frequency and short wave. REM sleep is sometimes called *paradoxical* sleep because, even though the muscles are very relaxed and the person is still asleep, brain activity is similar to a person who is awake. REM sleep is when we dream.

The stages 1–4 non-REM sleep and the additional REM sleep are different types of sleep and perform different functions. The stages 1–4 non-REM sleep revitalises the body and so is needed in abundance after strenuous physical activity, whereas the REM sleep restores the brain and is needed after strenuous mental activity.

In the course of a long sleep period, you alternate between the two types of sleep. Your body and brain ensure that you obtain sufficient of the required type of sleep each night, according to your needs.

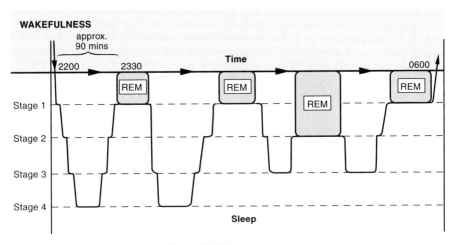

Figure 5-7 **Sleep patterns**

The first onset of REM sleep usually occurs about 90 minutes after commencing sleep, and recurs at about this interval throughout the sleep period as you rise out of deep sleep and sink back into it. Your brain is being rejuvenated during REM sleep, and it is important that REM sleep is not disturbed. Disturbance can be caused by alcohol, drugs, stress, or being forcefully wakened. Alcohol-induced sleep, while perhaps removing or escaping conscious stress, does not refresh because it reduces REM sleep.

## Sleep Patterns

Individual sleep patterns vary: different people require different amounts of sleep and prefer to go to bed and rise at different times. The need for sleep also varies with age, as an older person may need less sleep, but on a more regular basis; this can cause problems for older pilots involved in long-haul international operations crossing many time zones. Daytime operations close to home might be easier from the sleeping point of view.

In very general terms, we need around eight hours of sleep in a 24-hour day – eight hours of good rest and revitalisation in preparation for sixteen hours of activity. Some people need only six hours; others need ten. Some people prefer to retire to bed at 9 p.m. and rise with the sparrows, while 'night owls' prefer to retire at midnight or later and rise late the next morning. For the purposes of our study of sleep patterns, we will consider a person who goes to bed at 2400 hours and, after eight hours of sleep, rises at 0800 hours. You can move these hours forward or back, or reduce or increase them, to suit your own particular case. Unfortunately, there seems to be a maximum limit on the number of sleep-hours you can credit. Once you get to eight sleep-hours' credit, that is it. No matter how hard you try to sleep longer and gain more sleep credits, it will not be successful. In broad terms, we can say that one high-quality sleep hour is good for two hours of activity.

Eight sleep-hours will prepare you for the sixteen hours activity of a 24-hour day. After this time of wakefulness, your sleep credits will have been used. Your credits are now zero, your energy level will be low, and you will begin to feel tired and ready for another sleep. If you do not go to sleep, you will go into a sleep *deficit*, which will probably cause a significant decrease in your alertness and performance capability. An ideal, uninterrupted sleeping pattern for a person with regular habits is illustrated in the following diagram:

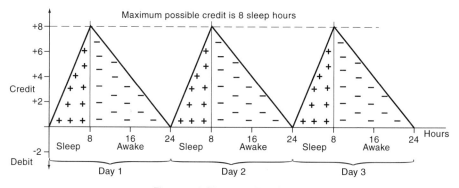

Figure 5-8 **Sleep credits/debits**

## Disturbed Sleep Patterns

It is not always possible to achieve the desired 8–16–8–16 sleep pattern due to the demands of work, family, illness or social life, in which case compromises have to be made. If you reduce the sleep-hours credit, then you also reduce the hours of useful wakeful activity available to you before you are due for another sleep, or before you start to slip into a sleep deficit. If you are deprived of sleep you will not perform as well as when you still have some sleep-hours in credit.

A very common sleep deficit occurs when you 'party on' late into the night, well beyond your usual bedtime. This can also happen to you if you work through the night and use up all your sleep credits. If you have the luxury of being able to sleep in until late the next morning, then you can recuperate and move out of the sleep deficit fairly quickly, provided your sleep is restful and not disturbed.

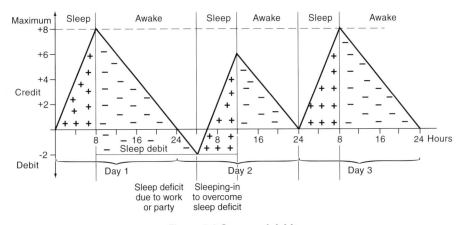

Figure 5-9 **Corrected debit**

An alcohol-induced sleep gives the impression that it is a deep sleep – but it is not. Your REM sleep will be reduced, your mental rejuvenation will not be as good as usual, you will probably wake earlier than you would otherwise, and most importantly, when you wake you may not feel refreshed. This is an important point to note for pilots who, in the past, may have used alcohol to relax after a stressful flight and to induce sleep. Trying to build up a store of sleep-hour credits by sleeping long hours the previous night also will not work. Once you get to the eight hours' credit, you will most likely wake up. Perhaps you could increase your energy level for a party, however, by taking a late afternoon nap after you have used up some of your sleep credits, and raise them back towards eight sleep-hour credits, which should then get you comfortably well into the night.

## Interrupted or Reduced Sleep

If you are woken after only four hours of sleep instead of your usual eight, then (in very approximate terms, and on the basis that one sleep-hour prepares you for two hours of wakefulness) you have only eight hours of activity available before you begin to get tired. If you go beyond this time of wakefulness, then your performance is likely to deteriorate.

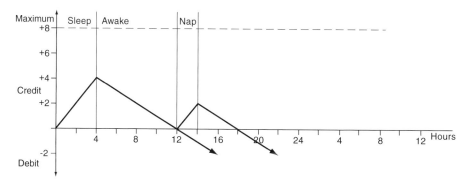

Figure 5-10 **Naps**

You may be able to recuperate to some extent by taking an afternoon nap, but this may not be as effective and restful as sleep at a normal time, and your sleep credits may build at a slower rate. With a nap, you also run the risk of sinking into a deep sleep from which it may be difficult to awaken before the sleep cycle runs its full course, the result being that you do not feel rested at all.

## Irregular Sleep Routine

For a person with a regular lifestyle, the *need* for sleep and the *ability* to sleep generally coincide, and going to bed when tired and falling asleep occurs naturally. This is usual for most of us working normal day shifts, and is also usual for the perennial night-shift worker whose body rhythms have adjusted to lifestyle. A night worker's sleep pattern of 8–16–8–16 may be the same pattern as for a normal day worker, but it may occur at different times of the day.

For the *irregular* night-shift worker, however, or the pilot who has to crawl out of bed at an unusual time to go flying, it can be quite a different matter. The body rhythms are synchronised for the normal eight hours of sleeping between 2400 and 0800 local time, followed by the sixteen hours of wakefulness between 0800 and 2400, and suddenly this pattern is broken. Going to work in the late afternoon after a normal night's sleep will not feel too bad but, sometime after midnight, fatigue will make its presence felt. This is a similar situation to 'partying on'. A late afternoon nap before work, or a nap in the early morning during a break from work, may prove helpful.

Going to work in the early morning, however, is a different problem. The body is crying out to continue sleeping, but the pilot has to force the body rhythms into wakefulness, and head off to what might be quite demanding activity. Trying to get eight hours of sleep at an unusual time prior to commencing work may not be possible.

The need for sleep and the readiness of the body for sleep depend not only on tiredness due to the time awake, but also on the time of day according to your body rhythms. The intermittent shift-worker may have trouble going to sleep, staying asleep, and then waking and feeling well rested. A few short naps during his period of 'wakefulness' might be necessary to overcome the sleep deficit.

### Sleep Disorders

*Insomnia* is an inability to sleep, or to obtain restful sleep. There are different types of insomnia. The most common one is *nervous insomnia*. Most people experience this from time to time, especially when they are anticipating something potentially stressful that is about to happen in the near future, such as an examination or a flight test. Nervous insomnia might disrupt sleep for one or two nights, often to a lesser extent than the person thinks. It is not a serious problem, with a quick recovery from any resulting tiredness or fatigue.

Acute or short-term insomnia resulting from stress or illness, or disturbed body rhythms (jet lag), is also usually not serious, with a quick recovery within days when the cause is removed. If the cause is due to unfamiliar surroundings, it is referred to as *situational insomnia*. If, however, you are in familiar surroundings and cannot sleep, it is referred to as *clinical insomnia*. *Chronic insomnia* is another matter; this is when the person is unable to obtain restful sleep for a period of weeks or months due to long-term unresolved stress, or due to illness. This continued sleep deprivation may require medical attention. Other sleep disorders besides chronic insomnia that may require medical attention include the reverse problem, that of an inability to stay awake even when well rested, as well as very heavy snoring, and breathing interruptions during sleep.

### Sleeping Drugs (Hypnotics)

Drugs used to aid sleeping are called *hypnotics*. They may assist sleep, but some of them also have fairly serious side-effects that could affect the skill and performance of a pilot. They should not be used by a pilot without advice and supervision from an expert aviation doctor. Subtle effects might also be very dangerous, since it is less likely that they will be noticed. Be cautious with the use of painkillers, decongestants to combat the effects of a cold, antihistamines to treat hay fever, antibiotics to combat infection, stomach tablets, or pills to combat gastro-intestinal infections.

## Body Rhythms

The regular sleep-wakefulness rhythm of 8 hours' sleep 16 hours' wakefulness is only one of our body rhythms. Others include the rhythm of internal body temperature, and the digestive rhythm with its regular hunger pangs and elimination of waste products. These body rhythms usually have a frequency of approximately 24 hours, and so are often called the *circadian rhythms,* from the latin *circa* (about) and *dies* (day). There are many of these circadian rhythms, and they seem to be connected to one another, in that a change in one leads to a change in others, not necessarily at the same rate, nor with the same amount of ease. In fact, it can be very difficult to change some body rhythms and have all body rhythms synchronised normally. Long-distance east–west travellers know this from struggling to get their bodies into a new time zone and not fall asleep when everyone else is operating at peak efficiency. The sleep–wakefulness rhythm is perhaps one of the rhythms that is easiest to change. There are other rhythms, such as internal body temperature, which are very tightly bound into a regular rhythm and which are much more difficult and take much longer to change. Our performance capability and our enthusiasm to perform is closely tied to our body rhythms – especially that of internal body temperature, which rises slightly by day and falls at night.

## Sleep–Wakefulness Rhythm

The sleep–wakefulness rhythm seems to have a natural time span somewhat greater than 24 hours, more in the range of 25–26 hours, but it is regularly pulled back into a 24-hour time span by a succession of time-of-day reminders known by the German word *Zeitgeber*. *Zeit* (pronounced 'tsight') means time, and *Geber* (pronounced 'gay-ber'), means giver, so that a zeitgeber is a time-giver – a reminder of the time of day.

Typical zeitgebers are the rising and setting of the sun, the everyday ringing of the alarm clock, the 8 a.m. breakfast pangs, the need to use the toilet before rushing off to catch the 8:23 train, lunch time, the ever-present wristwatch and clocks, the afternoon tea break, knock-off time, the 6 p.m. evening meal, the late-night news, and so on. Each person will have their own series of zeitgebers throughout the day pulling their sleep–wakefulness cycle into line, with the sun as a very powerful natural zeitgeber. The rising of the sun is a strong force moving us into wakefulness; darkness is a reminder that sleeping time is coming. The natural length of the sleep-wakefulness cycle can be observed by removing all of the zeitgebers – for instance, by placing a person in a darkened room and removing all time clues. The result is a sleeping pattern that becomes later each day, as shown below.

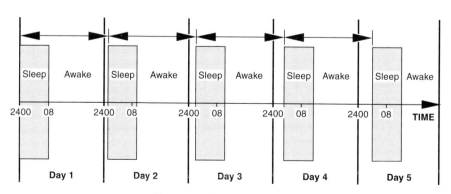

Figure 5-11 **Constant pattern**

With zeitgebers, however, the sleeping pattern will be continually realigned with the space clock of the sun-rise/set.

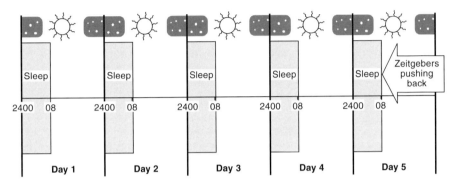

Figure 5-12 **Alignment of the body clock**

People who live in high latitudes, such as Scandinavia, Northern Canada and Siberia, have to cope with the loss of the sun as a zeitgeber. In summer they have continual light, and in winter they have almost continual darkness. Stress levels, sleeping patterns, and fatigue may change with the seasons in these latitudes.

## Melatonin

The underlying cause of light patterns affecting the body clock is the biochemical melatonin. Melatonin is secreted by the pineal gland in response to the absence of light. At the close of a normal day, fading light causes the melatonin to kick in, and bring about a general slow-down in your system, leading to drowsiness and enabling sleep. When the first rays of light are detected, the pineal gland switches off the melatonin flow and you progressively become less under-aroused. In other words, melatonin is a mild, naturally produced sedative. It can be artificially produced, and is often prescribed as a soft tranquilliser. With artificial light, we have pushed back the onset of drowsiness and lengthened the working day at the other end. Melatonin is foremost amongst those influences that adjust your body clock 'back' from its preferred 25 hours. However, as can be seen, its effects will vary with latitude and exposure to artificial light.

## Body Temperature

Internal body temperature averages at about 36.5 °C (98 °F), with a regular circadian cycles of 0.3 °C above and below this. Its natural cycle is about 25 hours, but again zeitgebers realign it to a 24-hour cycle.

The circadian rhythm of internal body temperature is a very strong rhythm that cannot be easily altered (as can other rhythms like the sleep–wakefulness cycle). For this reason, body temperature is often used as the yardstick. A high body temperature is linked to alertness and good performance; a low body temperature is linked to low mental performance and drowsiness.

The sleep–wakefulness cycle usually runs in parallel with the body temperature cycle. Your body is usually ready for sleep at a time of falling or low body temperature, and ready to be awake at a time of rising or high body temperature.

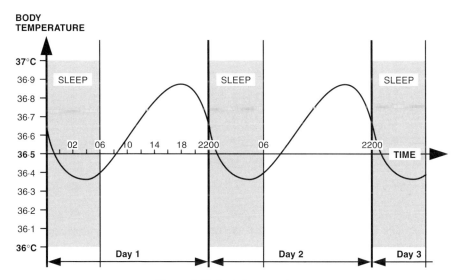

Figure 5-13 **Body temperature**

## Performance Cycle

Peak performance capability and alertness occurs at the time of an increasing or high body temperature, which is when you are usually wide awake; low alertness and performance capability occurs at times of low body temperature, which is when you are usually asleep. Different types of performance (such as *psychomotor* performance, hand–eye coordination, mental agility, reasoning ability, and reaction time) vary somewhat differently throughout the day; however, we can generalise and say that alertness and performance capability vary with body temperature.

If your sleep–wakefulness pattern is disturbed, the temperature pattern will remain the same. If you are forced to be awake at 4–6 a.m., your alertness and ability to perform well will be impaired somewhat because of the low point in your body temperature cycle that will occur as normal. The lowest body temperature occurs about 4–6 a.m., when you are usually in a very deep sleep, and if you have to work at this time, you may have great difficulty in staying awake.

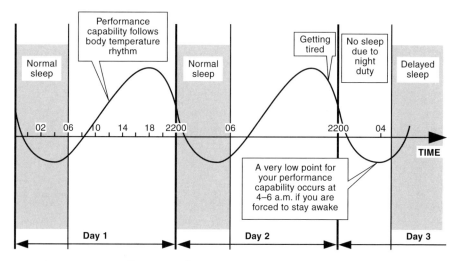

Figure 5-14 **Capability versus sleep pattern**

It is possible to modify the performance cycle by lifting it, rather than by shifting it in terms of timing. Your performance graph will be raised if you are feeling well, if you are well rested, if you are highly motivated, or if you are well practised in the skills that you wish to use. Even the low-performance points are raised, indicating that, if you are forced to stay awake during the normal sleeping hours, your performance will be better if you are fit and well.

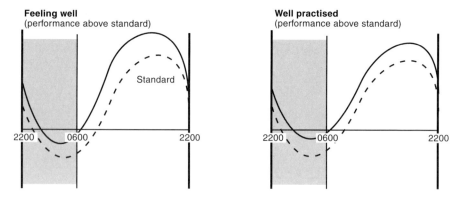

Figure 5-15 **Enhanced performance**

Extroverts and night owls usually have their performance cycle moved slightly to the right, compared with introverts, to match their other body cycles. Similarly, perennial shift workers have their performance cycle moved to match their body cycles, which run to a different body clock compared with daytime workers. Their peak performance may not reach that of a daytime worker because of the inevitable disturbance to the sleeping periods of a night-shift worker caused by normal family life, and sunlight and darkness.

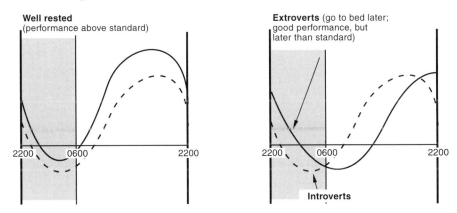

Figure 5-16 **Modified cycles**

The ability to maintain a high level of performance decreases significantly if you are fatigued or deprived of sleep. This applies in particular to physically passive but mentally active tasks, which is often what a long-haul pilot is involved in when the aeroplane is on the cruise – systems monitoring, maintaining a navigation overview with correct radio communication – while the autopilot handles the physical task of maintaining height and track, and the autothrottle maintains speed.

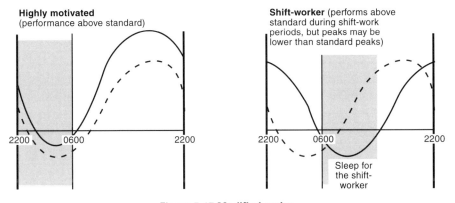

Figure 5-17 **Modified cycles**

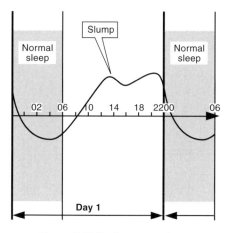

Figure 5-18 **Performance slump**

## Early-Afternoon Slump

Most people will recognise the previous activity model as accurate, but it is not the whole picture. In reality, most of us experience a slight 'downturn' in the early afternoon, connected with the subtraction of body energy from the overall system in order to digest lunch. In some countries, the habit is to sleep through this period. Other cultures – *mad dogs and . . . stay out in the noonday sun* – fight off the minor drowsiness involved and do not break the day. The version of the model below shows the slump.

Pilots can diminish the slump effect by eating lightly in the middle of the day. However, dietitians recommend a steady intake of high-energy (high sugar content) snacks through the morning, with lunch the main meal of the day and a light dinner.

The slump will be more pronounced if you are already tired. However, you should be able to anticipate this, and plan not to be facing difficult choices during the depleted energy period. On most days, for most people, tired or not, the slump is not beyond their ability to overcome by 'forcing the pace', as we have seen before. We will also see that it can play a significant role in time zone adaptation; that is, in recovering from the effect of jet lag.

## Jet Lag – The Desynchronisation of Body Rhythms

The long-haul pilot and the passengers are subject to the normal fatigue of a flight caused by a dry, oxygen-deficient atmosphere, vibration, noise, lack of exercise, and the stresses associated with any flight. This is the case especially on east–west flights where there is the very significant problem of crossing time zones and finding yourself in a place where the local time differs from home time. The rising and the setting of the sun, and the habits of the local population are on local time, and out of synchronisation with your body clock, which is still on home time. You feel like going to sleep just as darkness turns to light with the rising of the sun, and just as everyone else is waking up ready to start the new day. The early-morning sounds of garbage collection, milk delivery, trains running, church bells ringing do not match the way your body feels. The problem is whether to try to bring your body into the new time zone or not? This usually depends on how long the stay will be. For a pilot who will fly back home the next day, there is no point. For a long stay, such as a holiday, then the attempt is probably worthwhile making.

There are many body rhythms and cycles, the body temperature cycle being only one, although perhaps the most important one. Some rhythms can be brought into local time at the rate of about one hour a day, which means that, if the time zone change is four hours, then after four days this body cycle will be aligned with local time. Different body rhythms, however, change at different rates. Moreover, any disturbance of one body rhythm may lead to disturbances in other body rhythms. As some body rhythms operate on a 25–26-hour cycle, their phase changes by an average of 1–2 hours per day. It therefore takes much longer to move into local time – up to eight days for some rhythms if the time zone change is four hours. This means that as your body attempts to transfer into a new time zone, many of the body rhythms that are normally synchronised are now desynchronised and may be a little abnormal within themselves. This is known as *circadian disrhythmia*.

The result could be headaches, poor sleep, disturbed eating patterns, constipation, giddiness, poor mental performance, and even slight depression. Hunger pangs and toilet habits still based on the old home time could also disturb your new sleeping pattern as you try to move your body clock into the new time zone, making you generally tired all day long, and delaying further your move into the new time zone. The time between about 4–6 a.m. on your body clock, irrespective of what the local time is, will also be a period of low alertness and poor performance capability, which could be significant if you are in the middle of an important meeting or taking part in an activity that requires alertness.

Accidentally falling asleep is not uncommon. It may take three weeks or even longer before all the body rhythms are back 'in synch' again, and before you are operating at peak efficiency in the new time zone. Exposing yourself to sunlight, and allowing the powerful sun zeitgeber to influence your body and mind, may speed the process a little.

## Time Zones
The Earth is approximately 24,000 nautical miles in circumference at the Equator. A one-hour time zone is therefore about 1,000 miles across. Longitude affects our *diurnal coordination*. An example is the difference between Brisbane and Mt Isa. Brisbane is on the eastern edge of the time zone, and it experiences early daylight while Mt Isa is still in the dark. (In other words, Mt Isa has 'permanent daylight saving'.) Light patterns and their effect through the pineal gland will vary depending on where your place of sleep is in the time zone.

## Adjustment of the Body Clock
The adjustment of the body clock is easier if you travel west. This is because travelling westwards you are travelling with the sun, and the hours of daylight that you experience will be longer than normal – the day will appear to be longer than 24 hours. Because many natural body rhythms have a period of 25 hours if they are not realigned by zeitgebers, they have a natural tendency to move towards the new time zone at the rate of about one hour a day. Conversely, when travelling eastwards, the days are shortened, and the body rhythms have to be realigned to less than 24 hours, against their natural tendency to lengthen.

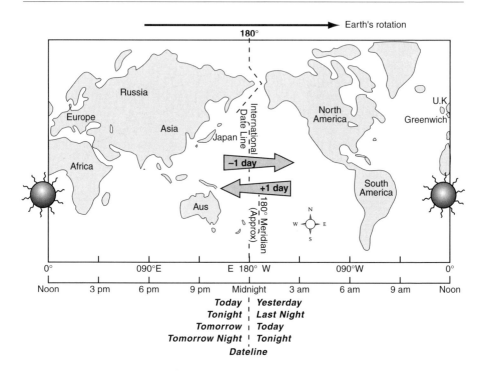

Figure 5-19 **Time-zones**

Although travelling north or south does not mean crossing time zones, there can still be jet lag problems, due to the usual fatigue from a long flight, and also due to the somewhat displaced zeitgebers. In winter, for instance, a Scandinavian or a Scot might be used to the sun rising at 10 a.m. If the northerner travels south to somewhere in Africa, the local time might be the same, but the sun now rises at 5 a.m. This change of an important zeitgeber may unsettle some of the body rhythms.

### Inhibited Body Clock Adjustment

We have previously noted the mid-afternoon energy slump. When a person is jet lagged, this can cause a worst-case recovery situation. Say, the jet lag gave you poor sleep last night and you feel fatigued. Come the middle of the day, the temptation to have a beer or two with lunch and then an afternoon sleep will be very strong. If you do that, you disable any possible effect melatonin could have had in resetting the body clock.

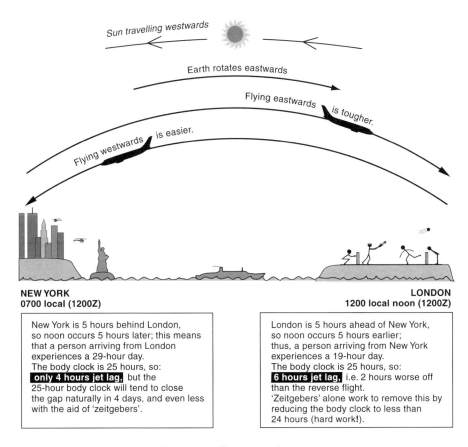

**NEW YORK**
**0700 local (1200Z)**

**LONDON**
**1200 local noon (1200Z)**

New York is 5 hours behind London, so noon occurs 5 hours later; this means that a person arriving from London experiences a 29-hour day. The body clock is 25 hours, so: **only 4 hours jet lag,** but the 25-hour body clock will tend to close the gap naturally in 4 days, and even less with the aid of 'zeitgebers'.

London is 5 hours ahead of New York, so noon occurs 5 hours earlier; thus, a person arriving from New York experiences a 19-hour day. The body clock is 25 hours, so: **6 hours jet lag,** i.e. 2 hours worse off than the reverse flight. 'Zeitgebers' alone work to remove this by reducing the body clock to less than 24 hours (hard work!).

Figure 5-20 **Time zone changes**

The best thing to do is to fight the desire to sleep during the day – physical exercise is a good antidote for the craving. By forcing your body to match the new diurnal pattern – holding off the need to sleep until closer to 'normal' bedtime – you will much more rapidly adjust. An afternoon sleep is guaranteed to result in early morning wakefulness, and more days of the wretchedly uncomfortable feeling of being out of phase.

# Fatigue

Fatigue is a very deep tiredness, and perhaps no longer caring, that usually comes from:
- a lack of restful sleep;
- a lack of physical or mental fitness;
- excessive or prolonged physical or mental stress and anxiety; or
- desynchronisation of your body cycles (jet lag).

All of the things that cause stress, such as noise and vibration, high temperatures or a lack of oxygen, domestic or work-related problems, can lead to fatigue. The essential immediate cure for *acute* fatigue is sleep. *Chronic* long-term fatigue may take longer to eliminate, and may require professional advice. A pilot suffering from chronic fatigue, be it due to physical or psychological reasons, should not continue flying.

## Symptoms of Fatigue

Symptoms of fatigue include:
- lack of awareness – radio calls that go unanswered or checklists that go unchecked;
- diminished motor skills – sloppy flying, writing that trails off into nothing as weather reports or clearances are written down;
- obvious tiredness – drooping head, staring or half-closed eyes;
- diminished vision – difficulty in focusing;
- slow reactions;
- short-term memory problems – unable to remember a clearance long enough to repeat it or to write it down accurately;
- channelled concentration – fixation on a single, possibly unimportant issue, to the neglect of others and to the neglect of maintaining an overview of the flight;
- easy distraction by trivial matters or, the other extreme, fixation – either extreme could indicate fatigue;
- poor instrument flying – difficulty in focusing on the instruments, fixation on one instrument to the neglect of others, drifting in and out of sleep, diminished motor skills with poor hand–eye coordination and acceptance of lower standards;
- increased mistakes – errors, poor judgement and poor decisions, or no decisions at all, even simple ones like 'Will I turn left or right to avoid this thunderstorm?'; and
- abnormal moods – erratic changes in mood, depressed, periodically elated and energetic, diminished standards.

A lack of restful sleep can lead to fatigue. Being fatigued is different from being sleepy or drowsy – it is being deeply tired to the point of being unable to attend satisfactorily to your flight duties for sustained periods and perhaps not even caring. Fatigue is stressful and damaging for a person. A routine flight can be fatiguing, with the pilot being exposed to mental and physical stressors such as noise, vibration, reduced oxygen, high or low temperature, low humidity, physical restraint, navigation problems, bad weather, technical problems, difficulties with passengers, and so on. The additional influence of poor sleep and disrupted body rhythms, imposed upon the natural tiredness of the pilot, can have a very serious effect.

## Chapter 6

# Information Processing

The bare minimum amount of information we must know to be able to control an aircraft under normal circumstances within an organised system of flight regulation, airspace management and air traffic is considerable. You need to have this vast array of information at your disposal. On top of that we have to cope with unexpected situations. The way you process this information determines how well you fly and how well you manage the flight. Do the one well and the other is made easier.

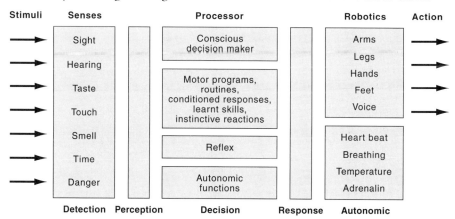

Figure 6-1 **Information processing**

The main feature (characteristic and limitation) of our brain, as a central decision-maker, is that it can only functions as a *single-channel* computer, which means that we can consider only one problem at a time. Decisions made in the brain are therefore not made simultaneously, but sequentially. They are placed in a queue – according to priority.

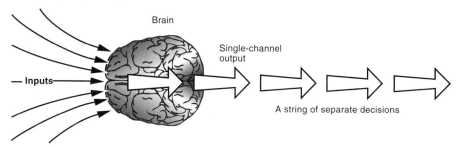

Figure 6-2 **Single channel**

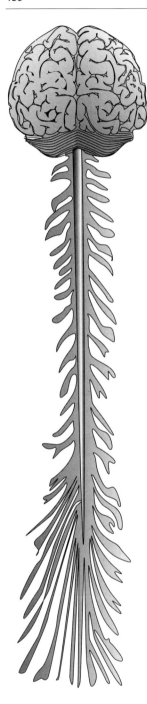

## System of Nerves

The nervous system equates to an electrical, digital signalling system. Nerves are effectively wires that run through the body, conducting electric impulses in both directions. The *central nervous system* comprises the brain and the trunk cabling of the spinal cord – like a bus bar. Groups of smaller nerves then radiate through the body and form the *peripheral nervous system.*

Nerves feed information to the brain – sensations of touch, movement, sound, sight and so on. The brain receives these messages. It then fires electrical signals in the other direction, to trigger and control muscular movement.

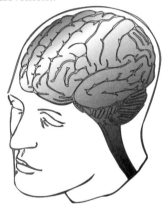

Figure 6-3 **Central nervous system**

Nerves pass all electrical signals to and from the brain. Nowhere is the concentration of nerve cells greater than in the brain itself. There is a vast filigree structure of nerves – and neural networks – in the brain. Nerves gather and distribute information. Information is sorted and moved around within the brain depending on its nature. For example, the brain processes arithmetical calculations in one location, visual images in another, and triggers movement somewhere else. Emotion is processed in an entirely separate, though connected, place: the *frontal lobes.*

With information processed and decisions made, command and control instructions are sent out, to organs to function, glands to manufacture chemicals, muscles for movement, etc. That part which is done under your conscious control is called *thinking*. These are all *cognitive functions*. This huge amount of activity consumes oxygen and produces a great amount of heat.

## Basic Model of Information Processing

How the brain processes information is fascinating. There are six fundamental stages:
- stimulation – sensors receive a signal;
- perception – recognise, classify, remember it;
- analysis – work out what to do about it (make a decision);
- action – do something (or nothing);
- feedback – check results; and
- correction – to achieve acceptable standards of accuracy.

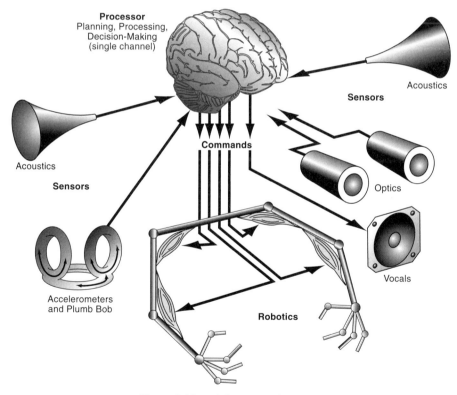

Figure 6-4 **Inputs/processor/outputs**

But, of course, we are talking of much more complex functions.

## Information Processing Model

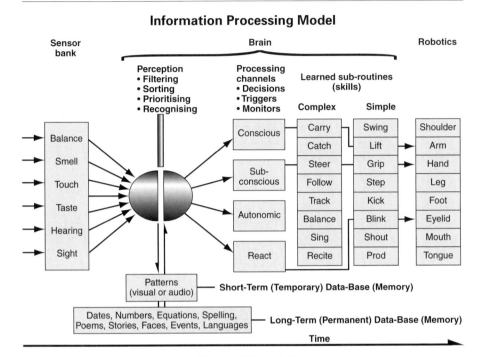

Figure 6-5 **IP model**

Note that the model shows a time line representing the never-ceasing passage of time. Everything takes time. Action takes time and so does thinking – the cognitive processing. Time is your most precious resource because it is always limited. Just how valuable, and how important the management of time is to a pilot, will become clearer. As we walk through the model, please bear in mind it seeks to simplify a host of infinitely varied and richly complex functions and activities that make up what we know as human thought. Referring to the basic functions laid out in the model's design, we will now follow information processing through the various stages and along different routes or channels. We will begin at the left where the senses detect some form of *stimulus* or *stimuli*.

## Stimulation, Sensation and Perception

### Stimulation

An enormous amount of stimulation from the external world is presented to us in the form of visual images, sounds, smells, tastes, and touch. These can be sensed by our *sense organs* – the eyes, ears, nose, taste buds, and *receptors* in the skin and muscles. We can also use receptors within the balance mechanism of our inner ear to sense accelerations and balance, and to determine which way is 'up'.

Not all physical quantities are sensed, however. For instance, whilst our inner ear can detect accelerations, which are changes in velocity, it cannot detect velocity itself. Being stationary or travelling at a steady speed of 80 kph feels the same, and with your eyes shut you might be unable to tell the difference, but you would certainly know if you were accelerating from 0 to 80 kph and decelerating from 80 to 0 kph.

The receptors are capable of detecting particular changes in the environment (either outside the body or within), and triggering electrical impulses in the sensory nerves. The sensitivity, and the attention of the receptors in each sensory organ, is different. For instance, those on the retina of the eye are sensitive to minute changes in light, whereas the receptor cells in the taste buds on the tongue respond to more coarse chemical changes, and the receptor cells in the skin are sensitive to heat, pain and touch to a varying degree.

There is a *sensory threshold*, below which the stimuli will not be detected by the particular receptors. For instance, very soft sounds, or sounds outside the frequency range of our ears, will go undetected. Similarly, electromagnetic radiation that does not lie within the visible light spectrum, or that is very faint, will go undetected by the light receptors in our eyes. The sensory threshold is a measure of the sensitivity of our sense organs and is often tested in pilot medicals – especially those of sound and vision.

If the stimulation is continuous or repetitive, then the receptor cells run the risk of *adaptation*, which is showing a gradually diminishing response to that particular stimulus. For instance, the adaptation of touch receptors in the skin causes the presence of clothes to be no longer felt just a few minutes after putting them on. Similarly, after long exposure to a steady sound, such as an aeroplane engine or wind noise, the pilot may become completely unaware of it. Nevertheless, it could still be damaging.

## Sensation

Sensors such as the optic nerve and the auditory nerve, carry sensed information towards the central nervous system (the brain and the spinal cord), where the messages are integrated, i.e. perceived. The sensory information is stored only briefly in a *sensory memory* before it is discarded and displaced by new information (unless we decide to retain it and process it).

Each sense has its own memory, with the time of retention varying between the senses. For instance, a visual image in the iconic memory lasts only about one second before it fades – illustrated by waggling a pencil in front of your eyes and noting that the blurred image of where it has just been quickly fades. Movies make use of this memory, enabling you to see a series of individual still pictures (*freeze frames*) as a moving image (called *iconic* – after icons or images).

Sounds last considerably longer in the memory than visual images (this is sometimes called *echoic* memory, like a mental echo). Sounds last about five seconds before they begin to fade, and this is time enough for us to recognise, half way through a radio transmission, that it is being directed at us and to be able to recall its beginning. It is also time enough for us to be able to count back the number of times a clock has struck, or to recognise a tune.

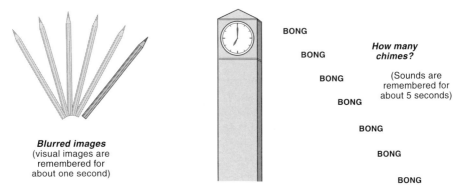

**Blurred images**
(visual images are remembered for about one second)

BONG

BONG

*How many chimes?*

BONG

(Sounds are remembered for about 5 seconds)

BONG

BONG

BONG

BONG

Figure 6-6 **Sensations versus memory**

## Perception

Perception involves the senses receiving some information about the environment, and then the brain analysing it to make it meaningful. For instance, a group of sounds may become a sentence with meaning, and a sequence of visual images may become an aeroplane moving across the sky. Senses are continually collecting new information to facilitate a continually updated mental model of the situation.

When you choose to process an image (sound, etc.), you have answered the *'read, don't read?'* question with a *'yes'*. That's fine, but then it must be recognised. The quickest way to do this is to see if there is a corresponding set of electrical pulses in stored memory. If there is – and the chances are there will be, then you accord recognition to the sensation, be it touch, sound or visual image. The process of making sense of what we hear, feel or see is called perception. When perception takes place, electrical pulses are carried as signals to memory and compared or matched to check if there is a similar pattern of impulses. This pattern matching is especially important to a pilot. It comes with training and experience. If or when a matching set is found, that image is accorded recognition. In one case, it is the runway. It could be a pattern on the ground matching a map, or the sound of an engine matching the normal (expected) starting sound.

Perception takes place in short-term memory. However, a good example of the perception cycle is when you meet someone for the first time at a social event, and can't remember their name five minutes later. The image of the heard name will dwell in short-term memory only briefly, unless you make some effort to store it more securely. If what you are hearing or seeing (person's name, runway image) is new to you, there will be no corresponding signal pattern to match it. If it is important, you will need to repeat its input several times to have it stored. However, what we perceive can be biased, confused and misled.

## Experience

The amount of sensed stimulation that is actually perceived and integrated depends, to some extent, upon our experience and expectation.

If we recognise the stimulus through previous experience, then we can more readily absorb it and integrate it into a model of the world around us. For instance, through experience we know that red-hot metal can cause pain, and when we feel pain and then see that our finger has just touched a piece of glowing metal, then we have no difficulty in forming a mental model of the situation – hot metal has burnt our finger.

Another example of useful experience is to do with radio messages from air traffic control. Pilots can understand the pattern of these messages through experience, but other people cannot: all they hear is a jumble of distorted sounds amidst static. Some radio messages are even difficult for pilots to understand, but an expectation of what the message will contain often helps. However, this expectation is a double-edged sword.

## Expectation

We all jump to conclusions and finish the sentence in the way that we expect or want it to end. We must guard against hearing what we want to hear or expect to hear, rather than what is actually said and meant. In the lined-up position on the runway at a controlled airport, for instance, we expect to hear, *'Cleared for take-off'*, and this is also what we want to hear. We are mentally prepared for take-off. The actual instruction, however, might be, *'Cleared for a Tumut 35 departure'*. We may not have even heard the words after, *'Cleared for . . .'*.

Anticipating an event or message is beneficial, provided we do not have a mind-set that precludes other possibilities and causes us to interpret a stimulus to be what we expect it to be, or want it to be, rather than what it actually is. We are all prone to this, especially when under high levels of stress.

During an early cross-country flight, trying to convince yourself that the ground features below match the mental model of your position (i.e. where you think you are) when in fact they do not is a common feeling. Expectation and anticipation can help us, but can also lead us into trouble if we are not disciplined enough to continually reassess the information that our senses present to us. The inflexibility of only hearing what we expect or want to hear, and see what we want to see, is known as having a *mind-set*.

## Sensory Confusion

When we hold our hand under a water tap marked C, we expect to feel cold water. English language speakers have become acclimatised to associate the letter C with cold. There is also a convention, though not consistent, of hot to the left and cold to the right – this is a function of the ergonomics that has also become confused (we will consider this later). Many travellers to Italy are thrown into confusion when they feel hot water rather than cold coming out of the tap marked C. C in this case represents *caldo*, the Italian word for *hot*, while F, for *freddo*, would be labelled on the cold tap. This mixing of signals can cause sensory confusion in our brains.

Another example of sensory confusion occurs when our eyes present an image to the brain that does not agree with the signals from our balance mechanism; for instance, after recovering from a prolonged spin, the wings of the aeroplane appear to be level with the horizon (eyes), but we feel as if we are still turning (balance mechanism). In this situation, we need to show sufficient discipline (the result of training) to take note of the signals from our eyes and over-ride those from the balance mechanism.

### Attention and Motivation
Attention refers to the (limited) control that you have over what sensed stimuli you choose to process – usually being the stimuli that you consider to be relevant to the task in hand. You can consciously focus your attention on a particular item – for instance, if you are specifically looking out at night for lightning flashes or for other aircraft – or your attention can be drawn to a particular item by external events – e.g. when you overhear your name being mentioned, your attention will almost automatically be diverted from your current activity to what is being said about you in this distant conversation.

**Selective Attention.** Selective attention refers to the sampling of stimuli, the selection of some of them for further processing and the remainder being discarded. The selected stimuli are usually associated with the topic currently of interest, which might be controlling the flightpath and airspeed of the aeroplane. Most of the time, however, if stress levels are not too high, there is sufficient additional capacity to notice stimuli not associated with the current task, such as emergency signals (bells, horns), your name, or your aircraft callsign.

Consciously selecting the most important stimuli for our immediate attention is known as *precoding*, and it usually depends upon what we think is important, how strong the stimulus is, and also upon our mental state (e.g. stress level). It is like the casualty department of the hospital where the patients are placed in an order of priority according to seriousness, urgency and trauma.

**Divided Attention.** Whilst concentrating on one task at a time, it is not possible to devote all attention to the one task – to the total exclusion of all others. There are often secondary tasks that have to be considered, such as raising the flaps following take-off (when your attention has to be diverted briefly from the primary task of monitoring and controlling the flightpath), or when making a radio call in the middle of responding to an emergency. Switching our attention from one set of stimuli to another is known as *divided attention,* or *time-sharing.*

### Stress
Usually we can switch our attention between tasks quite quickly, but stress and over-concentration on one task (single-mindedness, or one-track mind or mind-set) can inhibit this. Calls from air traffic control often go unnoticed when pilots are dealing with an emergency and their attention is narrowed to this one task. On some occasions, attention has not been divided enough to monitor the flightpath

concurrently with handling an emergency, and even though the emergency was resolved, the aeroplane crashed. Pilots under stress have also failed to hear warning signals, and have landed wheels-up or flown unexpectedly into the ground when warnings were there, but not perceived.

*The pilot turned base with the undercarriage still retracted. The tower controller called and warned the pilot but he continued the approach and landed wheels-up. When asked why he didn't respond to the tower's calls, he replied that he couldn't hear them because of the noise of the undercarriage warning horn. He heard the noise but did not perceive, accept, nor recognise the message that the noise was designed to convey.*

### Abnormalities in Perception

Perception is the process of receiving information through the senses, analysing it, and making it meaningful – it is a recognition process. This process is, on occasions, subject to certain abnormalities, which include:

- *hallucinations* – false perception of something that is not really there, i.e. imagined and not real, with no actual stimulus, only an imagined one;
- *illusions* – false perception due to *misinterpretation* of the stimuli, e.g. psychological illusions due to misinterpretation of signals from other people, optical illusions due to deceptive qualities in the stimuli received, such as sloping ground when we expect flat ground; and
- *agnosia* – a brain disorder that interferes with the correct interpretation of sensation, and that would disqualify a person from holding a pilot's licence.

Problems in perception also arise when we receive conflicting information from different senses, such as between our eyes and our balance mechanisms during a prolonged turn.

## Decision-Making

Once the stimuli are received and perceived, the brain is now in a position to make a decision. The message is now processed – decoded, recognised, understood, classified, acted upon and stored for future use. If it is a new image, the brain decides what it means and what to do about it – if anything. If it is a recognised image, there may be a previously learnt response to the same image/situation stored somewhere in memory. The snapshot of the runway is being referred to long-term memory, and its relative position is judged. The brain seeks an exactly matching image of the same or similar runway in the same relative position – that you have seen before, and that your instructor has previously told you is too close. The situation clearly calls for action. You need to turn away from the runway to begin to adjust the spacing – but you only need to authorise the action consciously, that is, if you want to do it. The mechanics of the control inputs have already been learnt, and, once decided, the action is a routine. The piloting is being done at a subconscious level.

Let's consider how we store information in memory.

# Memory

Memory is the capacity to classify, sort and store information and then retrieve it when needed. Memory is amazing. Events from years ago can be brought immediately to mind, words not used for a long time fit readily into sentences, which are correctly structured according to rules of grammar learnt in school, perfumes and tunes not experienced for decades can be recognised immediately – and can trigger associated situations or events.

Precisely how the memory functions is not fully understood, but it seems that memory consists of electrical signals passing between millions of brain cells, with different types and levels of memory, based on the period for which the information is retained and available for use. An equivalent might be the RAM and hard drive of a PC. The operating system (Unix, Mac OS or MS-DOS) are equivalent to the programs and processes we learnt and that control how we process the data stored in our memory (storage) banks, i.e. they are the result of our upbringing, education, training and our (acquired) self-discipline. These different types of memory can be categorised as:

- the sensory memory, where sensed items remain briefly (1 second for visual images, 5 seconds for sounds);
- the working memory;
- the short-term memory; and
- the long-term memory.

For practical purposes, the short-term memory and the working memory are considered to be one and the same.

## Sensory Memory

The sensory memory retains images, sounds, and other stimuli, for just a second or two – long enough for us to select which ones to attend to – before they are lost.

## Working Memory

The working memory contains the information that we are currently using, and which may be drawn from the long-term memory, with electrical signals passing back and forth between the memory and the central decision-making part of the brain. The working memory does, however, have limited capacity (like RAM). In the working memory, we work on the information that we have chosen to attend to. We either:

- rehearse it, i.e. repeat it a number of times in an attempt to remember it, as in rote learning; or
- encode it, by trying to understand it, or relating it to something we already know.

Encoding (understanding) is usually a better way of remembering something over a long period than rehearsal (rote learning). As mentioned earlier, some models treat the short-term memory and the working memory as one and the same.

## Short-Term Memory

The short-term memory in the brain is capable of holding only a few items for a brief period, typically seven items for 15 seconds, before they are forgotten. For instance, when you hear a telephone number spoken, or read the number in a telephone book, and then immediately dial it without error, you are using your short-term memory. If you delay the dialling for say 30 seconds, and do not rehearse (i.e. repeat) the number to hold it in your short-term memory, you will most likely dial a wrong number.

Similarly, a message from ATC to *'Change frequency to one three two decimal one'* will remain in your short-term memory long enough for you to select the frequency. Any delay, however, or any excess of additional information, and you will probably forget the frequency. Well-trained air traffic controllers pass only a single piece of information at one time, especially when they are aware that a pilot is inexperienced or may be under stress.

An ATC route clearance may contain four or five or even more items, and so is best written down as it is received. Your short-term memory may not be able to cope, both in terms of number of items and also in time of retention. ATC clearances must be read back by the pilot to ensure correct understanding. You can try this out by reading the next sentence once, and then repeating it aloud as a read-back:

*'Adelaide Clearance Delivery, Alfa Tango Charlie, Cleared to Parafield via Port Adelaide, one-thousand five-hundred, squawk zero four one seven, call Departures one two four decimal two, airborne.'*

Not so easy is it? Hence the need to write down clearances as they are being given. The seven items for 15 seconds is very variable between people (some might only be able to remember three items for 10 seconds), or for the same person under different levels of stress or tiredness.

It is possible to increase the capacity of the short-term memory, not by trying to remember more items, but by combining several items into one, a process known as grouping information, i.e. making clusters or groups of information instead of individual items. For instance, when you are given a new telephone number, such as 315 3023, it is better to remember it, not as seven pieces of information 3-1-5-3-0-2-3 but as two groups 315 3023, or three groups 315 30 23. This still leaves some capacity in your short-term memory, if needed immediately, say, for a name, before the number of items reaches 7 or thereabouts. Similarly, the radio frequency 132.1 could be remembered as one item instead of four.

Mnemonics can also be used to group information, such as in checklists. It is a lot easier to remember the mnemonic *PUF* on short final than it is to remember each of the items individually: *propeller, undercarriage* and *flaps*. Seeing a written instruction and then saying it aloud helps considerably. We can actually check ourselves when we hear ourselves speak. It is a very useful tool. Further, visual patterns of groups of letters or numbers are well retained. We see and hear and recognise in patterns. We are a very visual species – especially pilots. The design of the cockpit displays, controls and warnings can exploit this very effectively or can waste this talent.

## Long-Term Memory

The long-term memory is where information is filed for later use after being rehearsed or encoded in the working memory. The information may have to be retrieved several minutes later, or as long as several decades later.

Information seems to be stored in two areas, one involving *meaning*, such as the use of language, and the other involving *events*. The information can be reconstructed and brought together in the working memory when needed. Unfortunately, the reconstruction is not always totally accurate, as we all know when comparing our memory of an event with someone else's, or even with our own diary.

Items that are encoded (entered) and categorised into the long-term memory are thought to stay there for ever, although there may be problems and delays in retrieving the information, especially if it has not been recalled or used for some time. Periodically recalling important information from the long-term memory, i.e. practice, enables it to be recalled more readily when you really need it. For this reason, it is good technique to occasionally practise recalling items that should be known, such as limitations and vital emergency checks. Also, repetition will embed the correct pattern of thought. A singer, having learnt the lyrics, may recall them correctly many years later.

The information stored in the long-term memory is of value when the brain is trying to evaluate new information that has just been sensed. Usually, the brain will try to associate new data with data already stored in the long-term memory. Totally new information, bearing no relation to anything previously sensed and stored, will probably take longer to process mentally than familiar information, because the brain cannot associate it with anything.

An example of this could be when attempting your first visual approach, with no experience of how the runway should appear, or how the aircraft should feel. You have to think everything through from first principles. With experience, however, you will be able to compare the current situation with previous earlier situations.

### Meaning Memory

The meaning memory part of the long-term memory is also known as the *semantic memory*. It is where information is stored in terms of words. Knowledge stored in this part of the long-term memory includes the meaning and use of language, remembered items such as home telephone number and address, vital checklists, and so on. New material being learned and entered into the meaning part of the long-term memory should be given our full attention. We should try to understand it thoroughly, organising the various pieces of information logically into word messages so that our brain can encode it accurately and then store it. Association with items already in store helps with the encoding process. Learning in situation – for instance, learning checklists in an actual cockpit or simulated cockpit – often helps with encoding, and with the retrieval later on, since the information was learned in a familiar environment. The scenario is important reinforcement, like rehearsal for a ballet. Good encoding into the meaning memory makes later retrieval of the information easier and more meaningful. If the meaning of the information is understood, it can often be retrieved bit by bit through logic and located via several channels.

## Event Memory

The event memory part of the long-term memory is also known as the *episodic* memory. Interesting events and episodes are stored here. Visual images can also be stored in the *spatial* part of the memory. Unfortunately, images are occasionally not all that accurately stored, sometimes being coloured by our attitudes and expectations, i.e. what we think must have happened, what would have been logical to have happened, or what we would have liked to happen.

Accident investigators are often faced with expert witnesses of aircraft accidents, such as pilots, not remembering the event totally accurately. Their knowledge of aviation and their attitude and expectations as to what must have happened, or at least of what possibly happened, interferes with their memory of what actually did happen. Non-expert witnesses, having no prejudices or expectations, can often recall the details more accurately than expert witnesses.

## Memory Problems

Sometimes information cannot be retrieved due to poor encoding, and sometimes due to brain damage. *Amnesia* is the total or partial loss of memory following physical injury such as concussion, disease, drugs, or psychological trauma. It usually affects the event *(episodic)* memory, with the meaning *(semantic)* memory relatively untouched. A person suffering amnesia or brain damage may be able to speak sensibly with a good use of language, but be unable to remember events.

Having accessed our databanks, we can now allocate the appropriate action to the appropriate level of consciousness.

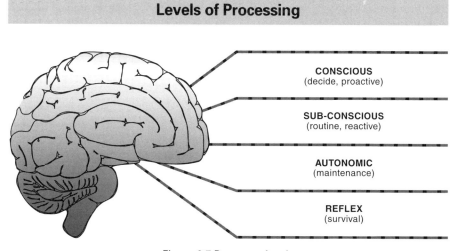

Levels of Processing

CONSCIOUS
(decide, proactive)

SUB-CONSCIOUS
(routine, reactive)

AUTONOMIC
(maintenance)

REFLEX
(survival)

Figure 6-7 **Processor levels**

## Conscious Control

Conscious control is the active intervention of the mind to take control of the situation. Rather than leave the process to automatic reactions or conditioned responses, the mind takes positive control and actively concentrates and participates in the control and decision-making functions.

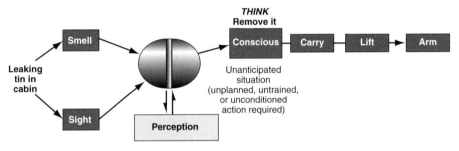

Figure 6-8 **Conscious processing**

The reasons for this intervention can be many and varied – from a situation for which the person has not previously been trained, to where the person is out of practice or where the risk levels are higher than usual and the consequences of error or inaccuracy are not acceptable (e.g. when you have to assume control from your student). When the conscious mind is participating, whether in an active control mode or a positive monitoring mode, the senses then function to check the outcome of the control inputs or decisions and make further corrections to achieve the desired result. This active cycle is called a control loop, and when the senses check the response this is called feedback or the feedback loop.

### Control Loop

The brain is always keen to follow up instructions, to see if the decision/action achieved the desired or expected result, and whether further action is required. Note that this feedback can be part of the conditioned response. Say the altitude you have achieved is within one hundred feet and that tolerance was acceptable to your instructor or Captain, then the skill will fly the aircraft within those tolerances. Your conscious mind can be on other things. If you were taught and self-disciplined to maintain altitude to within fifty feet, then the skill circuit will strive for that tolerance. If you were used to accepting a one-hundred-foot error and the situation required a fifty-foot accuracy, then your conscious mind would actively take control to achieve the desired result.

An example of the feedback loop is control of the radio volume. Say, the signal that came in through the sound channel was that the radio volume was too high – in relation to your acceptable level or for the particular situation. Signals have gone out resulting in hand movement to the volume control. While the action is under way, feedback signals will be returned to the brain, including your touch of the knob, how far it is rotated, and the eventual acceptable reduction in sound level. You can see there are distinct levels or styles of mental (or cognitive) function. Here, sound has been treated as an absolute, rather like temperature, in that if there is too much, do something about it. Obviously, modulated sound also conveys meaning – messages from the outside world. However, if the volume is what is capturing your attention, then meaning is not processed. The reason for that is the mind is a single-channel processor and sorts according to priority.

Feedback is manifested in many ways. The simplest relates to movement. If your brain wants your hand to move to a particular place, feedback images tell when it has arrived there and signals to move are stopped.

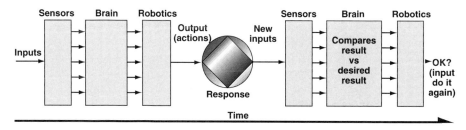

Figure 6-9 **Serial processing**

Hunger is a stimulus to eat. The 'that's enough' feedback message is often not as strong as it could be. Indeed, a lot of our decision-making – and other drives in life – is based on perception of a need, followed by the motivation to satisfy the craving. When feedback is potentially weak, knowing when a need is satisfied may be something we have to augment with conscious will, e.g. dieting.

Will-power (or won't power) is the control factor. It is based on the proposition that so much of what we do, can and should be is subordinated to conscious, positive management so that we make rational rather than autonomous choices. The exercise of this management function is crucial in flight.

## Management

The *sapiens* in *homo sapiens* means *thinking*. Like so many aspects of life that have become unremarkable and commonplace, the fact that we are thinking beings escapes the attention it deserves. It really is quite extraordinary (and perhaps false?) that, of all living creatures, we are the only ones that use complex reasoning. Certainly, some animals appear to be following logic and using rational processes, but these appear to be all learned behaviour, or conditioned responses. The Russian physiologist Ivan Pavlov would ring a bell before feeding his dogs. The dogs came to associate the bell with food. He then rang the bell and found that he could make the poor critters salivate with no smell or food in sight. They had developed a conditioned response, which would eventually disappear if left unfulfilled. Burrhus Skinner, an American psychologist, taught 'logic' to rats. Thorndike, an eminent scientist, observed how cats learnt. But apparently, none of the animal behaviour was the product of conscious decision-making. It was all learnt − subconsciously driven habit patterns. In humans, we exercise both active controls and learnt responses to manage rational processes and our resultant behaviour and action.

This crucial difference between us and the other species is evident in the manner in which we manage − or exercise control over − our information processing. The conceptual model shows a series of control points that represent the control function.

An image may be available to the eyes, for example, but we decline to 'see' it. In the same way, there are feelings and sounds that we will not process. That is, the processing is terminated before it gets to the 'perception' stage, through an exercise of will − of rational choice.

The IP model is hypothetical rather than an accurate layout of complex circuits and functions. While the control option has been placed at various points, it can exist at many more, as we shall discover later. Further, the impression should not be gained that control is invariable or omnipotent. In some manifestations it is strong, in others weak. Blocking an unwelcome smell or sensation of motion can be done − but it is not always possible. Exercise of the control or management function is, like so much else, a skill or (as we commonly apply) a discipline. It sets the standard that the skill seeks to achieve. If you practise with it − give it good solid workouts − it will always be at maximum strength when you need it.

The problem of time has been mentioned. Time control, or time management, is an essential feature of the overall control/management function.

Before moving on to review how your mind works to support you in flight, it is necessary to differentiate two closely related syndromes. In walking through the IP model, autonomous functions were mentioned. These are complex skills, habits, capable of being commenced and operated with a minimum of conscious time/effort. *Autonomous skills* should not be confused with *autonomic functions* − breathing and heartbeat.

## Skills

The time problem for pilots is hardly affected at all by reflex actions. In other words, reflexes are rarely useful in flight. They are not the handy little time-savers they are designed to be. Indeed, your interests might be better served by suppressing the reflex, or converting it to a controlled reaction. So there's still the problem of 'so much to do, so little time'. Another option for minimising the consumption of valuable time, in thinking through reactions to stimuli, is to adopt a wide range of skills, or skill sets, that can be consciously activated but autonomously operated.

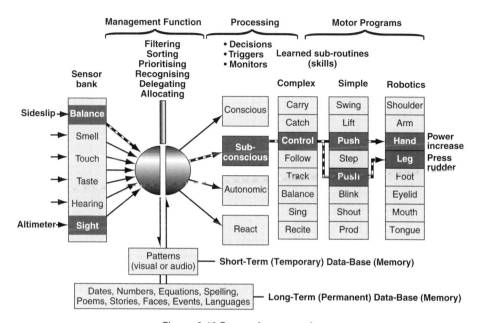

Figure 6-10 **Processing example**

For example, the reflex stimulus causes an action without thought. By way of contrast, once you have received and processed information – say you are at a lower altitude than you want to be – you need to carry out the remedial actions – power increase to anticipate the climb, then backstick to enter the climb. If you talk yourself through these actions, step-by-step, *('move right hand. . . ')* much time is used up. If you have memorised a string of actions that will do the trick, you can initiate them with only a single thought. Time consumption is minimised.

In this case, the demand was not especially taxing. You 'read' a problem, checked to see if there was a preprogrammed solution (the skill), and activated it. However, flying isn't that simple. And this process is still time-consuming. The need to exercise skills invariably arises in multiples – if you are to enter a climb, a power adjustment must precede, requiring a rudder adjustment, and so on. The demands are always pressing. You may have to adjust distance out as well as height, manage your situational awareness, and on and on. Minimising time for the activation of whole sets of skills is obviously going to be an advantage.

## Complex Skills and Sets of Skills (Motor Programs)

To see how complex sets of skills function, let's go back to that point on downwind in the circuit. Out of all of the components of the landscape image in the area where you look, you have selected the runway to *perceive* – and to pass the resultant image into the computer for processing. The fact is that you are too close in and are going to have to turn away.

We already know that talking through each individual step is too time-costly. However, if there is available to you an image of that precise situation, gained from earlier experience (or from another form of concentrated learning) and if it is also 'connected' to remedial action, 'turn right 5 degrees', or a string of actions, 'apply power, raise nose, trim', then the necessary action will occur without your having to think much about it at all. This autonomous function is so much like a reflex that it is often called a *conditioned reflex*. In truth, it is simply a habit, something you do without necessarily knowing you are doing it. In learning to fly, you have, through practice, inserted many such habit-programs into your long-term memory.

As you can see, this is the most time-saving controlled option of all. Note that the control switch is interposed at the commencement of the action path. Sometimes it is not there at all. When a pilot is operating at high levels of demand, conscious control is normally exercised as a power of veto. That is, at the instant your mind receives an image that matches an 'undesired situation' pattern in memory, the 'fix' slips into place. Your ability to stop an autonomous set of actions happening is limited, though, for you may not even perceive the problem you are reacting to. You will be able to recall many instances where you have suddenly found yourself doing something without knowing why.

Learning to fly comprises an extensive process of learning and storing sequences, thus automating sets of actions *(motor programs)* for various contingencies – walking and running are examples. In the airborne applications, your hands move the controls, all without your saying a single word to yourself, nor even perhaps being consciously aware of what you are doing. What has happened here is that the conscious mind has been bypassed. The perceived situation had been referred to memory, checking for a 'have we seen this before?' Note that there is no control switch on the return *message*.

When the stored image is happened upon, a string of electrical signals go out to the various places and the right actions automatically take place. The habit pattern is activated. This, however, is not always in your best interests, as there are bad habits.

When skill habits are activated, the autonomous actions take place *before* perception has consciously been registered. This pathway through the information processing model also shows autonomous – or subconscious – activity taking place *after* perception. The effect is pretty much the same, with a 'pre-programmed' decision taking the place of genuine, rational, choice.

Unthought decision-making can occur when what you have perceived – say a low fuel state – disagrees strongly with what you would prefer to it to be. You subconsciously continue as though the fuel was sufficient. You have thus bypassed the rational part of your brain. Strong emotion has this potential to render you 'blind' to the smart choice.

Note, however, that the model again contains options to use the control function at several places. You can choose to let your subconscious programs have the running, or you can choose to take conscious control. When emotion is involved, the options for choice may not be strong. As in the case of exerting control over an otherwise 'reflex' activation of a habit, you will need to learn how to positively manage inappropriate use of the subconscious mind – for example, to refuse to admit the truth of a situation.

## Subconscious (Learnt) Routines

**Learning the Skills.** Learning the basic skills of flying requires much conscious thought, concentration and decision-making (as did walking or learning to ride a bicycle). Practising basic skills over and over allows you to learn the responses needed for certain stimuli so well that, eventually, manipulating the controls of the aeroplane can be run by motor programs – and feedback will be included (to the standard that you were shown by your instructor) An experienced pilot, for instance, will almost automatically apply back pressure on the control column when sinking below the flightpath, and add power if speed is decreasing. A trainee pilot must think it through before acting, which of course takes much more effort. There is then a direct link between the level of skill, recent practice and, consequently, the workload needed to achieve the task to the desired standard.

Well-learned skills leave the central decision-making part of your brain available for other activities, such as navigation, updating fuel calculations, making and receiving radio calls, handling emergencies, making judgements and, in general, just managing the whole flight from start to finish – a task which requires a lot of conscious thought. Using an autopilot can also off-load routine mechanical tasks.

Your ability to fly consists of a tool-kit of learned, practised and retained skills. Skills exist in two forms: physical skills are the obvious example; however, ways of thinking, including how you manage your information processing functions and routines, and how you regard certain issues (i.e., your attitude to them), are also skills. They are cognitive skills, and are learned and maintained in the same way as physical aptitudes, i.e. learned through exercise and repetitive practice – and maintained through exercise and repetitive practice. While it is generally easy to see that you need to practise to keep your hand in at, say, sport, applying the concept of disciplined workouts to keep your cognitive skills in good shape is not so readily accepted. Here's a way to remind yourself about skill patterns: when you input data into an automatic teller machine, you are following a mental pattern. It is well learned. You can remind yourself of how well learned it is. Next time you use the machine, make the key entries with your left hand.

**Autonomic Activities.** Normal bodily functions such as breathing, the heartbeat, the digestive process, maintenance of body temperature, etc., continue under the control of the *autonomic nervous system,* which does not require any thinking on our part. Biological control systems and reflexes do not require learning and/or conscious thought.

## Reflexes

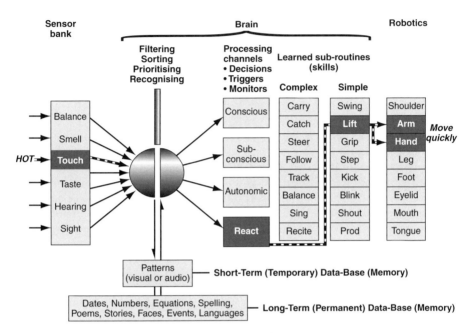

Figure 6-11 **Reaction**

Certain actions are so important that *immediate* – as opposed to *considered* – action is required. The classic is touching something hot enough to severely injure at the point of contact. There is no time to think about a response. You will be damaged and in pain before a conscious decision is made. The touch point must be withdrawn from the heat source immediately.

*Reflex centres* permit these unconsidered actions. Located in places such as the elbow and knee (there are many other centres), they short-circuit rational processes. Taking the case of the knee reflex point, all nerves from the lower part of the limb pass through it. For another instance, at the very instant your hand rests on the burning ember, the 'MAYDAY HOT' message arrives at the reflex point, the order to move is instantly issued – from the reflex centre, not the brain – and the hand moves or the eyelid blinks.

Reflexes bypass complex thinking, rational processing and conscious control.

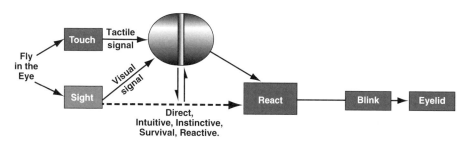

Figure 6-12 **Reflex action (bypass channel)**

A reflex action is an instantaneous, unconsidered, move. If you touch something hot or sharp (the stimulus), your hand rapidly moves back before your mind has even registered heat or pain, and well before the conclusion that withdrawal from the touching position might be wise, *vis-à-vis* past experience (memory of previous pain/injury). All of that computing processing has been bypassed. You know about muscular reflexes from medical examinations testing the reflex centres in your knees and from experiencing inadvertent contact with your elbow (the *funny bone*).

Note from the model diagram that the conscious control switch is interposed between the reflex and the action. Although reflexes are powerfully automatic, they do not have to be that way. You will know from experimentation that the knee reflex, when tapped, will not always 'fire'. By 'tensing up', you can override the 'flinch' response.

It is essential for a pilot to learn to control reflexes. For example, an automatic flinch that has you pulling sharply back on the control column could pull the wings off. You can practise overriding reflexes by, for example, when you hear a loud 'BANG!', not permitting the flinch to occur. You thus exercise conscious control over an automatic action. In this way, you convert a *reflex* (no intelligent control) to a trained/learned *reaction* (a thought-through, preplanned, trained, conditioned response).

Not all reflexes can be thus subordinated to conscious control. Just as you can no more stop your skin tanning from being in the sun, nor your pupils from dilating in the dark, there are sensations that are going to 'arrive' in your brain, unwelcome though they may be, at any time. Some are associated with movement. We will have considered examples of 'felt' sensations of motion in flight, and your likely reflex reactions, that you may or may not be able to dominate. Similarly, there are many *autonomic* body functions (e.g. breathing) that are associated with a reflex action (yawning).

Additionally, while reflexes are *hard-wired* into our nervous systems, and are thus 'dumb', the time problem suggests that we ought to be able to accomplish equally snappy responses under conscious control – that is, intelligently. We can. We can learn rapid responses by inserting into long-term memory images that are instantly recognised, along with matching decision that resolve any perceived problem. This cycle of *detect a need* and *apply a response* is called a *skill*. A cricket ball is heading your way, fast. Rather than process the stimulus–perception–analysis–action cycle, in time-consuming spoken words, you want to be able to reach out, automatically, arms moving so as to ensure the hands will intercept the projectile, and do all of the other things necessary to catch the ball. These are skills. Some are simple, others complex.

## Chapter 7

# Management of Time

Cognitive processes can only be active (conscious) in one channel at a time, e.g. when you focus your attention on hearing words, other conscious processes cease. Therefore, time limits the amount of attention you can allocate to receiving information and then processing it to make a decision. Since only one piece of data can be considered at a time, time itself becomes a constraint. To respond appropriately, the brain must allocate priorities, shed less important information, or delegate actions to trained responses.

Time is a resource and is consumed just like fuel, and like fuel it can run out. Time must be managed just as carefully. Managing time means you allocate blocks of time to discrete functions. That is, you allocate time to attention. If you wish to understand the meaning of words, you allocate time to receiving information through the hearing channel. If you wish to interpret an image, you allot time to the visual channel, and so on. Attention takes place or is directed *(pay attention!)* when you authorise the stimulus – an image, sound or sensation – to enter the brain for processing. In flight, with a multitude of items to keep track of, you variously allocate time in clumps, or batches, to the items in accordance with their importance and urgency.

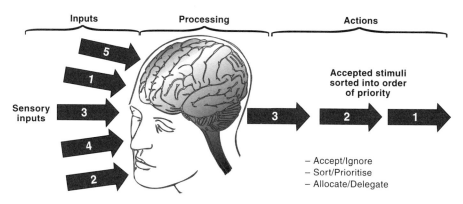

Figure 7-1 **Prioritising**

This process is called *situational awareness* (SA). You achieve situational awareness by managing the time you allocate to periods of attention, gathering pieces of information so you can assemble and update the total picture. For example, if you were on downwind in the circuit. Let's say three things concern you at one instant: height above the ground, distance out from the runway and fuel quantity. You would like to be able to:

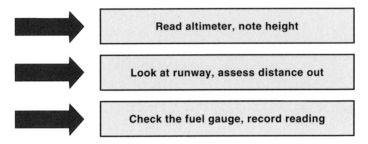

Figure 7-2 **Tasks**

However, it is not possible to do the three things at once. They can't be done in parallel. They have to be done in series and placed in order of priority. Discrete parcels of time have to be allocated to each information source to enable them to fit into the single-channel operation.

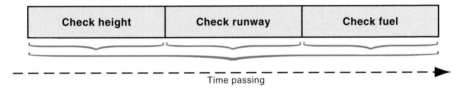

Figure 7-3 **Sequencing**

Furthermore, you also know that some readings take longer than others.

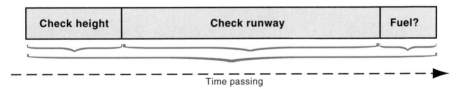

Figure 7-4 **Allocation of time**

And that's not the full story, either. Since in a linear processor – our single-channel computer – every function consumes time, it must have its own separate time allocation, or chunk. So you consume time when you manage the allocation of time between tasks. To exercise positive control and to manage priorities, the management function itself needs conscious direction, and thus time in which to do it.

The allocation of time to attention – where you look to take in information – competes with the time required for managing where the attention is being directed. You can establish this for yourself. When driving along, tell yourself to shift the focus of where you are looking. The very act of directing your attention to another source of information (or stimulus) itself occupies time. In other words, switching your attention from place to place takes time. It may not take much, but it is a consumer.

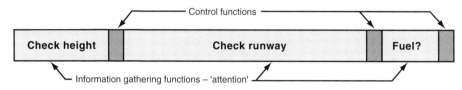

Figure 7-5 **Control functions**

As the demands on time accumulate, the time to act becomes increasingly limited. As there is only the single channel to process information in a multitude of apparent channels, the key to maintaining situational awareness is time management.

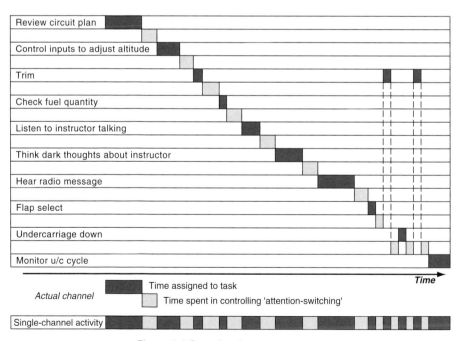

Figure 7-6 **Complex time management**

While the model given above is complex, the real world of flight is even more intricate and demanding. However, we can be trained. The crucial fact is that although we can operate as if our consciousness was multi-channelled (time-shared multiplexing), the mind really is single-channel. In practice, pilots group skills into virtual channels, e.g. fly the plane (aviate – in a trained response mode), keep track of position (navigate – by keeping track of position), communicate in recognised patterns of words and take time to look for traffic and plan arrival in between immediate tasks. The critical skill is switching between the channels in the correct order of priority at the time. It is this switching that provides positive management of the time resource (active situational awareness); otherwise, we can partially *lose the plot.*

## Virtual Channels

Faced with a multitude of task demands, pilots typically group demands by like type. Each group of like demands constitutes a *virtual channel.* As intimated, virtual channels are defined by functions/activities. Examples are:
- fly the aircraft *(aviate);*
- keep track of location, maintain situational awareness *(navigate);*
- keep other people informed and be informed *(communicate);* and
- manage the time spent in each channel *(allocate – decide).*

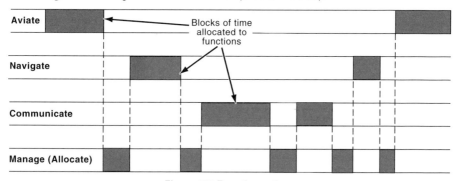

Figure 7-7 **Function – time**

As this model will be used extensively, please ensure you follow all that it tells you:
- although the mind works in the one channel, in flying, we group associated activities into virtual channels – separate control loops (under *aviate* for example, you might have working subroutines of *maintain altitude* and *turn left);*
- *navigate* encompasses all positional awareness functions, including time allocated to monitoring fuel state, location, progress according to the plan;
- keeping crew and ATC informed takes place using time from the *communicate* channel; and
- only one activity can take place at a time and, in between each activity, you need to *allocate* some time to direct your attention to the next task.

The *allocate* channel contains all of those control functions that choose where attention will be directed and for how long. It also represents the time used to permit stimuli to be admitted for processing and to authorise use of a reaction or skill. This is the operation of the conscious control in the information processing model (chapter 6).

There will be times where you just can't be looking at an information source for long enough to get the message. In that case, a series of rapid glances will permit you to get the reading you want. Consider low flying. The *aviate* and *navigate* channels are properly given most of the priority. You have an instructor alongside whom you need to keep informed by communicating frequently, thus ensuring that he/she knows what you are doing and planning. Now you need to take a fuel reading. But you feel that if you look inside at the gauge for long enough for it to register, you will not be paying sufficient attention to obstacle clearance.

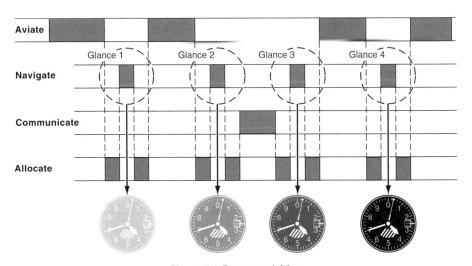

Figure 7-8 **Data acquisition**

Through a series of swift glances, you find you can assemble or accumulate a reading (hence the value of analog displays).

Note that the switching messages can be quite small, and thus not demanding of excessive time allocation. Efficient use of time enables rapidly switched attention like this. It is a valuable skill and can be practised. It is also a good illustration of the value of analog display – as we'll see in the chapter on ergonomics.

The less time spent doing one thing, the more is available for others. You don't have to be inside the cockpit to exercise this skill. You can practise rapid attention-switching – and time management in general – walking around, driving a car or cycling. Force the pace. Make yourself scan a whole series of information sources as rapidly as you possibly can.

## Stress

You will have experienced how your scan control can become disrupted under stress

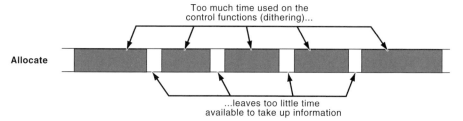

Figure 7-9 **Poor allocation of time – crisis management – saturation**

This sort of inefficient scan pattern – the mind slowed to a crawl – is usually the product of confusion. At other times, say, through boredom, the glance lazily focuses on the middle distance, going into idle mode (*empty space myopia*), and there is no scanning at all. It is important to note that the models used to illustrate time management and the control function are artificial. The reality is that the human mind functions in the one channel. However, for simplicity we use four virtual channels. But there is another essential aspect to consider: emotion.

## Emotion

Emotion (anger, fear, enchantment) is processed in the conscious mind. It is not, and cannot be, a subconscious process. It is a real-time activity. As long as emotion is present, therefore, time is consumed. In other words, there is less time for the other functions. The stronger the emotion, the greater the time stolen. As aviation presents more opportunities than most occupations to experience the grossest emotion of all – anxiety related to fear of death – then its effect is of major interest. Rather than depict gross apprehension as a separate dominant channel, it is best to see it in terms of how it affects your other preoccupations.

The engine stopping shortly after take-off could present a situation like this:

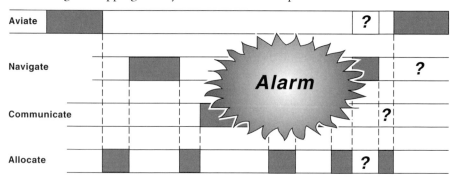

Figure 7-10 **Attention-grabbing (confusion)**

Emotion can totally obliterate logic. However, the more deeply learned and rehearsed are the skills, the better you will cope with an emergency. Moreover, by the very possession of those skills – you know they are there – the more confidence you will have that you are able to prevail over the problem. But you cannot fool yourself that you have the capacity when you do not. When the pressure comes on, and you say to yourself, *'I can handle this'*, if that is not true, another voice will come right back saying, *'No you can't'*.

The proficient pilot we also saw earlier is better equipped to manage an emergency, no matter what level of apprehension. More important, because of the confidence in the skills being there, practised and readily available, able to be put into action with an instant's thought, the anxiety factor, though tangible, is considerably diminished.

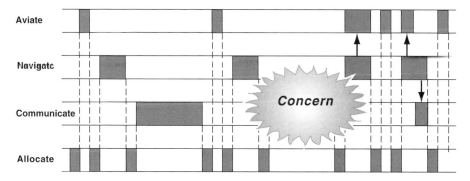

Figure 7-11 **Managed emergency (re-allocation of time)**

## Overload

Emotion has the capacity to paralyse through indecision (like a rabbit frozen in your headlights or a cat mesmerised by a snake). To ensure that you can cope, you will need to have tested and trained your resources – rehearsed the appropriate actions for that very situation. You will need to also understand the reason why emotion can disable your thinking and how it can be contained. The paralysis is an example of a known phenomenon: *mental* or *cognitive overload*.

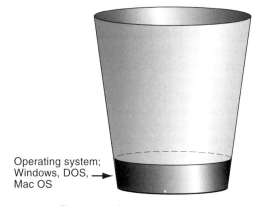

Operating system; Windows, DOS, Mac OS →

Figure 7-12 **Processing power**

As well as being a single channel, the mind has a fixed upper limit on processing power at any given time. In the case of a computer, the limit is imposed by RAM (random access memory). RAM is like a bucket that is progressively filled.

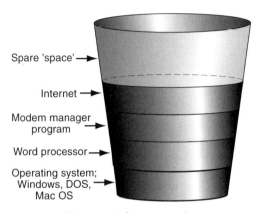

Spare 'space' →

Internet →

Modem manager program →

Word processor →

Operating system; Windows, DOS, Mac OS →

Figure 7-13 **Spare capacity**

As the computer starts up, the operating system is loaded into RAM. Next, you start up a working program, say, a word processor, and also activate your connection with the Internet.

The remaining RAM space is available for files that you either create, or download from the Net. If you load the RAM until it is full, as the last byte of the last file slides into memory, it has used the last available space. In other words, there is not even enough room left for a single keystroke or command to be processed, and the computer freezes. The human brain is similar.

## Human Cognitive Capacity

The schematic below represents your fixed processing capacity. You will recall that this is conscious processing, not subconscious. (Incidentally, our own 'computing power' is about 18 bits per second and is not a function of intelligence. We all, regardless of IQ, have about the same 'number-crunching' ability. Intelligence seems to be more a function of long-term memory and ease of access to it.)

Maximum 'cognitive capacity'

Figure 7-14 **Processing capacity**

During normal, day-to-day, activity, there is not much demand on the computing resource. A little, but not much. The mind is in idle mode.

Normal activity, low demand for information processing

Figure 7-15 **Small demand**

Flying can add a great deal to the demand for processing.

Figure 7-16 **Higher demand**

As noted earlier, emotion intrudes uncontrollably into the conscious mind. In this situation, a large amount of emotion is being processed, on top of normal, day-to-day workload demands. But there is still some space left in RAM.

Figure 7-17 **Demand plus emotion**

But what if you experienced the same *belt* of emotion while in a high-demand flight regime?

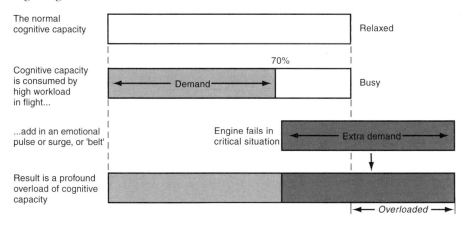

Figure 7-18 **Overload**

*The twin-engine passenger jet was in the approach pattern at 6,000 ft when it rolled to 90° of bank. The uncommanded roll could have been caused by a runaway rudder system component, or the wing vortex of a preceding heavy jet. Either way, the general view is that recovery was possible. Accelerating to a higher airspeed and application of aileron, assisted by some rudder, to get the wings level, then nose-up pitch to regain level flight, would have been the appropriate control sequence. The flight data recorder (FDR) shows that the only control input was full back stick. The aircraft stalled and crashed. All 132 on board perished. The cockpit voice recorder (CVR) tape reveals evidence that the pilots succumbed to emotional overload.*

The result is the same as the computer. All processing space is taken up. There is not even enough remaining capacity to manage the control channel. This leads to total loss of control – panic. Once control is lost under time-critical circumstances, it is never regained. However, you can maximise your resistance to anxiety, and ensure you can always stay well back from the panic threshold, by anticipating and rehearsing potential high-workload situations:

High demand,
but plenty of
spare capacity

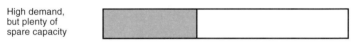

Figure 7-19 **Managing overload**

Through training, you are never too loaded in flight. That is, you know your checks until they are intuitive, and you have learnt your flight management skills as deeply. Through self-confidence, you know you will prevail in an emergency, and thus experience less anxiety (less emotion) when it happens:

The emotion is felt – as
it will be – but through
your self-confidence, it
will be less. Capacity is
not exceeded.

Figure 7-20 **Control through training and self-confidence**

The emotion is felt – as it will be – but through your self-confidence, it will be lessened. Capacity is not exceeded.

Note the importance of well-learnt and rehearsed skills under these circumstances. Note also that the decision-making role was attributed to the conscious mind (as opposed to subconscious routines, reflex responses, and autonomic functions). The *analysis-leading-to-decision* process follows *perception* in the processing sequence. It is also a function of experience, conditioning and training. The response time between perceiving a stimulus and responding correctly to it depends to a large extent upon how much mental processing is required. If the central decision-maker is involved, then the response time will be longer than if the response comes through a reflex or a skill not involving the central decision-maker: the more practised the skill, the less response time and the less conscious attention required. Be careful though when the circumstances require a procedure contrary to a well-learnt skill or routine.

## Skills Memory

Skills, once learned, are difficult to modify. This is why an *ab initio* student is taught from flight one to check the undercarriage. However, there is a contrary argument that says that teaching a student to check the undercarriage of a fixed-gear aircraft degrades the authenticity of the check and actually produces a valueless routine. Often skill-based behaviour is difficult to explain. Three main errors are associated with this memory:

- *Action slips* are where the central decision-maker selects the correct routine but the wrong one is accidentally carried out, e.g. selecting gear up instead of flap after landing.

- *Environmental capture* is where multiple or sequential skills usually exercised together are automatically carried out even though all were not required, e.g. selecting flap when turning base for a planned flapless approach.

- *Reversion* is where the pilot returns to a previously learned sequence, such as putting gear down on approach for a water landing in an amphibious aircraft.

*The Canso was a large and elegant seaplane of WWII. An amphibian version, the Catalina, was subsequently developed. A very experienced Canso Captain was undergoing conversion training at an airfield and consistently failed to lower the undercarriage. Eventually he learnt the routine until he could made reliable circuits and bumps on the Catalina's land-legs. At the completion of this quite stressful unlearning and re-learning of routines, he then flew back to the seaplane base, where he landed, shut down and stepped out into the sea. (It is true.)*

Skills are the result of well-learned experience and exercise, such as walking, speaking, writing, riding a bicycle, driving a car, and (eventually) flying an aeroplane. A child learning to walk, or to ride a bicycle, has its mind fully occupied. Nothing can intrude. Having learned to balance the bicycle, however, the child can navigate a little better, hold a conversation while riding, or perhaps even watch for traffic – all at the same time. Learning to fly is no different. But what if the skill that is taught is incomplete and only covers the motor functions?

## Flying as a Skill-Set

While a student pilot is concentrating on learning to fly safely and accurately, the central decision-maker will be almost fully occupied. There will be very little spare capacity for other tasks such as navigation and radio calls – or even listening to the instructor. Once the student has learned the motor skills and practised them until they are second nature, flying the aeroplane will occur with little conscious thought. In this case, a string of activities is run autonomously in the brain, leaving the central decision-maker available for higher-level decisions.

Strings (or sets) of skills are often initiated by the central decision-maker. You might make a decision to get up and walk towards the door, but once this decision has been taken, the central decision-maker can drop out of the picture temporarily and let the motor program run the activity. As well as initiating the activity, the central decision-maker will also return to monitor the motor program from time to time, to check that the proper skill sequence is in use, and to check progress and decide when to stop.

It is possible that, even though a decision to commence a certain autonomous sequence has been taken, the wrong program swings into action. This could be walking in the wrong direction, or raising the flaps instead of the undercarriage, something that is especially likely when flying a different aeroplane type in which the position of the two controls has been interchanged. Your automatic skill sets need to be periodically monitored.

Using the wrong skill routine can also be dangerous with respect to movements of the throttle, mixture control, pitch control, and carburettor heat in an aeroplane. More than one aircraft has landed short of the runway because the mixture control was pulled fully out instead of the carburettor heat, stopping the engine instead of protecting it from ice. Hence the need for the central decision-maker to monitor the program in critical situations or where the consequences of error are unacceptable. For instance, when about to feather a propeller, visually check which lever your hand is on before you move it – and have the co-pilot confirm that you have the correct lever.

Errors due to old habits, such as moving the wrong lever, are more likely to occur when a pilot is tired and under-aroused, or when over-aroused and in a state of stress. You will remember that there is an intermediate level of arousal where optimum performance occurs. If skills are not used regularly, they deteriorate, and an activity that was once run automatically by a single thought may now have to be managed by conscious decision-making. This will occupy the central decision-maker and, as a result, you can expect a temporary deterioration in the performance of other tasks. Professional pilots returning from a holiday break notice this, as do musicians and others who have to perform skilled tasks. We can certainly *do* more than one thing at a time, thanks to skill programming, but we can only *think* about one thing at a time.

## Action and Feedback

Action is initiated by a conscious decision from the brain (a thinking response) or by an autonomous sequence that is running (a skill-based or learned response). A series of electrical signals will be sent along motor nerves to the appropriate muscles for the action to commence. It could be speech, body movement, or a decision to stay still. The results of the action can then be observed by our senses, with important feedback hopefully being perceived, i.e. noticed, analysed, and understood. If the feedback indicates that action is not having the desired result, then we can take further action.

For instance, during the take-off or ground landing roll, we attempt to maintain the runway centreline by moving the rudder pedals. A student may have to think consciously about this; an experienced pilot will do it automatically.

In both cases, the result, as to how well we are holding the centreline, needs to be monitored every few seconds, and adjustments made if necessary. In any manoeuvre, there is a continuing process of *action-feedback-action-feedback-action*. The standard to which we strive is a function of our training, self-discipline, motivation and arousal.

## Standards

How well we fly is measured by accuracy and passenger comfort. How well we manage the flight is a function of situational awareness and anticipation. How well we put them together is a function of our personal attitude and our training. Airmanship is the traditional term used to encompass these elements but now we know that there is more to it. To be complete, pilot training must now be far broader, and far more conscious of these elements, than ever before.

## Response Time

The time it takes for any initial stimulus to be perceived, considered, and acted upon can take between a fraction of a second and several seconds, depending upon the complexity of the decision to be made, the action to be taken and the acceptability of that degree of deviation. In a control loop, such as an autopilot, this is known as the *gain* – high gain means a quick response to any deviation, low gain is a sluggish response. High gain is less tolerant of deviations but can mean a rough ride, and so autopilots have a soft ride or half bank mode for fewer disturbances and a more comfortable flight. Responding to a stimulus often requires a series of sequential decisions to be made; this of course needs time due to the single-channel nature of the brain's central decision-maker. On approach to land, for instance, the undercarriage has been selected down and a horn unexpectedly sounds.

Some of the decisions that now need to be made are:

- Establish a safe flightpath. In this case, a go-around is essential to gain time and place you into a position where you can sort out the problem. Continuing with the approach is pushing you to a higher workload, with more critical demands – on time.
- Silence the horn to remove the distraction – now that the warning has been noted.
- What does the horn mean? Is it undercarriage not down, or something else? It means that the undercarriage has been selected down, but is not actually down.
- Radio call. Declare emergency to tower, ATC or other traffic.
- Carry out checklist items.

Throughout the decision-making following a very simple unexpected event, you must continue to switch attention through aviate, navigate, and communicate to allocate priorities and to trigger skilled responses.

In a situation like that above, you removed the pressure of time by deciding to make a missed approach, and then allowing the learnt skill to fly the aircraft. Once the safe response was seen to be in progress, the conscious mind then established the next priority. Time was thus made available to solve the problem. In other situations, you may not have that luxury – for instance, in a take-off that is rejected at a high speed on a limiting runway. This will require a split-second decision and immediate actions.

If the pilot of a large aircraft suspects a problem during the take-off run, especially as the decision speed is approached, there are only two seconds to decide what to do, *'Stop or go?'* Stopping may not be possible if a tyre has blown and reduced the wheel-braking capability. Continuing the take-off may not be possible if the problem is with the flight controls, or if the problem is multiple engine failure due to bird strikes. The enormous pressure of limited time between input and a necessary decision can sometimes lead to a faulty decision and response.

The risk of making a poor decision, no decision or an incorrect response is minimised by maintaining a high level of knowledge, and by practising manoeuvres frequently so that they becomes a conditioned response. The decision/response is thus based on the probability of the best course of action and then accepting those odds. Full-flight simulators can play a big role here, particularly when practising critical manoeuvres, such as aborted take-offs or engine failure at $V_1$.

## Mental Workload

Best performance is achieved by a combination of high levels of skill, knowledge, and experience (consistency and confidence), and with an optimum degree of arousal. Skill, knowledge and experience depend upon the pilot and his or her training; the degree of arousal depends not only upon the pilot but also upon other factors, such as the design of the cockpit, air traffic control, as well as upon the environment, motivation, personal life, weather, and so on. Low levels of skill, knowledge and experience, plus a poorly designed cockpit, bad weather, and poor controlling will lead to a high mental workload and a poor performance. If the mental workload becomes too high, decision-making will deteriorate in quality, or maybe not even occur. This could result in concentrating only on one task (sometimes called *tunnel vision*), with excessive or inappropriate load-shedding.

The pilot's tasks need to be analysed so that at no time do they demand more of the pilot than the average, current and fit pilot is capable of delivering. There should always be some reserve capacity – to allow for handling unexpected abnormal and emergency situations.

At the design stage, the pilot to be considered is an average pilot. On such a basis, the level of skills and responses are established for use in testing so that the aircraft can be certificated as compliant. But there is a valid argument that the specimen should not be the average pilot, because half of the pilot population would be below this standard.

The legislators establish the minimum acceptable standards for licensing, but the marginal pilot, who maintains only the minimum required standard, is not really of an acceptable standard. We can each ensure that we are at an acceptable standard by honestly reviewing the demand that the aircraft and the flight placed upon us. If our capabilities, mental or physical, were stretched at all, then we need more practice, more study or more training – at least in that aspect that challenged us. Many pilots feel that, under normal conditions, they should be able to operate at only 40–50% of capacity, except during take-offs and landings, when that might rise to 70%.

This leaves some capacity to handle abnormal situations. You can raise your capability by studying and practising, and by being fit, relaxed and well rested.

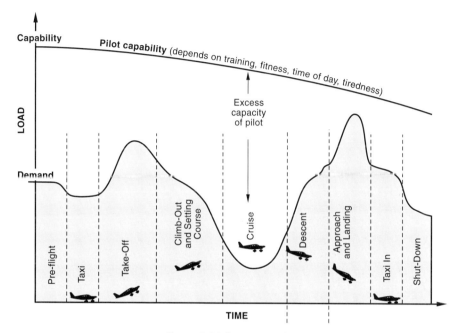

Figure 7-21 **Spare capacity**

## Mental Overload

Different parts of the brain can be overloaded:
- the *sensory memory* can be overloaded if there is too much stimulus, with too many important incoming signals to be perceived. A pilot coping with an abnormal or emergency situation, such as a ringing fire bell, might miss an ATC radio call advising details of conflicting traffic; and
- the *short-term memory* can be overloaded by excessive information or by time delays. It cannot cope with more than about 7 items, and these will only be retained for 15 or 30 seconds unless rehearsed (repeated). Incoming information will replace these items.

The single channel of the *central decision-making* part of the brain can be overloaded:
- if conflicting information is received;
- too many decisions are required in too short a time; or
- if the person is overstressed, unprepared or fatigued.

## Conflicting Information

Conscious decision-making is easier if all the information coming to the brain is in conformity and matches up. For instance, the clap of thunder that is heard is more easily assimilated if it matches up with a flash of lightning that occurred a few seconds prior. Unfortunately, the brain often receives *conflicting* information during flight, especially information that comes from the eyes and that which comes from the balance mechanism of the ears and bodily feel. Your balance mechanism and bodily feel might tell you that you are turning, but your eyes will tell you that the wings are level.

Good instrument training will ensure that you trust your eyes and what the instruments tell you over and above the other information. If, however, the situation is not so simple, say flying in cloud with a toppled attitude indicator or other failed instruments, resolving the conflict may be more difficult, and may lead to some stress.

## Learning

Learning is the process by which we acquire and store information and learn responses and skills for future use. It involves the formation or modification of already stored mental routines. As we have seen elsewhere there are different types of memory, e.g. short-term memory holds information for immediate use. Learning involves *semantic, episodic* and *motor memory.*

Episodic memory (being memory of events) stores information without any conscious effort, whereas learning flying theory and skills involves semantic and motor memory respectively. Information in short-term memory that is rehearsed sufficiently will transfer to long-term memory; it is also stored in long-term memory by a vivid occurrence. A fright teaches us better than all the warnings given by instructors. Retention is improved by preparing the information for storage using such tricks as mnemonics, summarisation and grouping. A reward motivates learning and recall better than punishment. Overlearning (over and over rather than too much) or extensive repetition is a very effective way of storing. There are three phases to skill storage in *motor memory*. Initially, it is a *verbal, perceptual* or *cognitive stage,* then the practical or associative phase and, lastly, the *autonomous* or automatic stage where the skill is perfected.

## Forgetting

Retrieval of information sometimes becomes difficult or impossible. This may occur due to low frequency of recall, distraction by new information, age, anxiety and lack of motivation.

Chapter 8

# Judgement and Decision-Making

## What Does a Pilot Do?

Fundamentally, the pilot's task is to process information; that is, to receive information, analyse it, decide on a course of action, make a control input, check the response, make an adjustment if necessary – and to keep doing this as the flight progresses. This cycle is called a *control loop* and, in this case, with a feedback mechanism, it is a *closed loop* – a continuously self-adjusting process. But this is just piloting. We also have a responsibility to command – to make decisions beyond the flightpath of the aircraft.

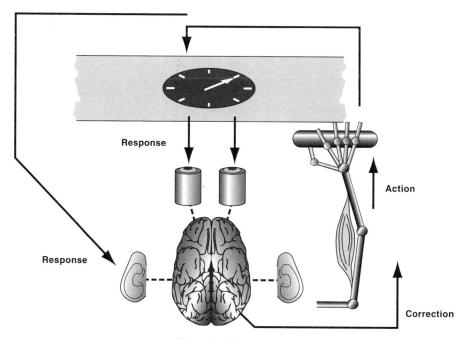

Figure 8-1 **Control loop**

The closed-loop system of flying the aircraft becomes an automatic function when we have been trained, are current, and are familiar with the particular aircraft and the operating environment. This is our piloting skill. However, the most important part

of the loop is our decision-making ability. That's where our human strengths and weaknesses lie. This process is conscious and depends on two vital elements:
- current, complete and correctly interpreted information; and
- judgement – the wisdom that comes from experience and training in choosing the best course of action under the particular circumstances.

Note that judgement in this context refers to wisdom, e.g. *sound judgement*, rather than visual estimation – judgement of angles or distance.

So what does the pilot need to know? The essential information is:
- the attitude and flightpath of the aircraft in terms of vertical and horizontal direction in relation to the airflow;
- the speed of the aircraft through the air;
- the three-dimensional position of the aircraft;
- the speed and direction of the aircraft relative to the ground;
- the status of the systems (engines, fuel, hydraulics, electrics, pressurisation); and
- the operating environment in terms of weather, darkness, other traffic, etc.

Assembling and maintaining the totality of this information, the so-called big picture, is *situational awareness* (SA). In addition, the pilot can only function effectively as the controller of the aircraft and, most importantly, as a decision-maker, if, along with the information, he or she possesses:
- the knowledge, experience and perception to interpret and process the information;
- the training, skill and recency to make the correct control inputs and to anticipate and assess the outcome;
- the discipline and attitude to make further changes to achieve a safe, correct and accurate result; and
- the time management skills to assign correct priorities.

The pilot's task is therefore total management of the flight, and this is done by flying the aircraft (*aviating*), by being responsible for its progress and position (*navigating*), by talking and listening to air traffic services and other aircraft (*communicating*) and by monitoring the systems, supervising the passengers and leading the crew. Thus the pilot has to be an aviator, navigator, communicator and, above all, commander (pilot-in-command). These functions take time, and as discussed, there is the need for this time to be managed. This is the sub-task of assigning priority management (*allocating*) according to importance, urgency and risk.

For the pilot or crew to be effective at all of these functions the training needs to encompass a much broader syllabus than flight and ground training. Life-skills such as inter-personal communications, self-discipline, teamwork, protocol, understanding, regard for others, wisdom from experience or example, self-esteem, patience, self-control, leadership and level-headedness all assume importance in the development of good flight crew. More and more of this needs to be integrated within the formal training curriculum. Much of it used to be classified within the term *airmanship*, but we are now in a position where the qualities of airmanship have to be formally taught.

## Judgement and Decision-Making as Information Processing

Earlier chapters dealt with information processing and the allocation of time to the information-gathering function. Now we'll consider what to do with the information that has been acquired.

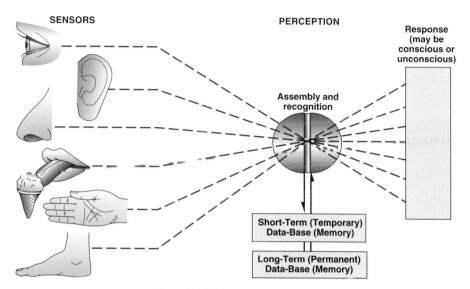

Figure 8-2 **Information processing**

We can only assess information that we have admitted for processing. If, for example, we have reacted to a stimulus reflexively, or autonomously, then we have bypassed the opportunity to evaluate information and to make a conscious decision. Judgement and decision-making thus require the conscious choice to admit information for processing. In other words, we must activate the perception function. Once we have a picture (data), we can do something with it.

## Perception – Attribution of Meaning

Admitting information for processing is a function of perception. Perception requires the sensors to notice or detect (to pay attention, i.e. to *see* rather than just *look*, to *listen* rather than *hear*). Then the brain needs to recognise (pattern-match) what is sensed. Of course, language *(comprehension)* plays a significant part in verbal information. If we cannot speak the language or recognise the visual image we do not perceive the message and therefore we cannot make a valid decision. Judgement and decision-making begin with perception. The *pattern-matching* relies on memory that comes from knowledge and experience. All sensations are considered and all memories interrogated.

We may well tie a song to a moment, a perfume to a lady, or an anxiety to a name. We may smile at the memory or shudder. That is the nature of stored imagery.

Having taken in the information, and recognised it, we then evaluate it in terms of meaning, importance, urgency and risk – what significance it has, in terms of the current situation. This evaluation is the basis of the next stage of prioritisation – the allocation of time – and again this is the most important function of all: active management.

*On downwind in the circuit, you look at the runway to assess your distance from the runway. If you had a radar to do that, the answer would be precise. Using the human eye, it is not. You know that the impression you get of that distance will vary depending on light conditions (poor visibility under cloud versus bright sunlight). Judgement is thus the process you exercise in allocating value to information. It is subjective by nature. As pilots, it is in our interests to try to make our judgement as objective (rational) as possible.*

## Allocation of Priority

We use information, be it derived subjectively or objectively, when we make a decision – but we do so in context.

*The left engine failed shortly after lift-off and the aircraft was at maximum take-off weight. It was able to maintain height, but as the pilot was about to feather the failed engine, the tower noticed that something was wrong and called. They asked the pilot his intentions and if he needed assistance. The pilot reached down for the hand-held microphone on the console. The aircraft struck power lines on the extended runway centreline.*

This was not so much a case of decision-making as an interruption of a trained response by conscious, but misdirected, intervention. Nevertheless, it does show how the traditional priority of *aviate, navigate, communicate,* came about. With a reasoned conscious decision, the risk of being caught versus the consequences of being caught-out, also interferes and interacts. Reasoned and conscious choices can only be achieved through *active* management of decision functions.

Rules are for the obedience of fools and for the guidance of wise men?

## Allocation of Importance

### Value vs Risk – Options/Rewards/Consequences and Odds

*What we stand to gain versus what we stand to lose – and what are the odds?*

Every decision has consequences and potential rewards. If we stand to lose a fortune, or to win a million dollars, the decision is stressed; if we are playing cards for matchsticks, the stress is less. If we have a high probability of winning we are less stressed; if the perceived odds are against us, we are again stressed. (Note it is *perceived* odds: confidence is a major factor). We can control the odds in aviation by training and by avoiding high-risk scenarios. We know beforehand where we are going to be tested and where we are at risk. We can be ready for it. The odds can be stacked in our favour.

# Context or Situation

## Scenarios

The context determines the importance, priority and urgency of making a decision and the risk or consequences of making an incorrect decision. A golf putt during a friendly game is an easier, less stressful decision than the final hole of a play-off in the Masters. In the city, the DON'T WALK sign, in red, presents an unmistakable, authoritative message. It is unequivocal, incapable of meaning anything else. Faced with this clear command, your decision to walk – or not to walk – say, at 2.00 in the morning, in the absence of traffic is a different decision made when the same warning illuminates during rush hour or when a policeman is watching. The same information does not always lead to the same decision – it depends on context. We can also develop a conditioned tolerance to disorder. If we break a rule and do not get caught, we are more likely to break the rule again, e.g. untidy bedrooms and red traffic lights. We will even do it on automatic drive. Like Pavlov's dogs, our conditioned response is motivated by punishment or reward (or non-punishment and non-reward).

## Rules, Protocols and Mores

The game of flight has rules – like the acceptable standards of behaviour demanded by the society in which we choose to live. These have been established by experience and by loss. If we operate within the rules the risks are less and so is the stress. Within the company or the cockpit we have behavioural standards and codes of conduct that are acceptable or otherwise. Stress and risk is reduced by following the party line.

## Conventions and SOPs

Formally, the company will establish procedures and formalities that, the chief pilot knows, will support the operational policies of the company. They are again based on knowledge and experience. Question them, by all means, but do so *before* contravening them.

# Indecision/Non-Decision

The other problems we all have are:
• not being able to decide one way or the other; or
• deferring, avoiding or not wanting to make a decision at all or at that time (pressing-on).

*There's the biblical story of Jacob's donkey being offered two carrots – one on each side – and dying of hunger because it couldn't decide which one to eat first. It turned left and right and couldn't makeup its mind.*

We seem to be, by nature, reluctant to make a decision – to commit ourselves. We like to keep our options, interminably, open. But, in the real world, time runs out.

Unfortunately, it takes luck, good judgement and experience to know when time is about to run out before it already has – and we cannot gain experience if we don't get a second chance to learn from the previous mistake.

## Emotions in Decisions

Emotion plays a significant, often a dominant, role in the decision-making process. We often decide on the basis of what we want to happen rather than what is most likely to happen. What we hope instead of what is likely. What we expect can also be ambitious or cautious – especially if we have pushed the boundaries and got away with it before. Thus decisions also depend on personality and confidence. What are the chances we perceive rather than what the odds really are. Do we by nature err on the positive side or the negative. And in terms of safety, the negative is not a bad thing. It is cautious and survival-oriented rather than goal/success-oriented. *We made it!* We must learn to make as much of a song-and-dance about sensible, reserved decisions and actions, as we do about taking a risk and getting away with it.

## Decisions and Stress

### Internal Pressures

Decisions not taken cause stress. While we are deciding, and are under pressure to decide, then the level of stress can become unreasonable. Avoiding a decision also causes stress because we know that ultimately it will have to be addressed. It won't go away. The solution is to make the decision and go for it. Stress is relieved by action – fight or flight.

### External Pressures

External pressures have a significant effect on our decisions. We have human wants, needs and fears: wanting to please, wanting to impress friends or siblings, wanting to earn more money or be promoted, needing to be loved, needing to be noticed, needing to be rewarded, fearing criticism or ridicule, fearing to lose a job, fearing injury.

A completely rational decision is made in isolation and such decisions can often only be made retrospectively: what we should have decided rather than what we did decide. Accident investigations are largely of this ilk because they do not – cannot – know the pressures under which the particular decision was made. We can rationalise why the pilot should have made the correct decision when we read the accident report. It's obvious. What is not obvious is the emotional strings attached to that decision. Making correct decisions sometimes takes considerable courage or, to use the old term, *moral fortitude*.

*The light twin was scheduled to go to another airport to pick up passengers and to fly them to Back of Bourke. Weather was poor, cloud down to 500 feet with showers.*

*An ILS would be needed to get in to the pick-up aerodrome. During the run-up, an alternator fail light illuminated. The pilot knew he would be expected to go on with the charter, even with one alternator out. He was a young pilot, keen to get hours up, quite concerned lest he lose this job, and the boss was a forceful, driving, personality. It was a hard decision, but he turned around and taxied back in. Here's a pilot who turned around and taxied back. How do you view his action – approve, disapprove? How would it be received down at the local aero club bar on Friday night – approbation, polite front but scoffing underneath, scorn?*

## Decision-Making Processes

You have been introduced to the concept of actively managing where and for how long your attention is directed at your various information sources. You know from your own practice that the key factor in managing your situational awareness is the control function. It manages the time-attention scan. In time-management mode, the effect of scanning can be likened to an empty goods train:

Figure 8-3 **Attention spaces**

Some of the space you will assign to physical skill tasks, e.g., enter turn, roll out of turn:

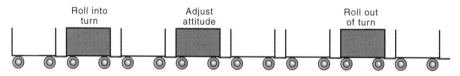

Figure 8-4 **Control inputs**

and into others, you will load information:

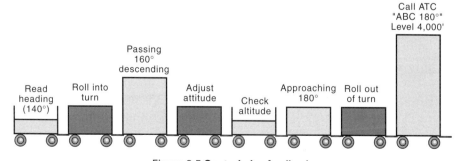

Figure 8-5 **Control plus feedback**

Note that the importance assigned each block of information differs. That's a reminder that even though the amount of time we take to acquire clumps of data may be the same, the level of importance, or the priority we assign to information, can vary considerably. This is perception and judgement at work. Also the sequence in which we decide to process the data (the priority) is a function of the urgency, importance and consequences of the process. In exercising judgement, we convert information into a chain of decisions. The information we choose to process, and the priority we ascribe is a matter of experience and training. This is *judgement*.

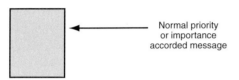

Figure 8-6 **Normal priority**

The analogy of the information presented by a DON'T WALK sign has already been used. The message is not capable of any other interpretation. It can only ever mean do not cross the road (or run – but we'll ignore that*)*.

*Don't walk* is the message you are receiving and red is the colour we have come to associate generally with *stop, warning, danger* or *fire*. The power of the command might have been somewhat less, had the colour been amber, not red. If it has been green it would have been absolutely confusing. We consider these aspects in *ergonomics*.

When observed during the day, with traffic on the road, the DON'T WALK message will have normal importance and we will probably comply unless we are

Figure 8-7 **Low priority**

late, there is a race against our teenage colleagues, we are trying to impress the girlfriend or we are trying to save a lame dog from being run over.

Such influences vary the intensity of the message received, in terms of affecting your decision of whether to cross the road.

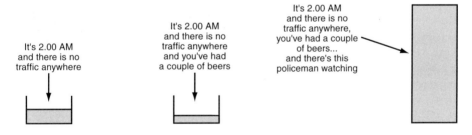

Figure 8-8 **Circumstance**

This was a decision based on a clear message, 'don't walk'. What if the message was less definitive but the external pressures were equally strong? While the time taken to make an assessment will remain the same – you look at the runway to check distance out – the result may vary considerably – bright sunlight, under cloud, at night, urgency to land, fuel state, fatigue. You have looked at the usual reference point, and received unclear answers. The potential for continuing despite the wise option of going around is considerable. And that is what the previous diagrams say: different information will be accorded different weight:

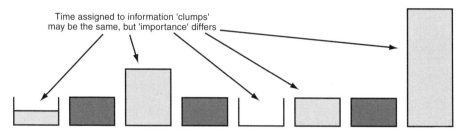

Time assigned to information 'clumps' may be the same, but 'importance' differs

Figure 8-9 **Attention – time versus importance**

## Priorities

In the example of the DON'T WALK sign, you saw how the weight of the message – i.e. the impact it would have on your decision – varied when it was in the colour red, as opposed to green, or whether a policeman was nearby. Obviously, there's a conditioned response in how we grade the import of messages. That is, our response might be automatic, semi-automatic (conscious decisions, trained responses), instinctive or fully conscious. The function of perception – the manner in which we assign priority to information is something that, as a pilot, we absolutely must subject to conscious audit and control.

## Motivation, Drive and the Error-Cancelling Force

*Being led from behind – by ourselves*

A model commonly used to depict the essence of decision-making comprises two circles. One is the desired state – the *goal*. The other is the actual state: *reality*. A natural force drives us to get from where we are to where we wish to be.

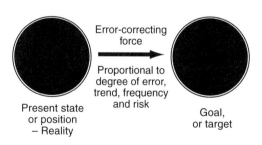

Error-correcting force

Proportional to degree of error, trend, frequency and risk

Present state or position – Reality

Goal, or target

Figure 8-10 **Present versus desired**

The error-correction process is a *closed* or *feedback loop*. The perceived information (where we are) enters the information processing system via perception, then the image is referred through the conscious process, checked against any image in memory (where we want to be and how to get there), and, decision made, instructions are sent to correct. As the aircraft responds, further perceptions are received via the feedback loop as a satisfaction factor – *have we corrected the error?*

This process can be exemplified in the case of an altitude reading. The desired altitude is, say, 1,000 feet. The present state is what you actually see on the altimeter.

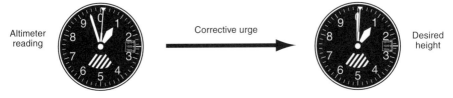

Figure 8-11 **Error correction**

The spontaneous urge to correct will exist in proportion to the magnitude of the error. A major error will register as strong dissatisfaction or unhappiness with the perceived situation and a corresponding urge to fix it. The urge determines the urgency and the magnitude of the correction – the *gain*.

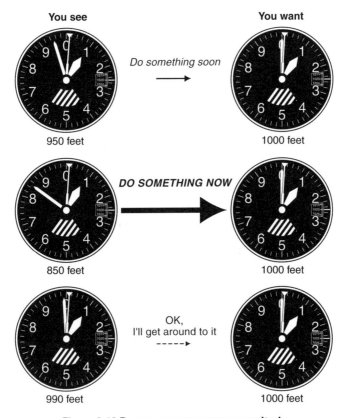

Figure 8-12 **Response versus error magnitude**

Similarly, as you monitor the effect of corrective action, through the feedback side of the decision loop, the drive to correct becomes weaker as your sense of dissatisfaction with the situation decreases.

As the situation improves, your concern abates, as does your sense of priority for its remediation. The power of the corrective impulse will thus exist in proportion to the error perceived – and how much you care about the error factor. In other words, though the reading is scientifically derived (the instrument is correct), your reaction to that reading is purely subjective. Subjectivity is the province of emotion – how you feel about the situation. Dissatisfaction and satisfaction are themselves feelings.

Research has shown that our decisions – all our decisions – are mostly made on an emotional basis. In the case of the altitude error, it may be that someone is watching.

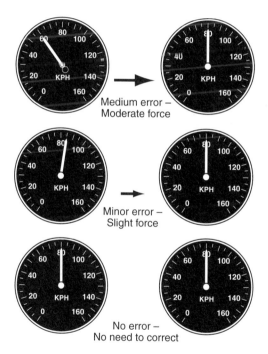

Figure 8-13 **Motivation versus error**

The error-cancelling loop has been reviewed. Two things are clear from that study:
- the greater the error, the more powerful the error signal, and the greater the drive to correct it; and
- the goal being sought is a mental image, a perception not a tangible reality, and as such a preferred state rather than an objective absolute.

The first observation is supported by the tendency to lock-on to a single reference point till the error is resolved. You may be familiar with that phenomenon. Here is how it plays out in terms of time management.

This model was earlier used to demonstrate how things can get busy for a pilot:

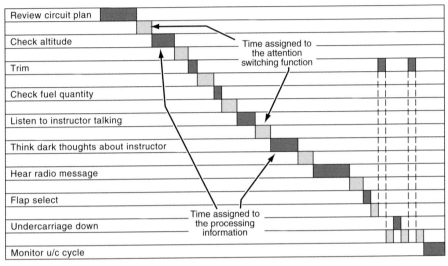

Figure 8-14 **Time sharing**

When a major error is detected, the urge to fix it can overpower all other interests. This phenomenon is familiar to all pilots. It might be called *single-channel focus*.

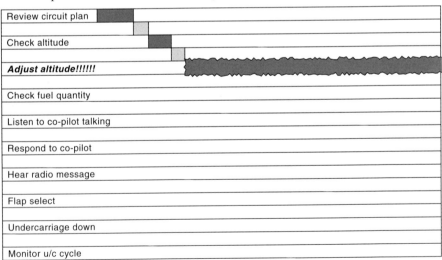

Figure 8-15 **Single-channel focus**

The impulse causing single channel focus is an elemental drive – or motivating force. It is no better displayed than in that common aviation problem of going on for too long under low cloud (destination obsession).

## Destination Obsession

The following section on destination obsession is a slight excursion from the main flow in the development of this manual. However, it is a serious problem and it is vital that pilots think it through in detail at least once a year – just before autumn's poor weather starts would be a good time. The story can tell you much about your perception and decision processes, building on from the preceding theoretical concepts. But it will only work to your benefit if you accept that something like this could happen to each and every one of us.

### Low Cloud, Pressing-On

The problem with pilots pressing-on under lowering cloud is well known within the aviation industry, and yet it just doesn't go away. (It continues to claim lives.) In a can-do world of solutions, you'd think we'd have been able to fix it by now, wouldn't you? But the solution to the problem remains elusive. What else do we know about it? Well, the idea that the pilots 'caught out' were all idiots is an unlikely one. The trap they found themselves in – and you can bet when the truth dawned, it came as a complete surprise – could maybe have happened to any of us? How it might occur is definitely worth a look.

The process involved obviously affects judgement of distances – distance from cloud and height above the terrain. It affects your judgement severely, and is called *adaptation*. All pilots know about it, though they may not have given it a name. Adaptation is taking place when, after a long flight at 5,000 feet, you descend to 1,000 feet and it seems to be very low – very low indeed. You'll get the same sensation at 500 feet after a long time at 1,000 feet, and so on. Students learning to low fly tend, progressively, to fly lower and lower, as they 'adapt' to the sensations of low flying. What at first had seemed 'low', now seems 'high', so down they go.

It is a commonplace experience in life. Adaptation has been experienced by everyone who found that, after hours of highway driving, maintaining built-up area speeds seemed like 'crawling'. And the folk who live near the train line who no longer 'hear' the trains, and so on. However, this is a particularly insidious aspect of human cognitive performance in flight.

With fewer cues available, those that can be read are accorded greater weight. They appear more pronounced, more compelling in their meaning. They invite greater reliance on what they are telling you through the judgement process. The main effect will be to deny a proper and accurate assessment of height above terrain and distance from obstacles and cloud.

The effect of limited visibility combines treacherously with that of adaptation. After all, if you can be fooled (as in the sensation of flying low after flying at higher altitudes) on a clear day, then under poor light conditions, and with restricted forward visibility, your judgement of height and distance will be so distorted as to be next to useless. (Ah, yes, but there's always the altimeter, isn't there? Well, maybe. For one thing, this may not be the time to be looking inside the cockpit. For another, you may not know the height of the hills out here.) You might not realise how very close to the trees or ground you have descended. But, by then, it's far too late. However, it has happened, hasn't it? We've all heard news reports of aircraft engine noise low overhead, often for long periods before the actual crash.

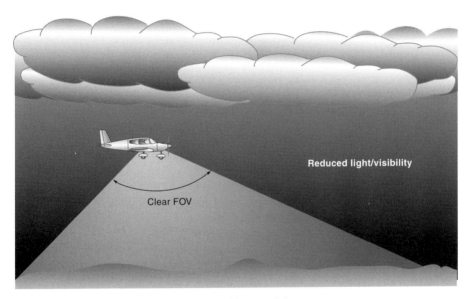

Figure 8-16 **Narrow vision**

Yes, pilots do press on too far under lowering cloud, lured by sensations of being actually higher – and further from the cloud base – and safer – than is really the case.

But there may be an even more dangerous trap waiting to catch you out. If the weather is associated with a front, there's a fair chance your last QNH is no longer representative of the real conditions. Barometric pressure typically drops with frontal passage, often considerably, and rapidly. If you have an 'old' QNH set, and the pressure has indeed fallen, then your altimeter will be saying you are higher than you really are. And, as noted, your visual cues won't be of any help at all.

All of which adds up the unsurprising conclusion that most, if not all, of those pilots who did go on too far under cloud had no idea how low they were actually flying until they hit something – or wound up in the 'soup' itself, blind in cloud. You can bet on it, can't you? That's what happened to them. One second they think they're OK, the next. . . Can you be sure it would never happen to you? As said earlier, these pilots were not fools. The adaptation force affecting their decision-making, distorting their judgement, must have been very powerful, indeed. And there will have been one more influence: *visual illusion*.

Many aircraft that have crashed under cloud against rising terrain having stalled while under full power. With the limited field of view, there is a tendency to use the ground as reference for level flight. The closer you get to the ground, without a strong nose-attitude vs. horizon reference, the more prone will you be to 'seeing' the fuselage's being parallel to the earth's surface as an indication of level flight. As the slope increases, therefore, so will the climb angle, until the inevitable stall. It's the same phenomenon as not being able to judge height any more – too few visual clues to form a situational awareness picture of any reliability at all. What that all adds up to is this: the further you go pressing on, the less you'll appreciate just how close you are to the cloud and the tree tops. But, of course, you should never have got there in the first place. But pilots do. The next question to sort out, then, must be how not to get there.

Figure 8-17 **Short-term response**

## Personality and Matters of Choice

The story about pilots pressing on in poor weather did not make for nice reading, did it? One of our defences against being discomforted by tales like these is the confidence that, '*It won't happen to me*'. On the other hand, most of us do know people who we would rate as more-likely-than-most to do such a thing. In other words, the idea that some types are more prone to taking higher risks than others is not especially controversial.

## Personality Type

That a cardiac surgeon should be the one spreading the word on personality types did not seem incongruous at the time. It was soon after the discovery that cholesterol in the blood stream could precipitate out of solution and leave fatty deposits on the walls of really important arteries, like those near the heart, with untoward results, such as premature demise from heart attack.

The sources of cholesterol were found to include dairy products. The news that people should restrict their intake of milk-based foods shook the foundations of the dairy-farmers and their industry. Their mayday was answered by a US hospital, who then sent out one of their top surgeons. He travelled the country spreading the word: it was not so much what you ate, but who you were, that led to cholesterol problems.

People, the theory went, could be broadly categorised as Type A or Type B. The former are your hard-charging types, serious achievers, action-oriented, and so on. As a result of a life-style packed with challenges and driven by the urge to succeed, the blood pressure was elevated. Higher blood pressure causes greater rates of cholesterol precipitation, and more of those unhealthy fatty deposits. Type B people, on the other hand, were more laid-back and relaxed, and less susceptible to the cholesterol problem and, as a result, live longer. (That women are more likely to be Type B than men contributes to the large disparity in average survival age.) The dairy industry breathed a sigh of relief. All that had to be done was to get the Type As to be more like the Type Bs. *'You just have to learn to slow down'*, the Type As were told. *'Sure,'* was the reply, *'immediately after I've climbed Mt Everest.'*

Are you an A or a B? You can test yourself. The car ahead of you at the traffic lights has not moved on within a microsecond of the green light. He's been sitting there in neutral while you were riding the clutch and revving the motor – then the chances are you are Type A. (The other bloke is a B. . .) Obviously, there are degrees of Type A-ness and Type B-ness. Some people are harder driving than others, some more relaxed, and so on.

There are more scientific personality tests than traffic light response. And they generally have more than just the two categories. One will assess you, and put you into one of 16 type descriptions. Amongst the determinants are the nature of your control over your own intuition and judgement, e.g. whether you'll make a quick decision on minimum information or await more data, whether you'll go with instinct or await more facts.

## The Virtuous Co-Pilot

*A healthy split (personality) – keeping ourselves honest*

The foregoing raises doubts about the reliability of human judgement. However, while healthy scepticism is very much in order, there is no need for despair. Control of perception is the key to getting the correct picture and perspective into our information processing apparatus, knowledge allows us to compensate for our human limitations, and, hence, the critical decision-making can be made reliable. In the absence of another crew member checking and assisting our judgement and decision-making, we need to develop a second self.

There's an old joke about lawyers. A man asks his accountant, *'What is two plus two?' 'Four'*, shoots back the answer. He addresses the same question to his lawyer, *'What is two plus two?' 'What would you like it to be?'* is the response. Decisions – the selection of a course of action from the list of alternatives – is a function of emotion. It is not too large a step to take, therefore, to see that information flowing through the perception process *might* – what do you mean *might*? Of course it will! – be biased to suit a given preference – how you would like the world to be, not the genuine present reality.

Let's revisit the pilot flying on under lowering cloud/rising terrain/fading light. Imagine yourself in that position. A particular decision point is passed, the decision is to *press on* – or is it a decision that has been deferred? Then another. None of us likes to admit having been wrong. You can see how later decisions to go on, or not to decide yet, are really reinforcement of earlier choices or habits, and not based on an objective appraisal of the facts.

Asking questions – *'Is the present low-light situation causing me to overestimate height above ground?'* – is a good technique. However, it is following the same pattern as the previous decision-pattern and is likely to come up with the same answers. It is better, by far, that you refer your perceptions to an independent arbitrator, get someone else's unbiased assessment, and get it as a statement containing reasons, not just impressions or feelings. What you want to hear from this in-flight auditor of decision-quality is something like:

*'The visibility ahead is degraded. You will experience difficulty in getting accurate assessments of height, distance and clearance from obstacles. You have too many reasons for pressing on to be able to make an objective decision. You've given it a good shot. However, by turning back, you will actually enhance your reputation as a professional – and reputations in aviation are everything.'*

You have already met the person you are going to rely on to sensibly audit your tougher in-flight decisions. You met him or her as your *virtual co-pilot* keeping your communications skills alive and well. In this manifestation, however, your alter ego will be your decision reviewer and, moreover, he or she will be a righteous and highly responsible person. It is you yourself, indeed, but in the guise of a *virtuous co-pilot*. It is the independent, reserved, objective part of you that asks, *'What would be your decision if you were not tired, pressured, late, worried about your job, under the influence of. . .?'* You have assigned your other, questioning self a QA role that is separated from emotional bias. *What would be the sensible, wise decision.* Then compare the outcomes. If they are the same you are in good shape. If not, have another look. Our virtual co-pilot is activated by *introspection* (self-examination), by second-guessing.

*Am I making the right (safe) decision? Am I right in deferring decision? Would my instructor/father/respected colleague make the same decision under these circumstances?*

As before, there is no point in this exercise or responsible self-management unless you speak these review conversations out loud. You will need to hear, in your own voice, how you propose to proceed, for otherwise the least sensible option will not reveal its true character. It really is a case of hearing is believing, i.e. your own voice describing that you are about to do something unwise.

*The pilot of the light twin became concerned about rough-running and surging of one of the engines after take-off. However, the symptoms disappeared. It was a planned two-hour flight with several passengers. All had connections to make. So, too, did the pilot within an hour of landing at the destination. An airline ticket to Melbourne for the next day's races had been bought in advance and was not refundable. Then there were the prepaid Melbourne Cup Ball tickets for the big event, that night. The ball was to be attended with the fiancé – and they had not seen each other for months. Turning back would mean that all of the arrangements, meetings and moneys would be sacrificed.*

*There had been a similar problem with the engine, a few flights ago. It had been ground tested, 'no fault found'. . .Yet she had the courage and sense to turn back and land immediately. That's professionalism. But in retrospect, do we reward such decisions?*

Driving forces, indeed. We must try to isolate the effect of such influences. We need to process facts, not feelings. We must consciously filter perception.

## Chapter 9

# Crew Resource Management (CRM)

*The Getting of Wisdom*

## Human Interfaces

### The SHELL Model

The overall concept of fitting the human to the task, and the task to the human, has been commonly represented by a model, called the SHELL model (Hawkins, 1984), where the letters represent:

* Software
* Hardware
* Environment
* Liveware (the human pilot)
* Liveware (other humans – inside and outside the aircraft)

Figure 9-1 **Interface model**

Design of the task, and the workplace, should take into account the interrelationships between each and all of these elements. We have considered, in some detail, the interaction of the human with the environment of flight. We will examine the interaction with the environment of the cockpit, and with the aircraft's software and hardware, under the category of *ergonomics*. We will here consider the most difficult interrelationship of human to human – liveware to liveware, person to person, personality to personality. Let's start with a look at what makes us, individually, tick.

## Personality

### Assertive/Aggressive/Compliant

*Is my obsequiousness to your liking, sir? (from a Playboy cartoon circa 1960s)*

Like most things in life the scientists have classified personality types. The two simple categories of *introvert* and *extravert* had been used to define an individual's personality. Then came a more subtle classification according to whether the individual personality was more driven by getting the job done, sometimes at all or any cost (called *task-oriented* or *goal-directed*), versus those more focused on pleasing others, even at the cost of their own happiness (called *relationship-oriented* or *person-directed*).

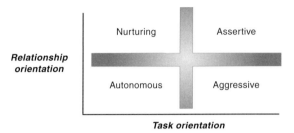

Figure 9-2 **Personality types**

Further, we can place certain personalities within one quarter of the grid. Studies of pilot groups have shown that the personality considered ideal for multi-crew flying fits into the top right-hand quadrant: that is, towards a combined, highly goal- and person-oriented personality. We can actually define our perfect first officer and that is the model we should therefore try to be.

The ideal might be:

- friendly;
- courteous;
- respectful;
- self-disciplined;
- positive;
- cheerful;
- polite;
- well presented;
- timely;
- confident but not overly;
- willing to suggest alternatives;
- ready to support and share workload;
- familiar and confident with the company SOPs and his or her duties;
- familiar with the aircraft and its systems;
- happy in the F/O role;
- happy in the company;
- willing to speak up, with respect, if the captain incorrectly enters an altitude, position or heading;
- supportive of the captain's decisions in front of the crew but willing to suggest alternatives privately – time permitting;
- assertive enough to take over to avoid an impending disaster – without respect for feelings, if necessary; and
- considerate enough to be understanding afterwards, but not to the extent that, if safety standards were prejudiced, the captain should be protected, from himself, by formal reporting.

Does such a person exist? The difficulty about identifying types of personality, especially those prone to accidents – and they can be readily identified – is that it is difficult, if not impossible, to get that individual to recognise the trait and even more difficult to get them to do something about it.

## Hazardous Attitudes

*Hazardous attitudes* are those that have been identified as being more prone to accidents than the norm. They include:
- anti-authoritarianism and rebelliousness (*I don't have to follow the rules – rules are for fools*);
- machismo (*I am a macho man and an ace pilot*);
- invulnerability (*I am unbeatable*);
- impulsiveness (*I make quick decisions and get on with it*);
- complacency (*She'll be right, mate*); and
- fatalism (*it's going to happen anyway, why try to fight it?*)

But who is going to admit to these traits? We must. It's our only chance.

Even more of a danger, in a multi-crew cockpit, is someone who will only say what they think the captain wants to hear (*the political animal?*) and speaks when they are spoken to. If they are not willing to stand up and be counted when things are about to go wrong they have no place in the cockpit.

## Denial

One aspect of our personality that determines our susceptibility to hazardous behaviours is whether we are prepared to admit that we have that particular attitude.

The refusal to admit can take several forms:
- outright refusal to admit (*I'm not like that, it can't happen to me*);
- avoidance of the issue (*Let's concentrate on something else*);
- rationalisation (*It'll be okay*);
- procrastination (*I'll just go on a little further*);
- seeing or believing what we want to happen rather than what is happening (wishful thinking – *It's clearing on the other side of the hills*); or
- ego, status or reputation (*I won't be beaten by this*).

Each of these is a form of *denial*. Denial is refusal – refusal to accept, admit, confront, change or decide. I would add one more refusal: refusal to reconsider, an attitude that could be called *mind-set*. This is the situation where we have made a decision, probably announced it or committed ourselves in some way (*I'll be home for dinner* or *I'll meet you in Canberra tonight*), and then we are reluctant, or will absolutely refuse, to change that decision. The thought of turning back would not even enter our minds. It is not an unusual characteristic of a successful businessman or woman that, once a decision is made, it must be seen through to its conclusion – to the end. The end, in our case, may be a little different.

Denial is seen as a major factor in accidents. If one considers the classic case, of pressing on into deteriorating weather, it is easy to see how these factors come into play.

## External Influences

As well as our personality, which could be called an internal influence, there are external influences which may influence, modify or totally dictate our behaviour, our attitudes and our decisions.

They include:

- peer group pressure (*bet you can't make it*);
- spouse/manhood/provider pressure (*they've got a Volvo*);
- organisational pressures (*it has to be there today*);
- financial pressure (*the car payments are overdue*);
- job security, advancement, promotion (*do you like your job – do you want to keep it?*); and
- religious or political pressure (*we must fight – to the death*).

# Motivation

### Maslow's Hierarchy of Needs

In the forties a researcher into management and leadership defined the main motivating factors which cause humans to aspire and work towards higher standards of performance. In 1943, Professor Maslow classified the following motivators in order of importance.

### Individual Motives

Motivation is what drives us. Motives are the reasons for doing something or deciding a course of action. Thus our motives influence the objectivity of the decision we make. At the base level, of Maslow's pyramid, our motive is survival – of the species, our offspring and ourselves as individuals. The motive for survival leads to the need for food, water and shelter and protection – safety or security. Having achieved these we may be motivated for comfort, money, status, power, fame, respect or love. The motive of passion can override all logical reason.

Up until then it was largely assumed that money (financial reward) was a significant motivator. Pay the workers more money and they will work harder. This only works to a limited extent. That's not to say that money is not important. In our modern society money is needed for food, shelter, clothing and comfort. Thus it is a means to an end. What Maslow discovered was that once the individual's need for money was satisfied the motivation of additional money – as an end in itself – was not as high as other factors.

Firstly the human had basic *needs* for survival and these assumed first priority – food, water, shelter, protection, procreation. After these were the needs for safety and security. Then came the *wants* – in some cases comforts and luxuries such as a car, fashion, baubles, bangles and beads. But there were much more powerful forces, we could call them *wishes, dreams* and *ideals* – the needs for recognition, happiness and respect by fellow workers and the needs for self-expression and self-realisation.

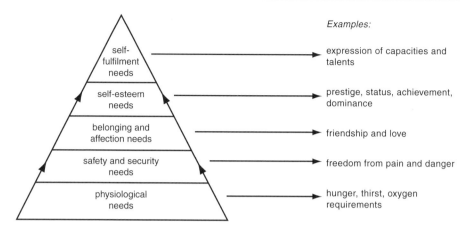

Figure 9-3 **Maslow's pyramid (hierarchy of needs)**

Our decisions are affected by these motivators, for example, the fear of making a fool of ourselves is a powerful influence that may override basic survival instincts – a bungee jumper standing at the brink may continue, even though terrified, because of the peer group mockery that would have to be faced if he or she did not jump. It is thought that many pressing on into bad weather decisions were made because of similar fears. Turning back is not macho – whereas it should be.

Another researcher, Herzberg, in 1959, proposed a *Two Factor Theory* based on the finding that some tasks are worth doing for their own sake, i.e. *job satisfaction*. He found that *motivating factors* could be quite different from non-motivating factors. Positive factors were achievement of a goal or standard, advancement, recognition, promotion, responsibility and the nature of the work itself – they enjoyed doing it, like we do. Negative motivators were quite different and included company staff policies, salary, job insecurity and poor working environment. He called the latter *hygiene factors*. He recognised their importance but noted that employees would put up with much if the motivators were there. Not that that should be an excuse for the company not to address those issues.

### Team Motivation

To achieve teamwork and higher performance, an individual within a group, and the collective group, must be motivated – otherwise why bother? Whether crew, armies or employees, there must be a factor that causes the team to try a little harder.

Firstly, there is the instinct and motivation to survive collectively (nationally, culturally, religiously) and, beyond this basic need, there must be some form of incentive or reward (gold medals, trophies). The rewards may be financial, symbolic, or congratulatory, and may be positive or negative, e.g. penalty and punishment for failure or a positive reward for success. It has been found that negative motivators are less effective in building a team – rewards gain more results than threats and punishment. It is no different from training a puppy. It will do anything to please you but it will soon do as little as possible if it is unreasonably punished. Humans are no different.

The rewards or recognition may also be public or private, stated or implied, and obvious or subtle. We are complex creatures. We have motivators within the team and then for the team. The task of the team leader is to develop motivators such that the cause of the team comes before the needs of the individual. In a situation where the team is not necessarily the crew, because it is always changing, then the 'family' really is the airline company itself. This is a vital realisation for managers.

## Performance Versus Motivation

The following model, which relates task performance to motivation and shows the relationship with skills, was developed from a simple model proposed by Frank Hawkins (*Human Factors in Flight*, Avebury 1993).

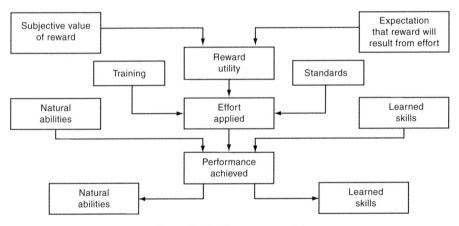

Figure 9-4 **Performance model**

When we are performing a task, the standards that we set are a result of motivation. Do we wish to please or impress the instructor or the wife? Were we taught to achieve certain minimum standards? Have we developed or inherited the self-discipline to maintain those standards and to reward ourselves in the absence of the instructor? Do we set and insist on the same standards when we fly alone? We each have to answer for ourselves.

# Mistakes

## Behaviour

We all make mistakes. Formal investigation of accidents classifies human behaviour, and therefore, behavioural errors, into three categories:

* knowledge-based behaviour;
* rule-based behaviour; and
* skill-based behaviour.

Thus the prevention of accidents needs to address these areas. This, of course, leads to a need for awareness and for specialised training.

### Knowledge-Based Behaviour

Knowledge-based behaviour is conscious, decision-making behaviour where the human operator assesses the inputs and decides on a course of action based on prior knowledge and deduction. It requires experience so that the long-term memory can relate to previous events and can evaluate outcomes and consequences. Because it requires conscious thought, it is vulnerable to other demands for the single-channel processor (the conscious mind).

### Rule-Based Behaviour

Rule-based behaviour is the trained sequence of actions memorised as a ritual such as checks and push-back procedures, approach and departure procedures, and emergency procedures. They require conscious decisions but save time and are made reliable by following a set sequence of events that has been rehearsed. Thus the likelihood of complete and correct actions is enhanced

### Skill-Based Behaviour

Skill-based behaviour is represented by those learned subroutines and subconscious motor skills that we learnt so well that they have become second nature – such as landing and attitude flying. Don't forget that the standards we accept are part of that feedback loop and are a result of our training and self-discipline.

## Potential for Error

### Knowledge-Based

Since knowledge-based behaviour relates to conscious decision-making then the potential for errors of judgement lies with:

* rushed decisions;
* lack of sufficient data;
* misleading information;
* wrong priorities/motivation;
* inexperience/immaturity;
* overconfidence/poor training;

- stress initiating inappropriate skill, e.g. retracting flaps instead of undercarriage; and
- misinterpreted or misidentified information.

## Rule-Based

Rule-based behaviour relies on the sequence of actions to be immediately available for recall. This in turn depends on regular and recent practice. It is vulnerable to:
- lack of knowledge;
- lack of recent practice;
- lack of discipline in following the sequence or checklist; and
- interruptions/distractions.

## Skill-Based

Skill-based errors arise from:
- lack of recency (on that type, in that role, at that place, in those conditions);
- lack of training/recurrency;
- lack of experience;
- poor training; and
- poor standards or tolerance to inaccuracy.

## Types of Error

Basically errors result from the human operator (*operator-induced*) or the equipment (*design-induced*). But it's not quite that simple. We don't operate in a vacuum. There are several further classifications into which errors, and accident causal factors, may be placed.

**Endemic.** These errors are inherent in the operation. In the realm of flight there are many identified potential risks. Also within the known patterns of human behaviour there are identified areas for potential errors – by our very nature. They cannot be removed but must be accommodated and countered by training, design of hardware and software and the operating environment.

**Systemic.** Theses errors result from aspects of an organisation that cause confusion about rules, procedures or responsibilities.

**Ergonomic.** These are design-induced errors caused by a deficiency in the man-machine interface – controls, displays, lighting or instruments, etc.

In terms of the pilot's actions there are three further possibilities:

**Omission.** This is a check or action not carried out or not done at the correct time (e.g. wheels left up or not confirmed down).

**Commission.** This is an action done when it was not appropriate (e.g. gear down above $V_{LO}$).

**Substitution.** This is an incorrect action that was done in place of the correct one (e.g. flaps up instead of undercarriage).

Some errors are *reversible*. Some are *irreversible* and alternative action is then required. Within these, there are further subcategories that identify the pattern of the errors (consider landing touchdowns):

* *Random.* Errors that occur with no predictable period or pattern (all over the place).
* *Systematic.* An identified pattern of error (consistently off-centre to the left or consistently short).
* *Sporadic.* One or two, out of the blue, and inconsistent with other patterns of behaviour (one or two, out-of-character, short touchdowns).
* *Sequential.* One incident that leads to another (heavy, fast landing, nosewheel impact, wheel-barrowing, nosewheel collapse, propeller impact, fire).

## False Hypothesis

The other danger with all human perception is that with, say, radio calls and vision, we see, hear and feel what we want or what we expect. This is called the *false hypothesis*. The greatest areas of risk may be represented by the following examples:

* You are cleared to line up and then you expect a take-off clearance: the airways clearance is misread as a take-off clearance.
* You have selected the gear down and there is a radio call. You are relaxed about the gear and don't bother to check that it actually is down and locked. On final you say, out aloud, *gear down and locked* and don't even look at the red light.
* You have completed a stressful flight and are turning off the runway. You reach for the flap lever and, at the same time, the charts fall onto the floor. You inadvertently retract the undercarriage.
* You have to get home and you know the fuel is marginal. You don't want to believe the fuel gauges now showing empty. After all, they are not very accurate, are they?

### Desensitisation

A similar situation arises with false warning systems. Early fire warning systems were notably unreliable – to the extent that they were ignored (they cried *wolf* too often). The odds were in favour of them being wrong. Thus, when they correctly warned of a fire, they were ignored. We became desensitised.

### Distraction

We are very vulnerable to distraction. If we are interrupted, or distracted, our probably of completing the task correctly is seriously prejudiced. Take the many examples of interrupted checks and wheels-up landings. Always stop the checklist and resume when the interruption is removed. This is where multi-crew is marvellous.

## Containing Systemic Errors

An accident generally results from a series of individually insignificant errors that were undetected, unreported and, ultimately, uncorrected. The errors may be institutional, organisational, operational, procedural, personal, cultural or attitudinal. One day they all line up and the chain of events leads to a calamity.

In fact, humans are remarkably free of error, and if we design an organisation with a healthy flow of communications and that encourages and rewards the reporting and correction of error, then the likelihood of accidents can be largely removed or negated. For example, how many of us have seen a pilot who has been described as *an accident going somewhere to happen* or a cockpit deficiency that could lead to misreading or a procedural routine that could be misinterpreted? If the organisation rewards such identification *and then acts to remove the potential problem*, then we have a healthy, active, safe organisation.

Professor James Reason of Manchester University (*Human Error*, Cambridge University Press 1990) proposed that an accident is the result of a series of events, or defects, both organisational and individual. Within an organisation there are several levels of supervision and activity, all of which influence the potential for error. Within each level there should be defences or shields that are designed to detect, report and break the error chain.

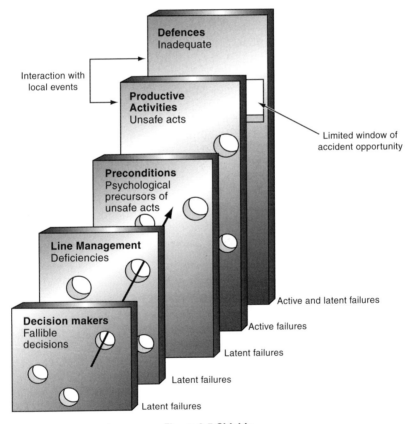

Figure 9-5 **Shields**

But each level has potential weaknesses and, if these line up, we have a chain of events that may lead to an accident.

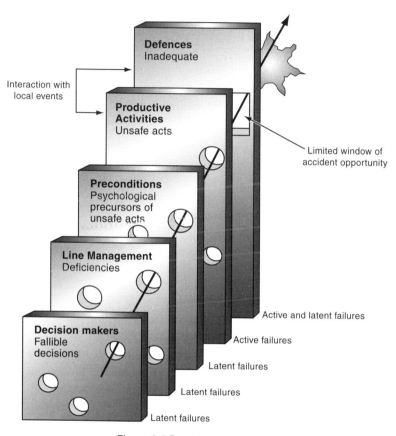

Figure 9-6 **Error (accident) chain**

There are two types of error or failure (failure to prevent an accident):
- *latent failures;* and
- *active failures.*

A latent failure could be a deficiency in a procedure or checklist or an ergonomic deficiency in the design of a control or displays. An active failure is a straight mistake.

A vital aspect of the defence mechanisms is reporting. The problem cannot be addressed unless it is identified. Much effort is now going into the development of an objective and fair reporting system that highlights any potential deficiency in hardware, software, environment or liveware. The reporting system may operate within the organisation or within the whole industry. For Australia, it operates via the CAIRS program.

## Containing Individual Errors

The ultimate management task faced by a pilot is decision-making. Our decisions are influenced by many factors. In the case of the individual, the last shield in the Reason model could be equated to a checklist – a formal objective review of how we reached a decision – before we commit ourselves to a decision. There are several suggested formal models (checklists) to aid decision-making but they all come to the same obvious and logical conclusions:

The *PILOT* model (Tony Wilson, 1993):
- Probe the facts.
- Identify the problem.
- Look for Solutions.
- Operate.
- Take stock.

*GRADE*:
- Gather information.
- Review.
- Analyse alternatives.
- Decide and do.
- Evaluate outcome.

*DECIDE* (Benner, 1975):
- Detect that action is necessary.
- Estimate the significance of the action – how important, how quick, the action is needed.
- Choose the way to go.
- Identify actions to achieve the chosen option.
- Do what appears best.
- Evaluate the effect of the action taken.

The basis, of course, is that any decision-making process should gather all available information, logically and objectively analyse and consider options and outcomes, make the decision and take action – most of all do *something* – unless there is a conscious decision to not act. Any non-action must also be the result of a decision. It must not be the result of avoiding or deferring a decision. Once action is taken, the normal control/feedback loop can operate and make adjustments if necessary. Above all, *make* a conscious decision. If possible take into account your own pressures and personality when you are reaching a decision. Have your inner self double-check your motives for the decision.

## Vigilance/Alertness/Awareness

Vigilance is our ability to maintain interest, attention and motivation over time. Humans are not good at long-duration, monitoring tasks. Thus error containment is largely conducted in three ways:
- by allotting tasks to the human or the machine where each can apply their best attributes, i.e. take advantage of the qualities, and counter the deficiencies, of each;

- by design and developing procedures, checks and policies that protect the operation from individual and endemic limitations and provide double-checks, and back-up systems, in those areas that critically affect flight safety, e.g. altitudes, clearances, landing checks, etc; and
- by training and monitoring the performance standards of all participants (liveware, hardware and software) in an objective, fair and constructive way.

## Crew Resource Management

Crew resource management (CRM) is the term used to describe the organisation and distribution of tasks associated with flight in a multi-crew cockpit environment. Recently it has come to include the complete crew. It has evolved and has been derived from human factors (HF) training, aircrew team management (ATM) and cockpit resource management (CRM). It is not a particularly definitive term as it encompasses many facets of human interrelationships – and that is essentially what CRM is – personal interrelationships. Of these interrelationships no aspect is more important than communications.

Most airlines process their crews through an initial and recurrency programme of CRM training but it is usually simulator based and lasts only two or three days a year – not much time to learn how to make best use of one's own and the crew's resources – skills, strengths *and* weaknesses. As soon as an individual becomes part of a team, whether of two *(doubles)* or more, then the interrelationship makes the overall performance greater or less than the sum of the individuals. We hope for the former and often experience the latter. Note how some tennis players are adept at doubles play whereas others can only perform alone. The game of flight requires a team player and that is why CRM has assumed such importance. Team playing doesn't happen naturally in all of us.

In sport we train as a team with set places (assigned by our individual strengths – bowling or batting, attacking or defending, full forward, or left behind), set plays to a large extent and a limited number of players. In the performing arts we rehearse with a script and with a set role for each player (based on individual strengths and talents) and we don't perform in public, or in competition, until we are very proficient and very consistent. In the military, crews and squads train as teams with set roles, positions and responsibilities (based on skills training and aptitudes – pilot, navigator, gunner, medic, and loadmaster – with each a specialist knowing his or her function in the team). The team trains and competes and is rewarded, as a team, for their performance. In the civil, multi-crew aircraft, we do not.

The airlines have a roster system and captains, first officers and cabin crew fly with all and any. There is no stable crew for more than a few days or a few weeks. This has both advantages and disadvantages. If you don't like the other crew member you don't have to put up with them for long – but nor do you have to learn to be part of a team – no matter who you are rostered with. You never develop as a team but nor is your performance measured as a team. You learn to *role-play* in a way appropriate to the type of personality with whom you are rostered to fly – but it's not quite the same.

Your simulator check-ride is not with your permanent co-pilot – as it is in the military. The crew performances are therefore averaged by the natural process of continual reassignment. Thus there are no exceptionally good nor exceptionally bad crews – at least not for long. They can only do this by operating within a stringent rule-based regime of protocols and standard operating procedures (SOPs) that provide standardisation – with little scope for exceptional performance one way or the other. This is the opposite of the *Right Stuff*. Here we are seeking consistent, reliable, predictable, safe and compliant individuals – and yet we expect exceptional lateral thinking and problem-solving under stress of an emergency.

Ultimately, each crew member is an individual and each is assessed, paid and promoted as an individual. Yet each individual is expected to perform efficiently as a member of a crew with strangers and without rehearsals before their public performance.

Thus the demand for people skills on the flight deck and in the cabin of today's airliners is more than in any other scenario. The essence of being successful under these circumstances is *give-and-take* and good communications.

## Communications

Communicating is our greatest social asset and our greatest potential weakness. Unless we plan to live as hermits we must learn to communicate and encourage, and welcome, others to do so.

### Personality

A major breakdown in communication occurs when one of the two members establishes a position of non-negotiation – as distinct from authority. There is rightfully only one captain. But when that captain makes it clear that he or she wants the other crew member to *'sit down and shut up'* (or *'sit up and shut down'*, for that matter), then there is little hope of constructive communications. A similar reverse role exists when the timid first officer conveys a grovelling desire to please – *'Yes sir, no sir, three bags full, sir'*.

### Language

The international language of aviation is English – or is it? The quality of spoken English varies considerably and the language itself is compounded by similar sounding terms and expressions – *take-off power* and *take off power*, or *wheels up?* and *wheels up!*, for example. Flight crews with mixed nationalities have to be especially wary.

### Body Language

The term *body language* encompasses all non-verbal means of communication – of which there are many:
• hand signals – formal and informal;
• gestures;

- stance;
- posture/leaning;
- arms and legs – crossed uncrossed open closed hands face up down;
- eye contact;
- facial expression;
- touch; and
- proximity – invasion or protection of personal space.

A good communicator, or better still, an honest communicator, will have body language that supports the tone and content of the verbal communications. We all intuitively assess the speaker and the listener by their body language. It is an advantage, and a potential disadvantage, of training in a side-by-side versus a tandem cockpit. In the wide-body jet, it also has its advantages and disadvantages.

## The Good Listener

Body language is all important on the part of the listener. It is their way of telling the speaker whether or not they are interested in hearing what is being said. By being visibly receptive they are saying that they place some importance on listening. There is nothing more frustrating than trying to communicate with someone who appears uninterested. Further, a good listener does not interrupt, nor distract, but pays attention and, if really interested, asks questions – providing feedback and therefore reward to the speaker.

There is a tendency to:

- drift into random thoughts;
- think about what we are going to say;
- look for a break in conversation to insert our point of view;
- finish sentences; or
- interrupt.

Listening is an active and conscious process. We have to learn to listen well and we have to concentrate to listen at all. *Now we're talking or, better still, we're communicating. (Now if only they would listen too).*

## Styles of Communicating

Communicating is more than transmitting and receiving – more than speaking and hearing. It's about getting a message across effectively. This is *expressing* and *comprehending* and, like our closed-loop flight control system, requires *feedback*. With the message comes emotion – what we say versus what we mean. We humans often speak with forked tongue – not to lie but to camouflage, hint, disguise what we really mean. On the flight deck we have to relearn to say directly what we really mean – but with the protocol necessary to achieve a positive rather than a negative result.

Communicating is a two-way process and requires the willing and active participation of both parties – one wanting to communicate, the other wanting to listen. The speaker needs to set the tone, language and content. The listener needs the environment, mood, and attitude to be paying attention, concentrating, overriding distractions, comprehending and above all ignoring preset ideas, and negative attitudes. Communicating effectively is a skill on both sides – a skill that can be learnt. The tone of the conversation is particularly important on the flight deck. Commands must be clearly non-negotiable. Instructions must be unequivocal. Nevertheless there must be an obvious channel for feedback, checking, doubting. It must be clear that such comment will not result in rebuke but in reward. Then there is proper communications. The style or tone of the conversation can vary from:

- shouting;
- talking down;
- criticising;
- telling;
- commanding;
- ordering;
- directing;
- instructing;
- advising;
- speaking on level terms;
- sharing;
- asking;
- seeking;
- active listening (*switched-on*); and
- passive listening (*switched-off*).

The style is selected for the occasion but, in the cockpit, the extremes are rarely, if ever, appropriate. Talking *to,* rather than talking *at,* is the goal. Talking *between* is even better. The captain sets the tone by his or her level of approachability. The F/O responds positively or negatively. The value of the crew depends on this initial positioning, gesturing and signalling. In some references (Wilson, 1993), the style of communications is classified as *push* or *pull.* The former is telling, commanding or advising, the latter is asking, questioning or responding. Both are appropriate under certain circumstances and the tone of voice and body language should be chosen to reinforce the style.

## Culture

A significant factor in the communications gulf is cultural. If you have grown up in a society that respects elders, seniority and social status to the extent that any criticism, questioning or non-compliance is considered disrespectful and intolerable, then you are in a position when there is effectively a master–slave relationship on the flight deck. If the first officer, for any reason, is not willing to genuinely question the decisions or actions of the captain when he or she believes that there is a safety problem, then that first officer is a waste of space. They may as well not be there and certainly don't deserve to be paid for their non-services. With respect, the company culture and the cockpit culture must learn to override the traditional culture – in the cockpit.

Even religious beliefs can affect the relationship. In some philosophies, what befalls us and the aircraft is *fate,* the will of God or Allah, and cannot be interfered with. There have been occasions where this acceptance has resulted in no action being taken to cope with what could and should have been a survivable emergency.

### The Gulf War

US researchers into communications breakdown discovered an inequity and coined the term, *trans cockpit authority gradient* (TCAG) where they found that a significant difference in seniority, age, experience, stature, status, reputation or assertiveness, between the captain and first officer, led to a communications *gulf*. Personality and culture plays a large part in setting the cockpit gradient. Gender can also play a part, but hopefully that will disappear quickly (the gradient not the gender).

## Crew Coordination

### Two Versus Three, or More, Crew

*The ayes have it — mutiny versus scrutiny.*

In older cockpits there were many cases of the voting system being used to make decisions — based on the voting power of the older members of the flight crew. Now we have a crew of two. One is, indubitably, the captain, commander and ultimate decision-maker — unless the aircraft is about to crash and action needs to be taken. Under those circumstances, there is such a thing as justifiable, momentary, mutiny. Otherwise he/she should be allowed to command — under our scrutiny. This is a healthy way to protect him or her against themselves. The captain will make mistakes — so will we. The task of the first officer is to notice and politely indicate the potential error before it affects the safety of the aircraft.

CRM is about forming a constructive and effective partnership whereby the crew of two perform better than two individuals. If we consider our role as fulfilling our part of the bargain, there will be little problem with CRM. We should be as proud that our captain commanded a good, safe, flight and that we were part of the team (crew) — as we receive praise when we land well and the passengers applaud (it does happen). We are not competing with each other.

### Challenge and Response

As well as the continuous routine checking of the pilot flying (PF) by the pilot not flying (PNF), there are several more formal occasions where actions are completed and checked. A normal procedure within the company will be for the pilot flying to set and read back assigned headings, altitudes and clearances, and for the other to check the FMS, flight director or autopilot setting that has been entered and then indicate that it has been checked and found correct. This completes the multi-crew control loop.

This is a serious matter. Integration of another human into the control loop is not easy. There is potential for better delegation and therefore less workload, but there is equal potential for increased workload and redundancy and even negativity. If the second crew member is not used or is not useful we are better off alone.

Each person's duties should be clearly defined with the workload being fairly divided. There must be systematic cooperation between the PF and PNF, with an open flow of information in both directions. The tasks being performed by one must be monitored by the other, in both normal and abnormal situations.

Another formal process is the litany of the checklist. Checklists are usually *performed* by the PF and *checked* by the PNF. In some cases, the cockpit is divided into left and right halves and both pilots perform the litany. In this case, the *check* is then done by the PNF. The checklist is a set procedure for the particular aircraft and the particular company. While the design and use of checklists is an art in itself (another aspect of *ergonomics*), the use of checklists is another matter.

The complement of the crew is a significant factor. If you are part of a two-person crew then you can readily establish a procedure where one carries out a series of actions and the other then completes an independent check. The important aspect is that it is a *check* list after a *do* list. The situation is compounded by cockpit design as we will see.

## Single Pilot Checks

When we are operating as a single pilot then the situation is not so pedantic. There are strong arguments that, when alone, there is less workload and less likelihood of missed items, if the checklist is memorised rather then read; that is, provided that the actions are checked as they are completed and that, if interrupted, the checklist is resumed at the point where it is interrupted or with the item that is not yet completed.

There are arguments for and against written checklists for the single pilot, but ultimately if they add to your workload, rather than reduce it, they are a burden rather than an asset and should be discarded. Further, there is a human tendency that, if we use a written checklist, it becomes a crutch without which we are insecure and unreliable. There have been as many missed checks with checklists as there have been with reliance on memorised items – besides it's not a good idea to be reading checklists in the circuit. One added protection for all single-pilot checks, clearances and settings is to say them aloud, checking that the pattern of sounds you hear matches the pattern of sounds you received or expected (you will confirm your correctness by hearing yourself say the item).

## Command Versus Control

The *captain*, the *aircraft commander*, the *pilot in command* or the *commandant de bord* is always in *command* and always remains ultimately responsible for the flight. The role of commander cannot be delegated – even when it is the F/O's sector. What is delegated, temporarily, is *control* of the aircraft and control of the flight. Just as if the autopilot was engaged, the human autopilot takes control. He or she becomes the *pilot flying* – but not the commander. In a two-pilot cockpit, the tasks are systematically organised and distributed so that one pilot has the primary task of piloting the aircraft, this person being known as the *pilot flying* (PF), supported and monitored by the *pilot not flying* (PNF). The systematic organisation of tasks and the distribution of duties between the PF and PNF will be found in the company operations manual and standard operating procedures (SOPs).

Like a script for a play, the duties and interactions of the crew members for each phase of the flight are itemised and choreographed for both normal and abnormal operations. However, in our case, we change roles. The captain always remains the pilot in command but may not necessarily be flying the aircraft. Thus we have a complex and diverse delegation of duties but not responsibilities. The pilot flying may or not be the pilot in command and vice versa.

On long-haul, the second officer may occupy the first officer's seat, and be flying the aircraft, while the first officer is acting as pilot in command while the captain sleeps. What we are witnessing is the process of on-the-job training by role-playing, and it works, provided it is well managed, standard procedures are followed and nothing untoward happens.

In this flexible two-crew situation, the decision-making is even more dependent on the relative personalities of the two individuals and the safety of the flight will be determined primarily by the leadership qualities demonstrated by the captain.

## Leadership Qualities

There is *management* and there is *leadership*. They are not the same. Perhaps we should be discussing CRL rather than CRM. The pilot in a multi-crew cockpit must have leadership skills if the operation is to function safely and efficiently.

Leadership differs from management as follows:
- A leader leads by example; a manager states what is required.
- A leader shows how; a manager states what is to be done.
- A leader takes risks; a manager delegates risks.
- A leader shares success and failure; a manager gets promoted.
- A leader rolls up her sleeves; a manager rolls up his trousers.
- A leader earns respect; a manager demands or pays for compliance.

Management as organisational structure and efficiency is essential, provided it encompasses rather than overrides the individual. In a corporate sense the individual is dispensable. In an aircraft crew, in an emergency, each individual is precious – worth their weight in gold, or opals, as the case may be.

A good leader will be:
- positive and cheerful;
- supportive of the company and its policies;
- self-confident – but only with justification;
- firm, fair, reliable, dependable and there – if needed;
- approachable;
- as loyal to the crew as to the company;
- honest;
- understanding and caring of others;
- non-critical and non-judgemental;
- able to communicate clearly and on even terms – with anybody;
- able to listen to others and accept their opinion or criticism;

- able to separate facts from emotions;
- able to persuade and encourage;
- able to coordinate and direct;
- able to inspire a team, on both technical and emotional levels;
- able to show sound judgement and to consistently make decisions that the rest of the team will know are in their best interest;
- able to breed confidence in others and help them to learn and develop;
- able to delegate tasks and responsibilities, but accept ultimate responsibility;
- able to establish priorities, *to sort the wheat from the chaff;*
- able to maintain a complete overview of the flight and manage it to a successful conclusion;
- able to fly well and safely according to standard operating procedures;
- able to show flair and an ability to deal with non-standard and unusual situations; and
- able to represent him/herself, the profession and the company, socially.

Multi-person decision-making has it advantages and disadvantages. When we make a sole decision, we are influenced by our personality and by external influences and pressures. When we try to make a decision within a group, even of only two, we tend to offer a view that not only solves the particular problem, but that may also impress or please the other member/s of the group. Conversely, some will choose a much more cautious approach and not take a risk until they hear the views of the other members. Thus there is an added layer of complexity.

Like most things in aviation, there is a mnemonic for highlighting the qualities of a good leader. In this case it's LEADERSHIP. A good leader:

**L**    Leads by setting an example. Shows rather than tells what is expected.

**E**    Establishes and defines the task, the team roles, the priorities, the *expectations* and the individual responsibilities.

**A**    Advises and explains intentions before acting.

**D**    Delegates, in a very clear way, flying and routine tasks so he or she can focus on broader decision-making issues.

**E**    Evaluates the response to his or her actions and decisions and makes adjustments.

**R**    Responds to crew inputs and explains why or why not – time permitting.

**S**    Sets and maintains priorities – no distractions nor interruptions.

**H**    Has a high degree of personal knowledge, skill and reliability (commands and deserves respect).

**I**    Involves and invites the participation of the crew in the problem-solving and decision-making process.

**P**    Praises (publicly, if appropriate) and credits good results – where credit is due.

Figure 9-7 **Leadership mnemonic**

## Setting an Example

*Do as I do not as I say*

There is an fundamental learning process for us humans – we follow and copy what we see our elders and wisers do. Our survival instincts, which in evolutionary terms are as strong as ever, tell us that, if we think the person we fly with, captain or instructor, is a good example, we'll copy her every move, radio call, decision and we will try to adopt her standards. We want to be exactly like her. She becomes our *role model* – our perfect pilot. If our role model is a less-than-professional pilot or if, in the case of many of us, our role model is ourselves, we have only our perceived ideal to aim for, and self-discipline plays a part in achieving, rather than just desiring, the standard. When we fly with a selection of other pilots we see the best and the worst. We respect the ideals but, unfortunately, also tend to recognise and adopt the accepted average as the easy way out. It's less work and less of a hassle. Besides, we are neither recognised, rewarded nor remunerated for being within twenty feet rather than fifty. It's better to aim for fifty and achieve it than to aim for twenty and not achieve it – especially when someone is watching – is it not?

## Leadership Style

When leading a team to accomplish a task, there can be a variation in emphasis between two extremes:

- total goal orientation, where completing the task at all costs occurs without regard to the human aspects of the team (common these days, but short-sighted as the *bottom line*); and
- total people orientation, where keeping every individual happy takes precedence over the group and, as a result, completing the task safely and efficiently (the company goes bankrupt).

The ideal leader/manager is a balanced person who will encompass both aspects in completing the task safely and efficiently, but in a manner that involves and rewards the team and takes advantage of their input and skills. This person will be a captain who is respected and liked by the crew and one who respects the needs and constraints of the company.

The totally *task-oriented* captain will be seen as a poor captain – perhaps a tyrant. He or she may be a short-term success because of the bottom-line results but he or she cannot prevail. The totally *person-oriented* captain may be seen as weak. Aeroplanes cannot be run by committees. Even though a contribution from team members is required, someone has to make the final decision, within a suitable time-frame.

The required management/leadership skills can all be learned and practised as a matter of daily life and in relationships with everyone with whom we have contact. Life is too short to be miserable or negative. Being a good captain is closely linked to being a good person in other aspects of your life.

## Who Is in Command?

The pilot flying may be controlling the aeroplane but the pilot in command (the captain) makes the ultimate decisions. He or she *always* retains ultimate responsibility and authority. The pilot in command must always be clearly, and unequivocally, in charge, even if flying duties (control) have been delegated to the F/O. Even in a single-pilot cockpit, the problem of who is in command can arise, especially if the pilot acts in a passive manner and allows others to make decisions for him – the person paying for the charter, the aircraft owner or the aircraft operator. Domineering and demanding crew members, spouses or passengers can sometimes exert authority, and occasionally, the pilot in command has to re-establish command.

Unsatisfactory clearances from ATC (such as a *'cleared for immediate take-off'* before you are completely ready, or a VFR clearance that would take you into cloud) can be rejected; this will be accepted by ATC.

The trainee crew member must learn the role of pilot in command and how to act in this capacity. It is, to some extent, a style, act or part, that can be learnt and rehearsed and, by playing the part, we learn the skill. There is nothing wrong with role-playing if it achieves a safe end-result.

The role of the pilot in command is indeed to be *in command*. This means being totally responsible for all aspects of the flight. It is more a task and responsibility for decision-making than of physically flying or navigating the aircraft. These routine tasks can be delegated. Command can not. Radio transmissions can be just as professional and confident. On the radio, a Piper is no different from a Boeing.

If you wish to delegate some tasks to others, then do so in a planned, briefed and responsible manner, and retain command of the situation by providing clear guidance and then monitoring their actions and their accuracy. If an assistant pilot, rather than a trained crew member, is operating the radios or operating some of the controls, such as the flaps or undercarriage, then be careful – you are still in command and, ultimately, are responsible for the safety of the aircraft.

Informal assistance, without overall direction from the pilot in command, can be dangerous. Do not allow uncalled-for assistance, even from a more experienced pilot, as it may interfere with your operation and how you want it done.

In a two-crew cockpit, always be certain who has physical control of the flightpath of the aeroplane by using the phrases *'I have control'* and *'You have control'* appropriately.

Always make it clear, by means of take-off and approach briefings in particular, who is to do what, when and to what standard. Explain what is expected of your partner and what are the milestones/checks and balances. Review also the completed flight and reward successful performance with at least a congratulatory *well done*, and a less-than-satisfactory performance with a debrief that addresses the issues (not the person) and suggests a solution for next time.

## Remaining in Command

### Group Decision-Making

Decisions are made in formal and informal ways. Mostly it is not consciously thought about – or is it? Decisions such as to turn left, turn off the stove, mow the lawn or put out the cat are made on the basis of information presented to us. These are routine decisions made within a framework of normality and where the consequences of a wrong decision are not dire. In flight, the situation is such that time is of the essence, the consequences of a wrong decision are indeed dire, the information may not be complete and the prior experience (memory) on which a decision can be based is limited. Thus pilots are very vulnerable to the emotional overrides that can influence the decision.

There is a risk in suffering from the disease *press-on-itis* – impress the peers, please the wife or the boss, or meet the deadline. The very great tendency is to avoid decisions altogether – put them off until later and avoid the immediate hassles. This is sometimes not possible and, even if it is, it often compounds the situation later when there is no more time. It can only be avoided by setting go/no-go gates that are not allowed to be passed without a conscious and loudly spoken decision (e.g. *I am at my decision point, the circumstances are. . ., I am experienced and current... or not, I am not pressured, I have decided to. . .*). This of course takes honesty and self-discipline; the honesty and self-discipline to want to be professional about being a pilot. There is a further complication. You are not alone. It is even more difficult to make decisions when you are part of a crew.

In principle, a group decision offers a broader experience base, more ideas, more lateral solutions. However, it has been shown that there is a likelihood of the group deciding on a course that carries greater risk than the individual would have chosen. This is known as *risky shift*. A group decision can and should provide a more reasoned solution, one more balanced and more probable. There is no reason why it cannot also provide a more lateral, innovative solution – if managed creatively. Look at the *think-tanks* that have been very effective problem-solvers. They can also take time.

It must be a controlled pooling of knowledge and ideas, and not a committee meeting. It is not a referendum and consensus is not the objective. It is a group exposure and discussion process and then a *command* decision. In many ways, it is harder to reach a decision within a group than it is to go alone and get on with it. There are occasions when there it no time for any other alternative but to go for it and to accept the consequences. Fortunately, in our case, we are generally considering a group of only two. To take advantage of the two-person crew, most decisions should be at least considered and announced out aloud and the other crew member given the opportunity to understand the rationale for the decision and to suggest alternatives, or objections, if appropriate, e.g. *I have considered the following factors and I intend to. . .*

There is the other problem of *deference* (bowing to the other's views even if their views are assumed) or deciding by popular opinion or by committee (*will they like me or would they agree?*). There is no place for these marshmallow decisions. Without *shooting from the hip* (deciding prematurely, without consideration of all the factors), it is generally better to make a decision and get on with it than to compromise, procrastinate, defer, wonder about it and wander about the sky or into the ground. In summary a group decision may offer:

* more options;
* better solutions than those produced by an individual or by the average member; but
* is likely to be more risky;

- take more time; and
- rarely be a better decision than would have been made by *ablest* member of the team.

## Conflict Resolution

A major cause of conflict and increasing discontent is an event or incident that leads to a breakdown in communications. When we do not speak we cannot resolve our differences. The first step then is to open the channels of communication and keep them open. Next tackle the issues rather than the persons – that way the channel will stay open. Witch hunts and scapegoats don't help. Keep the discussion objective and non-emotional. Invite the participants to contribute to solutions and then discuss options. Allow open discussion. Don't give directions or show preferences until all the facts are in the open. Finally make and state your decision – and, if there is time, explain why you chose that particular course of action. Don't make the decision on the basis of *what will they think of me if I decide this?* Do it because you know professionally that it is the best, wisest, safest course of action for all concerned under those particular circumstances.

## Discipline on the Flight Deck

*Control versus dictatorship – You are not allowed to use a baseball bat despite the precedent.* To stay in total command of the flight, you must ensure that you do not get into situations for which you are not prepared or trained, or for which the aeroplane is not equipped (perhaps night or instrument flight). You should know your own limitations and capabilities, and should assess the expected workload on this basis. You should be able to operate safely right up to the point where the workload and skill demand meets your capability, albeit with some reserve safety margin if the circumstances permit, (although be aware that, in this case, you will be close to your personal limits). If you feel that the workload at any point in the flight could exceed your capability, then do not continue or do not go. Say *'no'*, *'no more'*, *'no longer'* or *'never again'*. For instance, the workload associated with normal take-off and landing at your home airport has always been well within your capability, but today you feel tired (diminished capability), there is a gusty crosswind (increased workload) and there is pressure to get airborne by a certain time (stress). In this situation, you need to make a rational *go/no-go* decision. This could be the most important decision of the whole flight – or your life.

Sometimes the workload imposed by individual items are within your current capability, but a combination of factors (such as an unfamiliar airport, a radio communications failure, and difficult weather conditions including rain and a gusty crosswind) might add up to a total workload beyond your capability.

You must then put your priorities in order – the first priority is that you, as a pilot, and therefore the aircraft and its contents, arrive safely, and so if there is any doubt, don't try. You are responsible for the aircraft and its contents. You are obliged professionally to do your utmost to achieve this and you are committed by self-development, training, self-discipline and knowledge to meet this obligation. There is no such thing as a half-dedicated, nor part-time, professional pilot. It is a full-time, committed profession. We're in it together. Welcome aboard.

Chapter 10

# The Flight Deck

## Ergonomics and Flight Deck Design

Ergonomics is about milk cartons. How often do you open the wrong side? The carton design is noteworthy. They mark the side to open but then stamp the opposite side with a use-by-date or whatever. What was a clear and simple marker no longer works. This is misspent ergonomics. Our situation is a little more complex but the principles are the same – to make the task easier, simpler, more reliable, safer, more comfortable, more satisfying and more efficient. A visit to the flight deck of any recently designed aeroplane will illustrate that cockpit design is a complex art. Instrumentation, controls, lighting, and seating are a vast improvement over earlier cockpits – at least in most cases. As we understand ourselves, and our limitations, so we can better design our operating environment to accommodate those limitations. *Ergonomics* is the science that optimises the *interface* between the machine and its human operator/manager.

### Past Designs

Early cockpits were cold, draughty, oily and smelly places, often with poor forward field-of-view (FOV), no heating and poor lighting. Instruments were placed, and sometimes heaped, clustered and cluttered wherever there happened to be space – often in different locations in different aeroplanes of the same fleet, and often widely displaced from their associated control. Some displays were so small, poorly lit, or poorly placed as to be almost impossible for the pilot to read, or took undue attention to read or decipher.

The aircraft was designed from the outside in. The airframe/engine combination was selected and developed to meet the operational requirement, and then the crew was given a place from which to operate the systems. Many production aircraft have an airframe design and a cockpit layout that is more than twenty years old. These designs have served their purpose. They were certainly a big step forward in their time, and brought safer aviation to ordinary people and, while many have been modified to accommodate newer and better instrumentation, the design limitations are still there.

Only now with the focus on type ratings, and transportability of those ratings, are we seeing an aircraft where the inside of the cockpit is as important as the outside – we are designing the aircraft inside out, which is the correct way as far as the crew is concerned.

## Human Pilot and Machine

The pilot and the aircraft (previously called a *flying machine* or simply a *machine*) form a very important combination that depends on a good pilot, good controls and good cockpit displays.

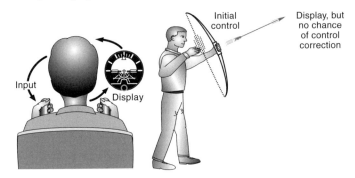

Figure 10-1 **Open-loop system** *(fire and forget)* **versus closed loop**

The pilot aircraft combination is a *closed-loop* system, in that the pilot makes a control movement, observes the effect as displayed on the instruments (or through the windscreen), decides if the response is what is desired, and then makes further control inputs to bring the actual even closer to the desired. It is a closed loop of *pilot-control-display-pilot* repeated again and again.

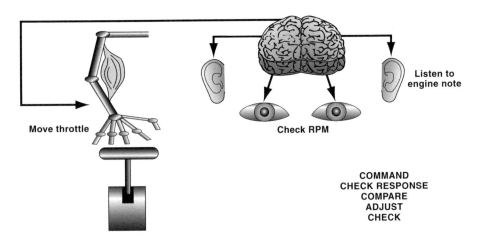

Figure 10-2 **Closed-loop (feedback/correction)**

When controlling the aircraft, you, the pilot, decide where you want it to go and then manipulate the flight controls to achieve the desired flightpath. You then observe the effect of the control movement on the flightpath by reference to the instruments and/or the outside environment. Next, you decide if any further action is needed – any fine-tuning – and then make further movements on the controls.

However, inaccuracy, or overcontrol, is not all our fault. The control system itself helps or hinders both our degree of control and our ease of control.

*The Sabre had one of the early hydraulically powered flight control systems. Called a bang-bang system, it had no subtlety. Move the stick and 3,000 psi moved the control surface proportionally – no arguments. There was no feedback, no stiffness with increasing airspeed (called q-feel), just a centring spring and a bob-weight to increase the stick force per g. The controls therefore had the same feel at 120 knots and 600 knots but the response of the aircraft wasn't quite the same. Indeed, at transonic speeds, the aileron deflection twisted the wing and the aircraft rolled the opposite way. But it was the pitch control circuit that was exciting. There was a lag, in response to control inputs, of about a fifth of a second and this is close to our human reaction time.*

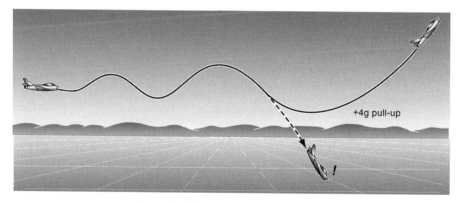

+4g pull-up

Figure 10-3 **Divergent control response**

*The combination of lack of feel and the delayed response made the aircraft difficult to control. A small pitch correction at high airspeed and low altitude, and the aircraft would initially show no response – for a fifth of a second. At these speeds and altitudes the pilot couldn't wait so would make a larger correction. The aircraft would now respond to the first input and it would be too much. The pilot made a reverse correction. Nothing happened. A larger correction was made. The response was now excessive. This input/delay/further input/over-response became a divergent oscillation. Engineers called it a PIO – pilot-induced oscillation. Pilots called it the 'JC' after the desperate assistance sought from heaven when it happened. The antidote was to pull to +4g to get away from the ground and to stop the oscillation.*

Due to long control cables and flexible tail booms, the Cessna 337 has had similar control loop problems in the landing flare – so had the Space Shuttle but for different reasons. In both cases the pilots adapted to the characteristics, or quirks, of the particular system. Alert, current pilots have the skills and familiarity to make the closed-loop system work so quickly that flightpath and airspeed deviations/trends are kept within accurate limits. For trainee pilots, the closed-loop may take a little longer to operate, and so flightpath and airspeed are not controlled as tightly (but will be, with practice and determination).

Another example of a closed-loop system is a radio-controlled glider which the operator can control from the ground. A glider without radio control, however, is uncontrolled once the glider is launched. There is no means of altering its flightpath, even though the glider is visible to the observer. In this case, the loop is not closed. Similarly, a golfer has no further control over the path of the ball once it has left the club face, even though it is apparent where the ball is going.

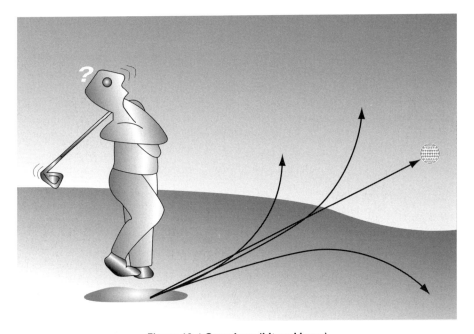

Figure 10-4 **Open loop (hit and hope)**

There are many closed loops in the cockpit – for instance, when controlling cabin temperature, the pilot adjusts the control then checks the cabin temperature gauge, or when adjusting the cockpit lights at night, the pilot dims them and then sees whether charts are still readable, then makes further adjustments if necessary. Action, feedback, and further action is a continual process in the cockpit.

In automatic flight, the pilot shares the tasks with the automatics to a certain extent, but there are further closed loops in this relationship, since the performance of the automatics must still be monitored.

## Designing the Pilot's Workspace

In designing the flight deck, account has to be taken of the limited space available, the size of the pilots, their need to reach and operate the controls, their need to see both the internal displays and the external environment, while strapped into a comfortable seat.

*Ergonomics* is patterned on the word *economics* using the Greek word *ergon* meaning work. The word *economics* itself has a Greek derivation meaning household management. In aviation, ergonomics refers to cockpit, cabin and galley design and the improvement of the crew/aircraft interface, taking into account human factors including physical dimensions, eyesight, hearing, comfort and expected human behaviour, reach, strength and performance, which, as we all know, is a variable    not only between people, but also within the one individual at different times. It is quantified and averaged for the pilot population or group for whom the aircraft is designed.

Figure 10-5 **The pilot's workplace**

## People Come in All Shapes and Sizes

People vary considerably in size and shape, with some very short people in a given population and some extremely tall people, but with most of us somewhere in the middle. Race, culture and diet affect our dimensions. Genetic properties come into play and so do social pressures. In Rubens' time, young ladies strived for voluptuous, milk-coloured bodies. Now we seek slim, tight and fit bodies. Also the relative dimensions vary within the total frame. A tall person may have a long torso and short legs, while a pilot of average stature may have unusually long legs, short torso and long arms.

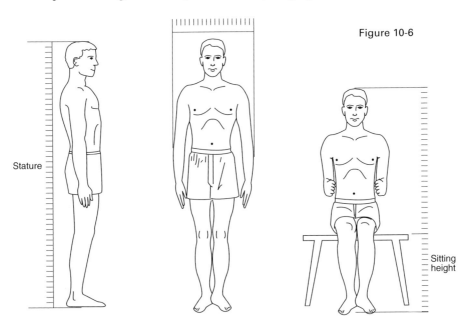

Figure 10-6

The task of the flight deck designer is complicated. It is impracticable to cater for 100% of the population, and it is generally accepted that the small number in the 5% at either end of the size-and-shape range may be neglected. The designer therefore plans for those who lie in the range from the 5%ile to the 95%ile of the population.

The science of human measurement is called *anthropometry*. Measurements can be static (joint-to-joint), contour (shape) or dynamic (such as reach or pull).

### Percentiles

A *percentile* is one of a hundred equal groups of a population distributed by some variable, e.g. the 95th %ile for the stature of Australian females may be 1.6 metres, meaning that 95% of the measured population of Australian females were below 1.6 metres in standing height (stature). The 5th %ile for the same group may have been 1.0 metre. So the designer uses the range of 1.0–1.6 metres if designing for 90% of the Australian female population.

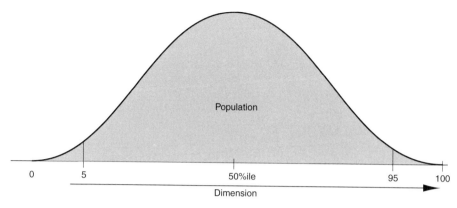

Figure 10-7 **Population/percentiles**

The flight deck is designed to cater for the male and female pilot population (5%ile to 95%ile) as measured. Recognising the importance of vision, the most important feature we must provide is a good *field-of-view* (FOV), and to do that, we must be seated.

## Design Eye Position

The pilot needs to be seated with the eyes in a position so that, with minimal head movement, there is:

- an unobstructed view of the *main instruments*; and
- a good view of the *outside environment,* not only the general area ahead, but especially the area forward and down from the nose to assist in judging the final stages of the approach and landing.

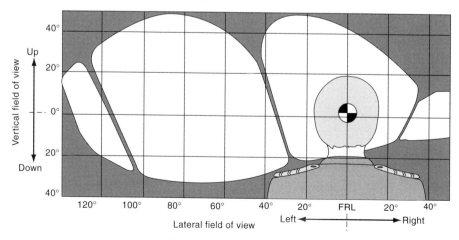

Figure 10-8 **Field of view**

Thus the cockpit is designed on the basis of the eyes being in a set position: the *design eye position* or *point* (DEP).

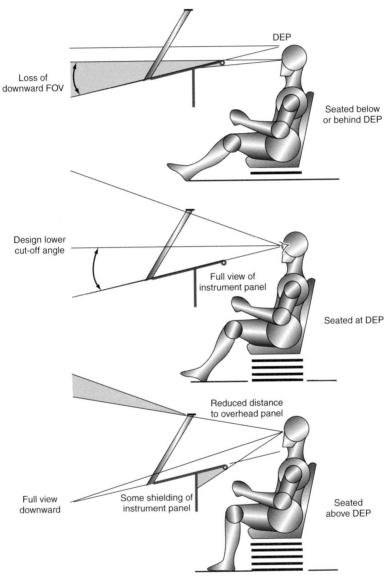

Figure 10-9 **Design eye point**

Instrument approach criteria are based on the pilot being at the DEP.

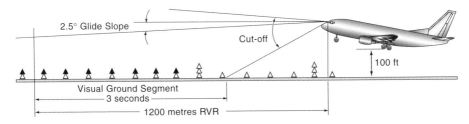

Figure 10-10 **DEP versus approach light acquisition**

The pilot must be able to see 3 seconds of distance over the ground at $V_{REF}$ within the 1,200 metre minimum visibility.

### Seat Design and the DEP

The seat should be able to be positioned fore and aft, up and down, and the backrest tilted if desired, so that the design criteria for operating the aeroplane are achieved: the eyes in the DEP, and all vital controls within reach and capable of being moved to the full extent of their travel without undue stretching.

The seat, having been designed to be moved and altered in shape to suit a wide range of pilots, must then be capable of being locked into position so that it cannot move in flight. With the seat adjusted so that your eyes are in the design eye position, you should now adjust the rudder pedals. You can do this while parked, but you may not be able to check full movement until taxiing, since, in many aircraft, moving the rudder pedals not only moves the rudder but also the nosewheel. The control column should be checked for full movement to ensure that it will not strike your knees or stomach. If the seat is already at the DEP, the abdomen has to go.

### Restraint

There are different seatbelt designs. To be effective, they must all be fastened correctly. The simplest is a lap belt where the belt should be fastened firmly over the hips with the buckle kept away from the soft abdomen if possible, so that bone structure (the pelvis) and not soft body parts carry the load. The belt should be flat and not twisted, so that it will not cut into the body under the pressure of deceleration or turbulence.

Many aircraft have a lap belt with an inertia reel shoulder strap that comes across one shoulder and fastens into the buckle. The inertia reel allows the pilot to lean forward under normal conditions, but under conditions of rapid acceleration or deceleration, such as in turbulence, the shoulder strap locks and restrains the upper body. The inertia reel is tested by pulling sharply on the shoulder strap – it should lock. Larger aircraft usually have lap belts for the pilots, with a fifth crutch-strap to hold the lap belt down and to prevent the pilot from slipping under the lap belt *(submarining)*, plus inertia reel shoulder straps over each shoulder. During turbulence, the shoulder straps can be mechanically locked.

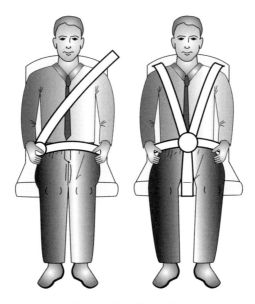

Figure 10-11 **Restraint**

## Design of the Controls

Getting used to the controls can be quite a steep learning curve for a trainee pilot or a pilot converting to a new type, but by using a certain degree of standardisation and good design, the task is made somewhat easier. There has to be some flexibility of design available to the aeroplane manufacturer, otherwise there would be no progress.

Some general principles of control design for all aeroplanes are:
- controls should be within reach of the pilots and capable of being moved to their full extent without obstruction or without undue force being required;
- controls should be standardised where possible, so that controls in one aircraft resemble those in another and are placed in similar positions;
- controls for different functions should be different enough to avoid confusion, so that the throttle is not confused with the propeller pitch control, or the flap lever with the landing gear lever;
- controls should be logically designed and placed, especially when they are to be used simultaneously or sequentially; and
- controls must be consistent in response and reliable.

## Control Column

*The most important interface*

Most aircraft have a standard control wheel, or *yoke*, placed centrally in front of each pilot. It may have subsidiary functions such as a radio transmit button, electric trim, and an autopilot disconnect (go around) button.

There are non-standard designs involving totally different shapes, such as the ram's horn in the Concorde, the joystick in older aeroplanes and most aerobatic aeroplanes, and the sidestick in the Airbus 320 and 340 placed not directly in front of the pilot, but to the side, as its name suggests.

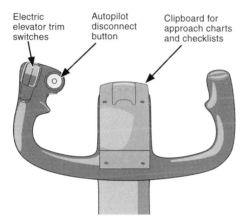

Figure 10-12 **Control yoke ergonomic features**

The sidestick is not just the province of modern airliners – the Millicer Airtourer, a light aircraft designed in the 1960s, had a sidestick placed between the two pilots.

Converting from one type to another will take time, but is made much easier by the fact that all operate in a logical sense – fore and aft for pitch, or for fast/slow, and sideways for rotation or roll. However, the left-to-right-hand changeover is a little more difficult.

Figure 10-13 **Sidestick**

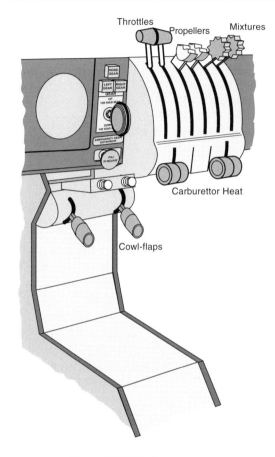

Throttles
Propellers  Mixtures

Carburettor Heat

Cowl-flaps

Figure 10-14 **Centre console**

## Thrust Controls

The throttle/thrust levers are usually placed centrally. International convention is now that forward movement or pressure will increase thrust/speed, and a rearward movement will reduce thrust.

Similarly, on aircraft with a constant-speed propeller, the rpm control (propeller lever) is moved forward to increase rpm, and rearward to reduce rpm. The idea of moving a control forward for increase, and rearward for decrease, is a general design principle. German aircraft in WWII had the throttle configured so that full back was full power. Variable-sweep wings caused somewhat of a dilemma. Should the cockpit control be a slide that is moved forward to sweep the wings back (like an oar) or slide back for wings back?

A jet engine is unusual in that with experience you simply place the lever in a set position and you will obtain a set value of thrust (you can do the same with a piston engine with a fixed-pitch propeller). The automatic fuel control will look after the surge boundaries. The new electrically signalled controls may be force sensitive but may not actually move. So the thrust setting is achieved by how long and how hard you push, rather than by how far or where you place it. The position of the lever no longer gives guidance. This philosophy has become the subject of an interesting debate.

## Aids to Communication

Communications within the cockpit, and without, are the greatest source of distraction, inefficiency, potential accidents and frustration.

Some aircraft use the same button for talking within the cockpit and for transmission over the radio. A second intercom/transmit selector is provided. As a result, many instructors have been in the position of unintentionally preaching to the world.

Some aircraft use a hand-held mike for transmission. It is usually retained on a bracket at the base of the control column or centre console. As well as requiring one hand to operate, thereby removing the hand from other duties, some can be accidentally operated by the pilot's knee. Any of these transmissions block the frequency.

It is not uncommon for the control column to have the same location of the transmit button for both pilots' seats. The column is standardised but the pilot in the right seat, often the flight instructor, has to change hands to transmit – the button being on the left horn of the yoke, whereas he or she is flying with his right hand. Clever design?

## Fuel Selectors

Fuel tank mis-selection has a notorious history, with many engines having stopped through fuel starvation while there was still plenty of fuel remaining. Faulty switching is often a result of poor design, and if you look at a variety of light aircraft you are sure to see very different fuel selectors. Some aircraft have all tanks in use at the one time, others have left, then right, some have all tanks off with the switch forward, others with it aft. Some have crossfeed. Some have transfer pumps. The fuel system is the one that must be well understood in any type conversion.

Which is yours?

Figure 10-15 **Fuel selector designs**

## Control Function and Design

Controls used for associated functions should be grouped together – for instance, the engine controls (throttle and pitch lever) should be near each other, but in an unambiguous relationship. Associated instruments should be adjacent and, where possible, aligned with the control.

If certain controls are used for related but different functions, and especially if they are located near each other, they need to be clearly differentiated. For instance, the throttle must look and feel different from the propeller lever, as must the mixture control and the carburettor heat control. This differentiation is now standardised by using different shapes, different texture (to provide a different feel), and different colours. Throttles have a rounded, smooth, black knob, propeller controls are blue, mixture controls are red and wrinkled, and carburettor heat controls are white.

Two controls that have been frequently misidentified are the undercarriage and the flap levers – a pilot error induced by poor design. In some older aircraft, the two controls were of similar shape and size, placed side-by-side, with the different colours not seeming to help fatigued pilots in darkened cockpits late at night.

Retracting the flaps immediately after take-off (reducing lift) instead of raising the undercarriage (thereby retaining high drag instead of reducing it) has obvious consequences. It is catastrophic if the slats also retract – which they generally do.

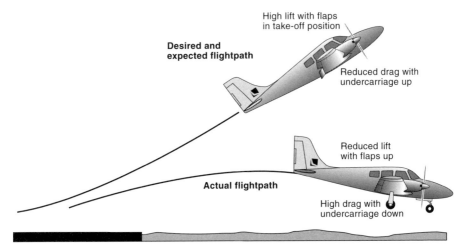

Figure 10-16 **Inappropriate selection**

There are still embarrassing moments after landing where the pilot retracts the undercarriage instead of the flaps. At least in this situation some protection can be provided by the *squat switch* (with weight on the wheels the switch isolates the undercarriage selector). Even so, we pilots can find a way around it.

*There was a trend in the sixties for fighter pilots to select the gear lever up before entering the runway. Thus, on lift-off when the weight came off the oleo, the undercarriage would retract by itself and the pilot could concentrate on formation flying. However, the microswitch was only on one leg and it was discovered with embarrassment that fast taxiing around the corner to enter the runway could be sufficient to relieve the weight on that leg. The gear would fold. Also in crosswinds or if the aircraft lifted-off early and then settled. Many settled on their drop tanks.*

In modern aircraft, the flap lever and the undercarriage lever are easily distinguishable, and are not placed side by side. The undercarriage (*gear*) lever has a knob that resembles a wheel, is on the front panel to be operated by either pilot and the lever is moved up for up and down for down; the flap lever has a knob in the form of an airfoil that resembles a flap, is on the centre console near the thrust levers and is moved fore-and-aft (forward to go faster) to select the desired position. The lever must be deliberately lifted through a series of detents, or gates, so there can be no inadvertent selection.

It all sounds so logical these days, but the lessons were learnt the hard way. Someone once said that there was an accident behind every regulation or standard – and that applies to cockpit layout, controls and displays as much as anything else.

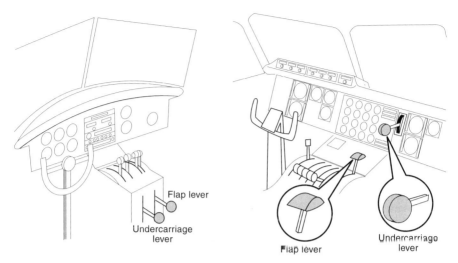

Figure 10-17 **Shaped and oriented controls**

## Emergency Functions

The reversionary or emergency modes are considered less important but some are horrendous in terms of safe operation. There are light aircraft where the emergency undercarriage requires 50 or 60 rotations of a handle that is located on the floor behind the pilots' seats – a challenge to instrumental flying, to say the least.

> *The F86 Sabre had an escape system that required the pilot to first jettison the canopy by pulling a handle connected to a lanyard at the base of the centre console and then activate the ejection seat. Several pilots were killed before it was discovered that the aerodynamic loads on the bubble canopy caused it to dish as it separated, The dishing decapitated the pilot. The solution was simple and elegant. The lanyard was replaced with a short rod, so the pilot had to crouch forward to reach it, and the ejection seat was modified to include a canopy breaker so that the pilot ejected through the shattered canopy and the frame remained with the aircraft.*

Well-designed cockpits enable a pilot to perform comfortably and efficiently. The converse is certainly true.

# Cockpit Displays

The function of cockpit displays (or instruments) is to convey information to the pilot. This information needs to be presented in a clear, unambiguous manner.
Well-designed displays are:
- easily seen;
- placed in a logical position, ideally adjacent to the associated control;

- standardised;
- reliable, and not prone to failure, but clearly indicating when a failure has occurred; and
- easy to interpret (difficult to misinterpret).

## Standardisation of Displays

*What does the pilot need to know?*

The AI may be supplemented in the future by a predictive flightpath vector. At present, to determine the flightpath you have to integrate in your mind information obtained from the attitude indicator, the altimeter and VSI, the airspeed indicator and the direction (or heading) indicator – quite a task, as instrument trainees know.

### Basic-T Layout of the Primary Flight Instruments

In earlier days, instruments were scattered around the cockpit, sometimes in a haphazard manner, as if providing information to the pilot was an afterthought. Even critical instruments, such as the attitude indicator, were placed in out-of-the-way positions, poorly lit, difficult to see and well away from associated instruments, such as the airspeed indicator, the altimeter, and the compass.

Figure 10-18 **Basic panel**

A major advance was made when designers and authorities agreed to arrange the primary flight instruments in a standardised pattern, known as the *basic-T*. The aim was to place the vital attitude indicator in the central position, since this is the instrument at which pilots spend most time looking.

The other important flight instruments are placed to either side of and beneath the attitude indicator, forming a T-shape. There is also logic in the representation on the AI and the plan position display of the DI or HSI below it. Slightly less important flight instruments are placed diagonally beneath it. This then allowed the development of the selective radial scan, which greatly enhanced instrument flying.

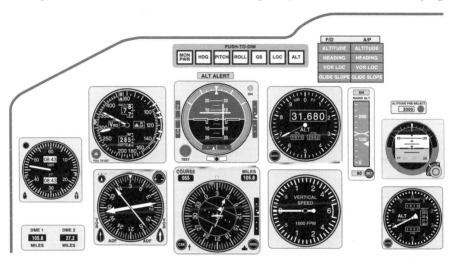

Figure 10-19 **Modern panel**

## Specific Instruments

### Attitude Indicator

The *attitude indicator* (AI) may also be called the *artificial horizon* (AH) and *attitude direction indicator* (ADI). There is no more important display, since it informs the pilot of pitch attitude and roll attitude relative to the horizon – the single most important piece of information for control of the aircraft. It is an analog (pictorial) display, showing the attitude of the wings and nose of the aeroplane relative to the horizon.

Usually the sky above the horizon is represented by the colour blue, and the ground beneath the horizon by black or brown. Less-than-perfect AIs topple when the angle of pitch or bank is too great – a really good AI gives correct indications even when an aeroplane is in an unusual attitude. Unfortunately, many lives have been lost because pilots have followed AIs that have toppled.

Figure 10-20 **Traditional AI**

The same attitude information that is shown on a standard AI could be presented on a digital (numerical) display, but a pictorial representation of attitude seems to convey the information more efficiently and more quickly to a pilot than just numbers. '*P+3 R25L*' is not as informative as a picture of the nose pitched 3° up, indicated by '*Pitch +3°*', and the wings banked 25° to the left, indicated by '*Roll 25 left*'.

On the standard AI, the gyroscopically erect horizon bar remains aligned to the horizon, while the index aircraft remains fixed within the instrument and moves with the airframe. As the aircraft pitches up, the AI case and the aircraft symbol move with it, and the horizon bar moves down within the instrument to remain aligned with the real horizon. As the aircraft rolls from wings-level into a left bank, the index aircraft and the AI case move with the real aircraft, and the horizon bar remains horizontal in space – aligned with the real horizon. Bank angle can be determined from the angle that the wings of the aircraft symbol make with the horizon, or from the bank pointer at the top of the instrument. The AI can be thought of as a porthole through which the attitude of the aircraft in relation to the horizon can be seen.

 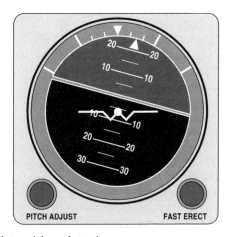

Figure 10-21 **Bank pointers (sky pointers)**

Unfortunately, even within the common design of the AI there are variations. For instance, some designs of bank pointer give a clearer picture than others. Some had ground pointers and now most have standard sky pointers. However, there are sky pointers and there are sky pointers. Note the above illustration shows the aircraft symbol banked to the left and the bank pointer also shows 25 degrees of bank to the left – the pointer is left of centre.

Now look at the display of the EFIS ADI.

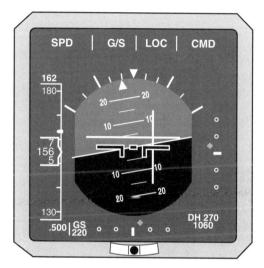

Figure 10-22 **Electronic attitude display**

Note the display shows the aircraft symbol banking to the right but the bank pointer is pointing left of centre. This can lead to confusion when you first convert from a GA aircraft to RPT.

Although we are used to a basic standard design of the AI, with its fixed index aircraft and moving artificial horizon, there are AIs in which the artificial horizon remains fixed in the instrument, and the model aircraft moves. This gives the pilot a view of the aircraft's attitude as if standing upright behind it as an observer.

This sort of AI is common in Russian-designed aircraft, and the pilots like it. However, this reverse-sense instrument has caused massive difficulties for experienced pilots converting to standard western AIs.

Most pilots acclimatise to the attitude indicator that they were trained on. This is a significant point about human nature. We are so adaptable that we can, with training and practice, accommodate almost any mode of operation. The difficulty comes when we have to change that conditioned and tailored behaviour.

## Heading Indicators

The modern *heading indicator* (HI) is placed directly beneath the attitude indicator in the basic-T layout. It is an easy instrument to interpret and to use intuitively – it is a plan view, and so up is forward, left is left, right is right. (It hasn't always been this way.)

To change heading from 360° to 340°, a left turn is required. The desired heading is to the left of the current heading, both in reality and on the DG.

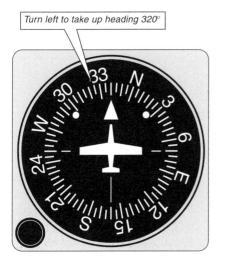

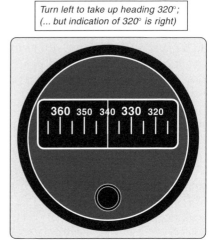

Figure 10-23 **Heading indications**

In contrast, the predecessor of the modern HI, the original *directional gyro* (DG),
was not an intuitive instrument.

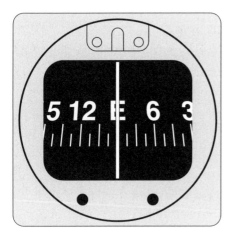

Figure 10-24 **Magnetic compass**

## Magnetic Compass

The magnetic compass is the *primary*
heading reference in an aeroplane,
therefore it is the magnetic compass, and
not the DG, that initially provides us
with the direction of magnetic north.
Why then do we not just use the magnetic compass for heading information,
and do away with the DG? The reason is
that, because of its design, the compass
has certain indication errors, and also a
non-instinctive relationship between its
display and the necessary direction of
turn to take up a new heading.

Indication errors will occur on the
compass during any acceleration, deceleration or turning, with the degree of
error being different on different headings, and reversed in the northern hemisphere compared with the southern hemisphere.

Instrument pilots know the frustration of having to apply *'undershoot when turning through north, overshoot when turning through south'* and by greater amounts at higher latitudes compared with lower latitudes near the equator. Moreover, this then is totally reversed when in the southern hemisphere. As if the pilot did not have enough to think about!

The non-intuitive display of the magnetic compass derives from its construction, and the fact that the pilot is really viewing the compass card from behind, and not from ahead or above. The card remains oriented in space, and the pilot moves the aeroplane around it, the pilot's view being confined to viewing the most rearward face of the compass card.

On heading 090°, 060° will be to its *right* on the compass card, even though a *left* turn is required to take up heading 060°. This requires some mental processing from the pilot if the intention is to turn in the correct direction – brain time that could perhaps be used on other problems.

Mental gymnastics are required from the pilot if wanting to turn in the correct direction (due to the non-instinctive display), and then roll out exactly on the correct heading (having allowed for turning errors during and shortly after the turn). For this reason, the usual technique of using the direction instruments is to:

- allow the magnetic compass to settle down in steady straight and level flight; then
- align the DG with it, and adjust heading according to the DG.

Modern heading indicators automatically align with magnetic north, but in all aircraft, including the most sophisticated modern airliners, you will find an old-fashioned magnetic compass as a standby – it needs no power other than the earth's magnetic field, and has only one moving part.

## Airspeed Indicator

The *airspeed indicator* (ASI) displays the vital aerodynamic quantity *indicated airspeed* (IAS), upon which the flying capability (manoeuvre potential) of the aircraft depends. As the pilot often needs to check IAS with a quick glance – for instance, when on approach to land – the indication and trend must be clear and unambiguous (hence analog display).

Traditionally, airspeed has been displayed on a circular dial, with the pointer moving clockwise to indicate an increasing airspeed, and anticlockwise to indicate a decreasing airspeed. Colour codes for various limiting airspeeds, such as maximum operating speed, stall speeds, and flap speed, are shown on the ASI or maximum weight. Some ASIs may be graduated in mph or kph instead of the usual knots.

One significant improvement was the counter/pointer airspeed indicator fitted to the Sabre. On the same principle as the counter/pointer altimeter it displayed the coarse airspeed and trend by needle position (which could be instantly interpreted) and precise airspeed, to the knot, on the drum (counter). Threshold speeds could be flown within one knot – yes, one knot.

Recent advances with electronic instruments (EFIS and HUDs) have made it possible to display airspeed on a vertically oriented *speed tape* that moves behind a fixed pointer. Limiting speeds and advisory speeds can be shown on the electronic tape for the actual weight and configuration, such as flap limit speed, stall speed, and buffet boundary. The debate as to whether the tape should move up or down, for increasing airspeed, occupied the engineers for years.

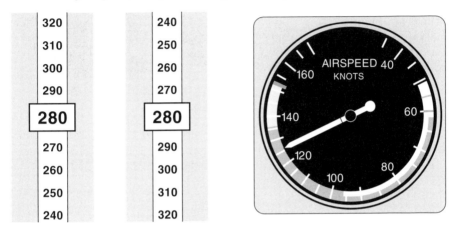

Figure 10-25 **Airspeed displays**

A disadvantage of the speed tape is that the total speed range is not always in view, numbers rather than the visual position of a needle has to be read and subtle trends are less obvious.

## Altimeter

Misreading the altimeter has led to many fatal accidents. It was once described as the only instrument that can kill you. Why should such a simple instrument be so dangerous? There is no doubt that the traditional three-pointer altimeter, whilst it works well technically, is often difficult to read correctly. In an attempt to promote safety, a magazine showed a series of photographs of three-pointer altimeters, and challenged pilots to read them correctly. Remember, just one misreading could be fatal. The accuracy was not good, but more disturbing was that when the answers were published in the next issue, some of these were also incorrect. These answers were prepared by people sitting in cosy offices and not in the cockpit of an aeroplane in flight. Such was the indictment of the three-pointer altimeter.

Many errors have occurred with the 10,000-foot pointer – the altitude being misread by 10,000 feet or more – making it a particularly dangerous instrument for high-flying aircraft descending in cloud or at night. Some pilots have hit the ground at 3,000 feet when they misread the altitude as 13,000 feet. Any pilot who still reads a three-pointer altimeter must thoroughly know how to use it – know which is the 10,000-foot pointer, which is the 1,000-foot pointer, and which is the 100-foot pointer – it is not obvious from the design. Always double-check the reading before approaching 10,000 feet on descent.

Figure 10-26 **Three-pointer altimeter**

Note that later three-pointer altimeters, incorporated a striped sector that appears below the centre of the altimeter when the reading is less than 10,000 feet. It begins to show at about 16,000 feet and is fully visible at 10,000 feet.

### Some Better Designs

A *digital* altimeter readout consisting only of numbers is a possibility. 13,430 feet is quite easy to read, and difficult to misread as 3,430 feet (as has occurred with three-pointer *analog* (pictorial) altimeters). Disadvantages of a pure digital readout, however, show up when climbing or descending; it is easier to judge the *rate* of altitude change (trend) from a moving pointer on an analog altimeter than from a series of changing numbers on a digital readout. It is also easier to maintain a constant altitude using a pointer and keeping it stationary rather than by watching numbers.

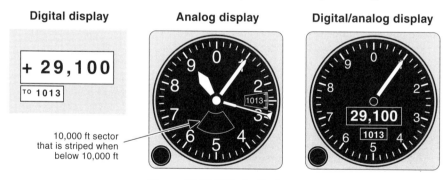

Figure 10-27 **Altitude displays**

A significant design improvement was to keep the 100-foot pointer, where one complete rotation equals 1,000 feet, and to replace the 1,000-foot and the 10,000-foot pointers with a digital display. This offers the advantages of the pointer for maintaining altitude or estimating rate of climb or descent, and removes the potential of misreading by 10,000 feet. This compromise has resulted in a successful and easy-to-use instrument – the counter/pointer altimeter.

It is also possible to have a vertical altitude tape rather than the traditional altimeter dial, with higher altitudes towards the top as is logical, and lower altitudes towards the bottom.

Rate of change of altitude can be judged by the speed at which the tape is moving behind the index mark (as well as from the VSI, of course), and actual altitude can be read from the numbers behind a pointer or displayed in an altitude box. Important altitudes or flight levels, such as selected cruising level, can be displayed digitally above or below the tape as appropriate.

| 39000 | Assigned altitude set by pilot (FL390) |
| 37400 | Moving tape scale, graduated in hundreds of feet |
| 37200 | |
| 370 00 80 | Digital display of the altitude, giving pilot an indication of rate of change |
| 36800 | |
| 36600 | |
| 1013 | Altimeter setting in millibars (mb) (or hectopascals – hPa) |

Figure 10-28 **Tape display**

**Mean Sea Level Pressure (QNH)**

Any indication of altitude is vulnerable to incorrect subscale settings. Hence any QNH setting is always double-checked as part of the pre-approach checks. There has not been an altimeter designed that can automatically set the pressure subscale to 1013, or to current QNH, because of all the variations, but there are some devices that can help avoid the consequences, such as:

- the altitude alert system, a light or sound that activates as you approach or depart a selected altitude, and that helps prevent incorrect altitudes being flown;
- the radar altimeter (RADALT), and the associated ground proximity warning system (GPWS), that warns of impending ground contact;
- the traffic alert and collision avoidance system (TCAS), that shows potential conflicting traffic on your map display.

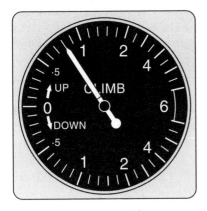

Figure 10-29 **VSI**

**Vertical Speed Indicator**

A typical VSI is an analog display with a pointer indicating rate of climb or descent against a static scale. On a glass display, the VSI may sometimes be associated with the altitude tape. It is easy to read. The traditional VSI is operated by changes in static pressure, and consequently senses a change after it occurs – it has an inherent lag. In modern instruments, an accelerometer compensates for the lag. This is the instantaneous VSI (IVSI). In many RPT aircraft, vertical speed is integrated from vertical accelerations sensed by the inertial navigation system (INS).

## Turn Coordinator

The turn indicator in most modern light aircraft shows the wings of an index aeroplane that can move only in a rolling sense, with a fixed pitch attitude. Whilst the real aeroplane is rolling into a turn, the wings of the index aeroplane move in the appropriate direction to indicate *rate of roll*. Once the aeroplane is in a steady turn, the position of the wings indicates the *rate of turn (yaw)*. The scale is marked to indicate a rate one turn (3°/second)

There is also a traditional instrument, the *turn and balance* indicator, the 'bat and ball', which uses a 'bat' to indicate rate of turn (yaw) – it does not indicate rate of roll. The turn coordinator is an intuitive instrument for a pilot to use. It can be used in a turn to maintain the desired rate and it can be used when straight and level to keep the wings level by not allowing any roll rate to develop, i.e. by keeping the wings of the turn coordinator's index aeroplane level, while keeping the balance ball centred.

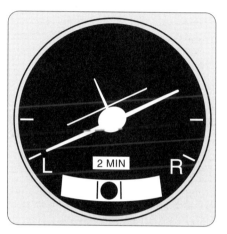

It is very important not to confuse the index aeroplane of the turn coordinator with the index aeroplane on the typical attitude indicator, which remains fixed while an artificial horizon moves behind it to give an indication of pitch attitude and roll attitude. To remind you of this, many turn coordinators are marked with the words 'no pitch indication', or similar. The limitations of the turn coordinator have been overcome by the general adoption of a standby AI in its place.

### Flight Director and Autopilot

The flight director (FD), or flight director indicator (FDI), is a device superimposed over the attitude display to provide the pilot with steering and pitch attitude commands to achieve the preset intercept or profile. It does not tell the

Figure 10-30 **Turn indicators**

pilot what the pitch and bank attitude is (which is the function of the underlying AI), but what pitch and bank attitude should be set to achieve the desired flightpath. By following the flight directions, you should achieve the desired flightpath. The flight director is set in exactly the same way as an autopilot, but the flying is manual.

The flight director receives inputs from various sensors, and integrates them into a simple guidance indication for the pilot. Some features are automatic and the pilot can program some in according to how it is desired to use the flight director. It can also be deselected, so that its symbology disappears from view and the raw attitude indicator remains.

Two typical designs of the flight director are:

- flying wings where the pilot manoeuvres the aeroplane so that the index aeroplane on the ADI is tucked into the flying wings of the flight director; and
- crossbars where the pilot uses the controls to place the nose of the index aeroplane directly beneath the intersection of the two crossbars.

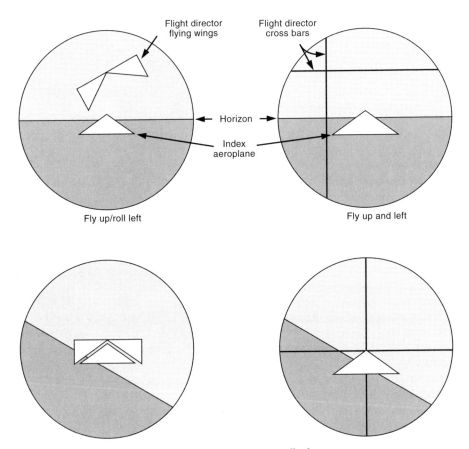

Figure 10-31 **Flight director displays**

The above flight director commands could be for an entry to a climbing left turn. The flight director command indicator moves within the instrument, and when the pilot has achieved the commanded pitch and bank attitude, it then overlies the index aeroplane.

The pilot can program the flight director to provide many types of commands, such as:

- maintain or change heading (by connecting the flight director to a bug on the direction indicator = heading mode);
- maintain or achieve a selected airspeed (by connecting the flight director to the airspeed system = airspeed mode);
- maintain altitude, or achieve a selected rate of climb or descent (by connecting the flight director to the altitude system = altitude or climb mode); and
- maintain a localiser track and a glideslope (by linking the flight director to the electronic instrument landing system, ILS = nav or approach mode).

Like GPS, modern flight directors are so good that pilots can become dependent upon them, but like everything, they can fail. Many strenuous flight simulator exercises have resulted from the simulated failure of the flight director. As a result, the pilot must revert to basic instrument attitude flying, using the basic AI and other flight instruments, and the basic radio navigation instruments, instead of relying on the flight director. This is known as flying on *raw data*.

## Mode Awareness

*Modus operandi*

One major issue that has come to light, with highly automated aircraft and cockpits, is the potential over-reliance on the automatics and the belief that they know better than we. In fact some engineers in aircraft systems design, and in the space programme, have suggested that the system is safest if the pilots do not interfere, i.e. there is more chance of them hindering the system than helping it. That could be statistically correct when everything is going according to plan and following predicted circumstances. However, there are notable exceptions. Fault diagnosis depends on predicted possibilities.

The point here is twofold:

- The human crew can only correct, monitor, and contribute to the total system if they understand its capabilities, limitations and modes of operation. If they don't then the engineers are probably correct. We have more chance of causing faults than fixing them. It is when the events are not predicted *('can't possibly happen')* or the circumstances are unusual that the human can contribute.
- Automatics are highly capable but blindly obedient fools that will happily fly you into the ground and they won't feel a thing. There is a pilot's counter to the engineer's argument – it is safer to disengage all of the automatics and to return to manual control and raw data if something unusual is happening. To make this decision you must know your own aircraft and its limitations as well as you know yourself and your abilities. That's practical application of human factors.

## The ADF and the RMI

The *automatic direction finder* (ADF) is simply a needle that points towards a ground-based *non-directional beacon* (NDB). Older-style ADFs have a fixed card to indicate relative bearing to the NDB, such as 30° left of the nose; this meant that a pilot had to use the heading indicator (or magnetic compass) in conjunction with the ADF if wanting to intercept and maintain a particular track to or from an NDB.

Figure 10-32 **Radio magnetic indicator (RMI)**

Humans cleverly learnt to imagine the ADF needle transposed onto the compass card (again only possible with analog displays). Mental gymnastics were sometimes required, especially in strong winds when drift became a major factor. Eventually, the designers physically incorporated the ADF needle within the heading display. This instrument is called the *radio magnetic indicator* (RMI). An earlier version has the ADF pointer backed by a manually rotatable card and aligned with the compass or heading indicator. Later the RMI allowed two stations to be simultaneously displayed – either NDBs or VORs.

## VOR and the HSI

A *radial* is a spoke that radiates from a beacon. The VOR was designed for air routes where the aircraft could follow a spoke from one beacon to the next. For free-ranging aircraft it is less user-friendly. It was further confused by the name *visual omni range*. It is not visual and it is not a ranging device. At the time there was also VAR (visual audio range), which was an audio tracking device similar in principle to the ILS markers. You followed dot-dash (morse code for A) or dash-dot (morse code for N) depending on which side of track you were. The original ILS had similar coding in blue and yellow sectors. Ask about the back-beam ILS approach.

The original VOR display showed angular deviation from the selected VOR radial, but it is not heading sensitive. It shows your position in relation to the selected radial irrespective of which way you are pointing. If you have the inbound course selected on the *omni bearing selector* (OBS), and you are flying inbound to the beacon on a heading close to that track, the *course deviation indicator* (CDI) is intuitive (operates in a *command* mode just like the flight director). Similarly, if you have a bearing from, and are heading away from, the station. If these conditions are not met, it can appear to be directing a left turn when in fact the radial is to your right. Terminology can be ergonomically confusing too. *Course* was the traditional term

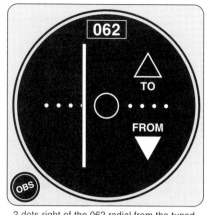

2 dots right of the 062 radial from the tuned VOR station (no heading information)

Figure 10-33 **VOR display**

for *heading* – '*Steer a course for home*' Here it means *radial* or *track*, not *heading* – '*Are you on course for home?*' – '*of course I am*'.

A significant advance was made when the VOR display (the CDI bar) was superimposed upon the heading indicator, the new instrument being called a *horizontal situation indicator* (HSI). This means that the VOR display is always oriented and is a command instrument at all times. Further, the CDI bar (and the ILS glideslope) can also be displayed on the AI with or without the flight director.

## Glass Cockpit

*Electronic flight instrument systems* (EFIS) are usually based on two multi-function electronic displays for each pilot that present attitude, flightpath performance and navigation information respectively and additional displays for systems monitoring. They are integrated with a Flight Management System (FMS) or Flight Management Guidance System (FMGS) for data input and pre-setting. The systems displays can also be used for checklists and emergency procedures (ECAMS). In some aircraft each display can be selected to display any of the available data, e.g. the attitude display can be used for navigation and vice versa. Weather radar and TCAS information can be integrated with the other data, and the preprogrammed FMS can be used to select all and any navaids that are available to update position.

Optimum flight profiles can be preprogrammed and the FMS can be coupled to the autopilot for efficient tracking. A vertical navigation mode (V-NAV) allows the pilot to program the optimum climb and descent profiles – was that five miles per thousand feet? The pilot can ask for the aircraft to arrive at the locator at a set altitude and speed and the autopilot will retard the throttles and commence the descent, perhaps 80 miles out, to achieve the entry window with minimal fuel consumption – or time – if that is your priority.

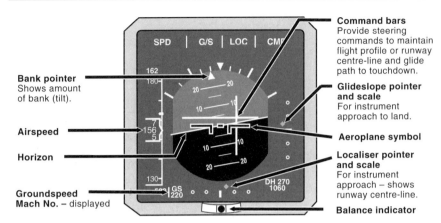

Figure 10-34 **Electronic altitude display**

The navigation display can be used in various modes, including VOR and ILS, but is generally operated in MAP mode whilst en route. In this mode, it shows the programmed route between waypoints in magenta, the *track made good* in white (which should overlay the desired route), the heading and the wind. Some displays are *heading aligned* (with the direction of the nose of the aeroplane at the top), others are *track aligned* (with the direction of travel relative to the ground at the top).

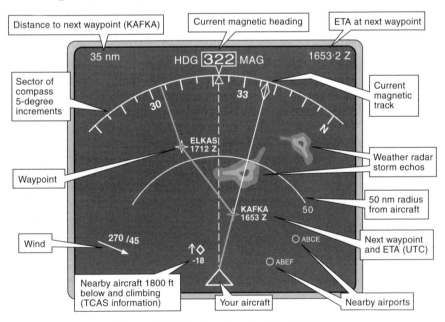

Figure 10-35 **Electronic navigation display**

Many other items can be brought up if desired, including nearby acceptable airports, VORs, ETAs at waypoints, a weather radar display, and TCAS information (potential collision threats detected by the *traffic alert and collision avoidance system*). Predictions of horizontal (turning) performance and vertical (climb or descent) performance can also be displayed.

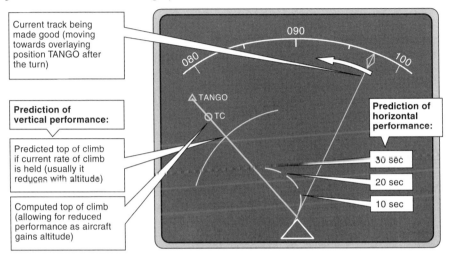

Current track being made good (moving towards overlaying position TANGO after the turn)

Prediction of vertical performance:

Predicted top of climb if current rate of climb is held (usually it reduces with altitude)

Computed top of climb (allowing for reduced performance as aircraft gains altitude)

Prediction of horizontal performance:

30 sec
20 sec
10 sec

Figure 10-36 **Navigation predictions**

## Head-Up Displays

A *head-up display* (HUD) is an instrument display that is projected ahead of the pilot so that instrument indications can be read while viewing through the windscreen. This is in contrast to the conventional head-down display, where the instruments are down on a panel, forcing the pilot to direct the eyes downwards from the windscreen to read them. Derived from the gun-sight, HUDs were developed to their current advanced capability by the need for low-altitude, high-speed navigation and weapons delivery. They simply use an electronic symbol generator from which the image is projected onto an angled transparent screen. The pilot sees the symbols superimposed on

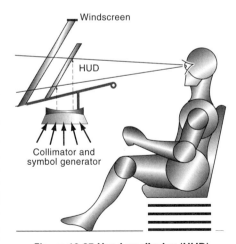

Windscreen
HUD
Collimator and symbol generator

Figure 10-37 **Head-up display (HUD)**

the view through the transparency. The projected symbols pass through a collimating lens (which parallels the light rays so that the image appears to be at an infinite distance).

However, there still seems to be a need for slight accommodation change of focus between the illuminated data and the outside world. It is a very powerful and useful instrument and no doubt will be the way of the future. They can display various flight parameters, such as airspeed, attitude, heading, altitude and vertical speed. The tendency is to display too much information and therefore clutter the display. Military HUDs have a *declutter* setting to shed all but essential performance data.

Figure 10-38 **HUD symbology**

Most applications for HUDs have been in military aeroplanes, but Air Inter used them for many years in the A320 with great success in achieving landings in very limiting meteorological conditions. The Falcon also has a HUD.

Aviation is by nature a conservative environment, and like fly-by-wire and side-sticks, the HUD is not yet generally accepted. Similar success can be achieved by conventional head-down instruments with good autopilots capable of performing autoland and roll-outs, and this seems to be the current trend. HUDs, however, will re-emerge in the future as aircraft performance and traffic densities increase.

Those who have used a HUD will attest to the value of a simple symbol of where the aircraft is pointing – the *fuselage reference line* (FRL) – or similar airframe reference. From this, the velocity vector (where the aircraft is going) and ground-referenced velocity vector (where the aircraft is going to impact) are added. Together they will change the nature of flight path displays.

## Flight Management System

The *flight management system* (FMS) is an alphanumeric (letters and numbers) keyboard with pages of menu items. It can be used to flight plan, preprogram and conduct a flight, depending on your company policy and personal preference.

There is a psychological barrier for older pilots adapting to the new technology, and companies need to pay particular attention to training for them to be accepted and used to their full potential. Conversely, there is a problem with younger generations accepting them as gospel and not questioning the outputs they provide. Like all electronic aids they must be kept honest by having simple manual and mental cross-checks. Computers are clever fools. And we still have to change hands.

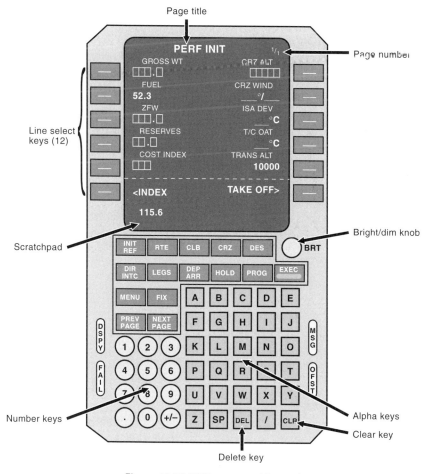

Figure 10-39 **FMS menu and keypad**

## Documentation and Procedures

### Cockpit Checks

Checklists are a vital part of modern-day operation. In the old days, it was possible to commit to memory the few checks that were needed, including normal checks, such as the *pre-take-off* and *pre-landing* checks, as well as *emergency* checks to cope with engine fires and other emergencies. But don't confuse performing with checking. The checklist is to confirm that actions that have already been carried out were done correctly and completely. Humans are often better at remembering the generalities whilst forgetting the particulars. It is also important to tie the check to a particular event or point – e.g. remember the general rule to do the pre-landing actions and then the checklist abeam the threshold (a *checkpoint*) or the PUF check when lined-up on final.

Checklists, if properly used, ensure that particular items have not been missed.

One human characteristic that we need to guard against when using checklists is to not see what we want to see, but to see what really exists. For instance, with the *'gear down?'* check, we all want and expect to see three green lights to confirm normal operation. On occasions, pilots have been known to respond, *'Three greens'*, when in fact that was not the case. They may not have even looked at the indicator.

Similarly they may have seen the gear selector was in the down position but the gear may have still been up. We must never respond to a checklist item mindlessly; always consider the response before giving it, even if it is an everyday, routine checklist. Another human failing with checklists is to skip items or be distracted or interrupted.

Checklists should be:

- easily found;
- easily read, day and night;
- concise;
- very clear and unambiguous;
- prioritised; and
- not add to the pilots' workload.

### Scan Approach to Checklists

Many operators complete a check in two stages:

- *scan-do* being a scan where the eyes and hands follow a flow pattern around the cockpit, noting and actioning the appropriate items; then
- *scan-check* being reading the checklist to verify the items.

### Manuals

Most of the information that a pilot needs to operate the aeroplane is found in a manual. A common problem in even the newest manuals, however, is that the information is often difficult to find, is often spread around various parts of the manual, and is often written in engineering terms. Bearing in mind these difficulties, it is vital that a pilot becomes familiar with the manuals for the aircraft type.

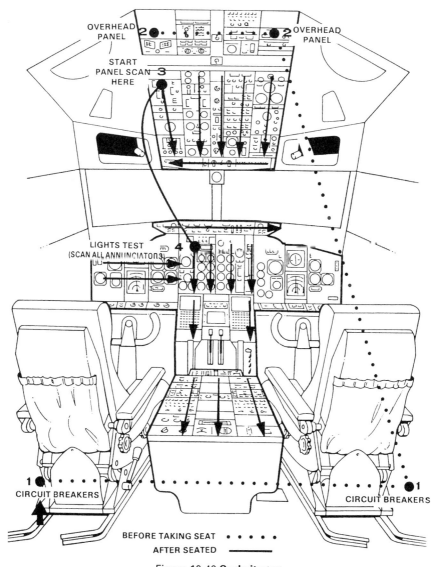

Figure 10-40 **Cockpit scan**

The requirements for a good manual, or set of manuals, are similar to the requirements for a good checklist, other than there is no need for a manual to be concise. The manual is the place for clear and full explanations and additional information, both for new pilots and for experienced pilots, whereas the checklist is a challenge-and-response action list for the qualified pilot.

For maximum effect, manuals should be:
* easily found;
* easily read;
* illustrated; and
* very clear.

## Standard Operating Procedures

In a multi-crew situation, each member of the crew should know what the others are doing, or what they should be doing. In a single-pilot operation, we need to know how the company wants and expects the aircraft to be operated. These procedures are contained in *standard operating procedures* (SOPs). This is not to say that pilots are locked into a totally rigid system, but rather that they participate in a standardised operation with no unexpected happenings. SOPs define the boundaries and the standards.

Most airline operators have an escape clause for pilots to improvise if they feel they need to, often by using words such as *'Non-standard, I intend doing. . .',* which may be a slightly unusual visual pattern to avoid a known area of turbulence, or it could be a faster and steeper descent to circuit altitude to make up time, and so on. The main thing is that each pilot knows what the other has in mind – before it actually happens.

## Units of Measurement

A significant cause of potential accidents in the non-standardisation of units of measurement. Now that we are in the twenty-first century and the third millennium, it is negligent to have international flight operations with non-standard units for mass, atmospheric pressure, altitude (in some cases), visibility, wind velocity and fuel volume.

Conversion charts, performance charts, loading charts and flight planning graphs and tables are all vulnerable to misreading – with potentially dire consequences. When we fly a European aircraft in the States, or a US aircraft elsewhere, we are effectively trying to fit a square peg into a round hole – as far as units are concerned.

Chapter 11

# Passengers

The pilot is responsible for the safety of the aircraft and its passengers. The pilot must also ensure that, as well as being properly prepared for the flight, the passengers are adequately briefed on safety matters.

## Pilot Persona

Passengers must have confidence in their pilot, and you, as pilot in command, can generate this. Passengers will feel more comfortable and less anxious if you, as their pilot, with their lives in your hands for the next few hours, are professional and confident both in your appearance and as you go about your duties. A scruffy-looking pilot, running late, and agitated, will not inspire confidence; a well-dressed, well-organised pilot will. No matter who the passengers are (parents or prime ministers), the pilot is in command during the flight, and the responsibilities of command begin well before the flight. Be aware of this, and conduct yourself in a manner that will inspire confidence.

The normal order of authority may have to change during this period. A person who has authority on the ground, whether a parent or the boss or some dominant person, must subject himself or herself to the authority of the pilot in command once a flight commences – and a flight commences well before the aeroplane takes off. In reality, the sense of already being under way may commence much earlier, during the flight planning stages the night before, or on the drive to the airport. It is important for you to be aware of this, and to assume the mantle of command right from the beginning, no matter how young or inexperienced you are. Passenger safety and the feeling of well-being should commence a long time before the flight.

Advise your passengers that you will need ten minutes or more without interruption to consider the weather forecasts and the other paperwork. They will respect this, and feel much better than if their proposed pilot bent to their every whim and did not pay attention to the other duties. Passengers will be aware of how you consider the preflight information and reach your go/no-go decision; you should do this carefully, efficiently and confidently. You should set the pace.

## Prior to Boarding

As the pilot, you should inform the passengers that at various times throughout the flight you will have important duties to perform that will require your full attention. For this reason, you may occasionally request that there be no interruptions and no excessive conversation during the periods while you are concentrating on *vital actions*.

Correct clothing is important to passenger comfort. Most aircraft cabins can be kept warm (or cool) in flight. Overcoats and other very heavy clothing need not be worn, although they should remain accessible in the event of an emergency evacuation. Passengers are forbidden to fly when drunk and should not fly if sick or affected by an upper respiratory complaint such as a cold. Pressure changes will occur as the aeroplane climbs and descends, and if the ears do not automatically adjust, chewing, yawning or holding the nose whilst blowing with a closed mouth may assist. Blocked nasal passages can hinder this process.

High noise levels and possible turbulence may be a little disconcerting. Passengers should be reminded if there are no toilet facilities on board. Baggage should be checked to ensure that it is not overweight and does not contain dangerous goods such as aerosol cans, pressurised cigarette lighters and matches, none of which should be carried. It is inadvisable to smoke or have any naked flame near aircraft, especially if refuelling is in progress. Normally, passengers should remain well away from the aeroplane as a precaution while refuelling is in progress, since the fire risk is somewhat greater. It is advisable to wash your hands after refuelling because the smell of fuel or oil, or indeed any other unpleasant smells, in the cockpit can be annoying.

Passengers should be warned to remain well clear of propellers, since even a stationary propeller can spring to life, and a rotating propeller may hardly be visible. For this reason, children must be very closely supervised. The safest approach to an aeroplane is from the left and behind the wing, with passengers remaining in a single group under the supervision of the pilot. Various attachments on the aeroplane, such as the pitot tube and radio aerials, are fragile and should not be used for support. Care should be taken when entering the aeroplane not to step where the wing or any part of the aeroplane structure could be damaged.

## Preflight Check of Emergency Equipment

A vital part of any preflight check by the pilot is to ensure that the required emergency equipment is on board and serviceable. The emergency equipment carried will of course vary according to the nature of the flight about to be undertaken, the requirements for a trip across the Sahara being different from those for a trip over northern waters in the middle of winter. The basic emergency equipment, such as emergency checklists and safety belts, will of course be on board at all times. Additional emergency equipment carried may include such items as a torch, fire extinguisher, emergency locator transmitter (ELT), lifejackets and life-raft for long overwater flights, survival kits, emergency flares, first-aid kit, and so on.

## On Board

Ensure that your passengers are comfortably seated and confirm that the front-seat passenger will not restrict full movement of any control with bags, cameras or legs. Any metallic or magnetic objects should be stored well away from the magnetic compass.

Seatbelts will consist of a lap-strap and sometimes a shoulder harness. The lap-strap should be fastened and adjusted until it is firm but comfortable, followed by the shoulder harness if one is fitted. The passengers must be shown how to fasten, adjust and release their seatbelts.

The passengers should know how to close, lock and then open the doors and windows or canopy. Once a door is closed by the pilot, the position of the lock and handle should not be altered. Aircraft cabins can become stuffy, so ensure that there is adequate ventilation and each passenger knows how to adjust the appropriate vent to maximise personal comfort. The intercom, if one is to be used, should be explained. The radio volume should be adjusted to a comfortable level.

Passengers need not be passive, but can actively assist in some aspects of flight, such as maintaining a good look-out for other aircraft and for landmarks, as well as passing the sandwiches around!

## Passenger Briefing

An important duty in taking care of your passengers is to brief them on the use of their safety belts, and on any relevant emergency procedures. This would form the basis of your standard passenger briefing. Additional items could be added to this standard briefing when appropriate. If about to fly over an expanse of water, for instance, you would include in your briefing an explanation of how to don the life-jackets. If the expanse of water was great enough for you to be carrying a life-raft, then you would also brief on how to remove the raft from its pack and inflate it, making sure it does not drift away from the aircraft. If you were about to fly at high altitudes, you would also brief on the use of the supplemental oxygen system. If you give the briefing in a friendly but confident manner, the passengers will be impressed by your professionalism, and be more relaxed. A typical standard briefing follows.

**Seatbelts**
*Remove any sharp articles from your pockets (such as keys, pocket knives, nail files, cigarette lighters). Position your seat and ensure it is locked in position so that it cannot move. To fasten your seatbelt, lengthen the strap if necessary, insert the belt link into the belt buckle, and tighten the belt by pulling the free end until you have a snug fit across your hips. If it is too tight, you will be uncomfortable; if it is too loose you may not be held firm enough in your seat if we meet unexpected turbulence. To release your seatbelt, pull upward on the top of the buckle. The shoulder harness can also be fitted into the buckle. It has an inertia reel that allows you lean forward, but will lock you firmly in position with any sudden deceleration. Your seatbelt must be fastened for every take-off and landing, but I recommend that it remain fastened throughout the flight.*

**Emergency Exits**
*In the rare event of having to leave the aircraft quickly, the exit to use is. . . Move away from the aircraft, and keep well clear of the propeller at all times.*

**Smoking**
*You must not smoke on the tarmac area, nor during take-off or landing. I would prefer no smoking in flight, because we also have non-smokers aboard and because it introduces the unnecessary risk of fire.*

**Radio**
*If you wish to listen in to the flight radio, we can use the cockpit speaker or you may use a headset which should make the communications clearer. The volume control is here. . ., and we can also use the intercom [test if possible].*

**Planned Route**
*We will taxi out and use Runway. . . which means a take-off into the [N, S, E or W], followed by a [right/left] turn. We will be tracking overhead. . . and. . . to our destination. . . The weather we expect en route is [good/may be a little bumpy].*

**Doors, Windows and Ventilation**
*Ensure your seatbelt is not hanging out, then close the door firmly and lock it. The window may be open for additional ventilation while taxiing. Normal vents are located. . ., and you can adjust them by. . . If you happen to feel unwell in flight, which I do not expect to be the case, advise me early on so that I can try to avoid bumpy areas or tight manoeuvres. Now we are ready for engine start and radio communication.*

**End of passenger briefing.**

Figure 11-1 **Standard passenger briefing**

Figure 11-2 **Life vest**

If you change your plans in flight, or if you have to carry out any unusual manoeuvres, then a quick briefing to your passengers will put them at ease. Handicapped passengers may need special attention, and a modified briefing to explain how they should leave the aeroplane in the case of an evacuation.

## Lifejackets

Before flying over any expanse of water in a single-engine aircraft, all occupants should don lifejackets. There are various types and the pilot must be familiar with their use. Most lifejackets are designed to be worn uninflated inside the aeroplane so that their bulk is minimised, both for comfort and for ease of departing the cabin.

The pilot should explain how to don the lifejacket, which is usually by fitting it over your head with the main part of the jacket in front of your body, then passing the straps around your back and tying them in front. Some jackets may require a different fitting technique for children. The passenger must understand how to inflate the lifejacket and use any attached items such as a light or whistle. It should be emphasised that it is best to inflate the lifejacket after having exited from the cabin so that the evacuation is unhindered.

Inflation is generally achieved by pulling a release on a small gas cylinder attached to the front of the lifejacket. If the gas pressure provides insufficient inflation, there is a tube through which the passenger can blow and further inflate the lifejacket.

## Life-Rafts

Immersion in the seas could result in death within a few hours – within a few minutes in extreme temperatures and winds. Whilst life-jackets are useful for flotation, they will not protect the body from icy water. For this reason, it is prudent, on overwater journeys, to carry a life-raft in which the occupants can be sheltered from exposure and remain fairly dry.

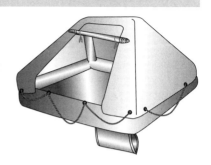

Figure 11-3 **Raft**

Most life-rafts suitable for light aircraft are stored in a small bag and weigh 10–15 kg. The raft must be inflated outside the aircraft, usually by removing it from its bag, ensuring that its cord is firmly held and placing or throwing the uninflated raft into the water. It may be advisable to swim a short distance from the aircraft before inflating the life-raft to avoid any danger of holing it. Pulling the release cord should then activate the gas cylinder and inflate the raft. A sea anchor (bucket) can be used to prevent the raft drifting too far from the aircraft, which will assist in the search.

The raft will have associated equipment such as paddles, a canopy (very important in minimising exposure) ropes, knife, dyes, flares, light, first-aid kit and possibly emergency rations. If necessary due to space constraints (and for faster evacuation of the aircraft), passengers should be instructed not to take luggage with them into the raft.

## Oxygen Equipment

If you intend to fly at high cabin altitudes, then the passengers should be briefed on the use of the on-board oxygen equipment. This will involve instructions on:
- removing fatty materials from facial areas exposed to the oxygen (such as face cream or cosmetics) since they could be combustible;
- no smoking when oxygen is being used because of the risk of combustion;
- how to don the mask and achieve a satisfactory oxygen flow; and
- the time of useful consciousness, which is only a few seconds at very high cabin altitudes, but longer at lower cabin altitudes.

The use of oxygen should be considered at cabin altitudes over 10,000 feet.

## Fire

Three things are necessary for a fire to occur:
- a fuel (e.g. Avgas, oil, papers, fabric, cabin seating, etc.);
- oxygen (present in the air);

- a source of ignition (cigarettes, matches, electrical sparks, etc.), but bear in mind that once a fire is burning it is itself a source of ignition.

Prevention is by far the best cure, and pilots are advised to pay attention to items and situations that are a potential cause of, or contributor to, fire. Any possible *fuel* and any possible source of ignition should be kept separate, e.g. when refuelling ensure that no person is smoking in the vicinity, that the aeroplane and refuelling equipment are adequately grounded to avoid the possibility of a static electricity build-up causing a spark, and that no fuel is spilled. As a precaution when refuelling, a suitable fire extinguisher should be readily available. In flight, if the pilot permits any passenger to smoke, then he must ensure that no hot ash or cigarette butt comes in contact with papers or even the cabin seating, which may smoulder or burn, possibly unnoticed for some time.

The risk of fire, as well as the detrimental effects of carbon monoxide in the blood, is another reason to discourage smoking in aircraft. Cockpit fires can also be caused by faulty electrical circuits, which can often be recognised by a peculiar smell. Further development of an electrical fire may be prevented by switching off the electrical power (master switch off, or pulling the appropriate circuit breaker).

## Extinguishing a Fire

The usual method of extinguishing a fire once it is burning is to eliminate one or more of these items (fuel, oxygen, source of ignition), e.g. blanketing a fire with dry chemical from a fire extinguisher to starve the fire of oxygen. If it appears that a fire has not yet started but is imminent, and the fuel and ignition source cannot be separated, it may be advisable to starve the area of oxygen by using an extinguisher.

| Paper, wood, textiles | Inflammable liquids & gases | Live electrical equipment |

Figure 11-4 **Extinguisher codes**

### Fire Extinguishers

Regular public transport aircraft must carry fire extinguishers; however, for private aeroplanes, this is only a recommendation and not a requirement. Many light aircraft are indeed fitted with a small fire extinguisher that is securely stowed where the pilot may reach it in flight. The usual extinguishants contained in these are BCF (halon) and dry chemical, both of which are capable of handling most types of fires. Other extinguishants in use include carbon dioxide, water and foam. There is a standard graphic code to differentiate between the suitability of fire extinguishers in fighting certain types of fire, and this is usually displayed on the extinguisher with an indication of its suitability for the specific categories.

Typically, a stored gas pressure discharges the extinguishant when a trigger is pressed. Each particular brand of fire extinguisher may have special requirements (such as to break a seal by twisting a handle, or by releasing a handle, or by breaking a lockwire), so the pilot should read the instructions and become familiar with the extinguisher, which might have to be used at short notice. Some of the more common types of fire extinguisher are discussed below. Some fire extinguishers are reusable either by recharging the cylinder or by placing the trigger and head mechanism onto a new cylinder, whereas others may have to be discarded once used. A serviceability check of the fire extinguisher may require checking pressure on a gauge, which may be colour coded, or on an indicator disc, which, if it can be pressed in, indicates that the pressure is low and the fire extinguisher unserviceable. There may also be a weight check to determine that no extinguishant has been lost, but this check is more likely to be done by a maintenance engineer during the periodic inspections.

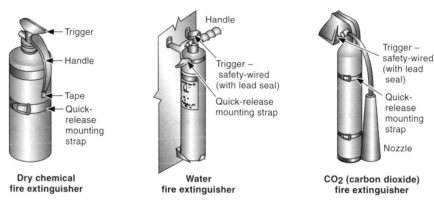

Figure 11-5 **Types of extinguisher**

### BCF (Halon)

BCF extinguishers contain halon 1211 (*bromochlorodifluoromethane*) and are often found on light aircraft. BCF is a very versatile extinguishant and is capable of combating most types of fires, including fuel, fabric and electrical. BCF is stored as liquefied gas, which comes out as a fine jet of fluid and develops into a spray. Its toxicity is low (so will not poison the pilot or passengers) and can be safely used in the cockpit, although it is advisable to avoid inhaling excessive amounts of fuel and smoke.

Bearing in mind that the BCF extinguishant gas will exclude oxygen to some extent, the cabin should be well ventilated once the fire is extinguished. A significant advantage of BCF is that (unlike dry chemical) it does not leave any residue, and so the cabin and instruments will not require cleaning after its use.

### Dry Chemical

A dry chemical fire extinguisher contains dry powder and carbon dioxide. It is very effective against most types of fire, including electrical and fuel, but is less effective than BCF against material fires (paper, textiles, wood). Unfortunately, dry chemical has several disadvantages. During its use it may restrict visibility in the cockpit and cause breathing difficulties, so ventilating the cabin is important once the fire is out. After it has been used, a powdery residue will remain that is corrosive to aluminium alloys and can be damaging to instruments, so thorough cleaning is necessary after dry chemical has been used.

## $CO_2$ Fire Extinguishers

Carbon dioxide fire extinguishers contain liquefied $CO_2$ that is discharged as a gas and used to combat electrical fires, engine fires on the ground and other fires. When sprayed at the base of the fire, the $CO_2$ blankets the fire and starves it of oxygen.

A typical $CO_2$ fire extinguisher will have a trigger with a lockwire that must be broken before use (an intact lockwire is also a check for serviceability), and a nozzle that should be raised before the $CO_2$ is discharged with the trigger. The nozzle pipe should not be held with the bare hands, since it will become extremely cold as the gas vaporises, and skin could be frozen to it. $CO_2$ will cause breathing difficulties and is best not used in the cockpit unless oxygen masks are available.

## Water Fire Extinguishers

'Wet' water fire extinguishers generally contain distilled water with an anti-freeze agent to retain serviceability at low temperatures and a 'wetting' agent. Water is suitable for extinguishing material fires (e.g. a smouldering cabin seat), but definitely should not be used for electrical fires or fuel fires.

## Foam Fire Extinguishers

Foam fire extinguishers are generally designed for outside use. One common type is inverted just prior to use, causing chemicals to mix and form foam under pressure which can then be directed at the base of the fire.

# First Aid

First aid is what its name suggests – the initial care of the sick or injured. It can preserve life, protect the unconscious, prevent worsening of a condition and promote recovery. First aid lasts until medical aid (doctor, nurse or ambulance officer) arrives or until the casualty recovers. First aid is useful knowledge for all citizens, but is especially useful for those who may find themselves in remote areas well away from medical aid (e.g. following a forced landing in an aircraft). The St John's Ambulance Association specialises in first aid and is highly recommended for its manuals and courses.

## Problems that May Occur in Flight

Minor medical problems may occur in flight and can often be handled without difficulty. It is most important, however, that this does not distract you from flying the aeroplane and adequately controlling its flightpath, which is your principal responsibility.

### Airsickness and Nausea

Airsickness may occur in flight, especially if the person is passive, in a hot stuffy cabin and is experiencing unusual motion, such as in manoeuvres or turbulence. Generally, passengers are more passive than the pilot, although it is not unknown for a pilot to become airsick. The affected person may feel nauseous and 'hot and cold', but will often feel better after having vomited.

To manage a person who feels airsick (ensuring that you, as pilot, do not neglect your prime responsibilities in controlling the flightpath of the aeroplane):
- loosen their clothing;
- ensure plenty of fresh air;
- lie the patient down or recline the seat;
- place a cool cloth on their forehead;
- comfort and reassure them; and
- have a sick bag handy in case of vomiting.

## Fainting
Insufficient blood reaching the brain may cause a person to faint and possibly lose consciousness temporarily. A temporary disturbance of the nervous control of the blood vessels can be caused by nervous shock (such as a fright or a horrifying sight), an injury, being passive in a hot stuffy environment or by a sudden postural change (like standing up after having been sitting for a long period). A person who is about to faint may feel weak and giddy, 'hot and cold', and have a pale, clammy skin, experience blurred vision and have a desire to yawn.

To manage a person who has fainted, or is about to faint:
- lie the casualty down if possible, with the legs raised; otherwise recline the seat;
- loosen clothing;
- ensure plenty of fresh air;
- allow the casualty to rest;
- have a sick bag handy in case of vomiting;
- place a cool cloth on the forehead; and
- if hyperventilating, have them breathe into a paper bag.

## Nose Bleeds
Nose bleeding may result from injury, high blood pressure, infection or excessive blowing of the nose. It usually occurs from just inside the nose on the central cartilaginous partition below the bone. Instruct the casualty:
- not to blow the nose;
- to breathe through the mouth;
- to apply finger and thumb pressure on the flaps of the nostrils (just below the bony part of the nose) for at least 10 minutes;
- to sit up, with the head slightly forward and loosen any tight clothing; and
- to keep cool with a good supply of fresh air and with cold towels on the neck and forehead.

## First Aid Following an Accident
The pilot is responsible for the safety of the aeroplane and its occupants at all times. On rare occasions, accidents do occur and the pilot must be capable of managing subsequent events adequately. The welfare of the group must take precedence over that of any individual, and if possible, the safety of the flight (whilst it lasts) should not be prejudiced.

## Prevention Is the Best Cure

Preventing an accident or incident is of course best. Food poisoning, for instance, can be avoided by careful choice of food. Pilot welfare is best achieved by staying on the ground if someone has diarrhoea or nausea, or if an upper respiratory or hearing complaint is being experienced.

Some good points of airmanship (common sense) in prevention are as follows:
• have the seatbelts fastened;
• do not allow smoking; and
• guard against fumes and carbon monoxide in the cabin by ensuring a good supply of fresh air.

## If an Accident Occurs and Passengers are Injured

In the event of an accident actually taking place do everything in your power to stop the situation worsening. Secure the aeroplane and evacuate uninjured passengers, taking any useful emergency equipment and supplies. Consider the welfare of injured passengers and whether or not they should be moved. Do not forget the welfare of the non-injured members of the party. If an unconscious passenger

Figure 11-6 **Think before moving**

is evacuated, then it should be done gently and firmly, with the casualty being placed in the *coma position*. This is a comfortable position that aids blood supply to the brain and allows any vomit to escape without blocking the breathing passages.

## Head Injuries

Head injuries are potentially very serious as they can result in brain damage, altered consciousness, spinal injury, bleeding, breathing difficulties, vision and balance difficulties. Even mild head injuries should be treated seriously. Indications of head injury may include headache, nausea, memory loss, blurring of vision, weakness on one side of the body, wounds, bleeding, bruising, clear fluid escaping from the nose or ear, twitching, noisy breathing, incoherent speech, congestion on the face, vomiting, dilated pupils or pupils becoming unequal in size, strange behaviour and abnormal responses of the injured person to commands and to touch. Treat someone suffering head injury the same as for being unconscious. Consider placing the victim in the coma position so that any bleeding, discharge or vomit can drain away. An open airway is vital. Ensure that the tongue or dentures do not obstruct the passages. Breathing should be monitored and assisted if necessary. Be alert for possible concussion.

## Bleeding

Bleeding is loss of blood from the blood vessels, and may be either internal or external. In either case blood is lost to the circulation and the ability to carry energy-giving oxygen around the body and to the brain is reduced. Blood loss can lead to faintness, dizziness, nausea, thirst, a weak and rapid pulse, cold and clammy skin, and rapid breathing. Fortunately, bleeding will often stop of its own accord, but if it does not, severe bleeding can lead to shock and eventually to death. Severe bleeding, therefore, is extremely serious and must be controlled before less serious injuries are attended to.

External bleeding is best controlled by placing a bulky dressing (or your hand if nothing more suitable is available) over the wound and applying firm pressure to it for 10 minutes or more. Raise the injured part and rest it to decrease the blood flow. Profuse bleeding may be reduced by pressing the sides of the wound together or by applying a constrictive bandage or hand pressure to block the blood flow through the arteries, say, above the elbow or knee. This should be a last resort and the pressure should be released every 10 minutes or so to ensure some blood supply to the area. Bleeding from the palm of the hand may be serious and can best be treated by clasping a firm pressure pad (e.g. a bandage roll, a handkerchief wrapped around a stone, or two or three fingers of the other hand) and elevating the hand above the head to reduce the blood flow to it.

Internal bleeding may result in pain, tenderness, tight stomach muscles and the above-mentioned signs of blood loss. To manage internal bleeding, rest the casualty completely. Elevate the legs comfortably (if not broken), loosen tight clothing and allow no food or drink. Seek urgent medical assistance.

### Fractures

A fracture is a broken or cracked bone. There will be bleeding, either internally or through an open wound, causing a loss of blood to the circulation. The area where the break has occurred may be painful, tender, misshapen or swollen, bruised and unable to be used normally. In managing a casualty with a fracture:
- control bleeding and cover wounds with a sterile or clean dressing;
- immobilise and support the fracture with a sling, bandage or splint, and prefer-ably support the injured limb in an elevated position:
- for *splints* use any suitable material that is long, wide and firm enough to give sup-port and immobilise the joints above and below the fracture (use can be made of the upper body to splint a fractured arm and of a good leg to splint a fractured leg);
- *padding* may protect the skin and bony points and allow the splint to fit snugly; and
- *bandages,* in general, should be broad and supportive; and
- check frequently to ensure that blood circulation to a fractured limb is not impaired, that bandages have not loosened, and that splints are still supportive, and look for signs of shock.

### Burns

Burns are a serious injury. Extensive burns to the body or to the respiratory tract (due to breathing hot air or fumes) are potentially dangerous and may be fatal. To manage a casualty with burns, first extinguish the fire if possible and/or remove the casualty from danger, making sure that you do not become a burns casualty yourself.

- Put out burning clothing by smothering with a non-inflammable blanket or jacket, or possibly a dry chemical fire extinguisher (directed away from the eyes).
- Remove or cut away any clothing near the burnt area unless it is stuck to it, in which case leave it alone. Remove any rings, bracelets, watch bands, etc., before swelling starts. Cool the injured area if possible under cold, gently running water (cooling may take up to 10 minutes).
- Do not prick blisters and avoid touching the burnt area. Do not apply any lotions, ointments, oily dressings or fluffy material. Apply a sterile non-stick dressing and bandage lightly.

A conscious casualty seriously burnt should be given frequent small amounts of water, weak tea or milk (about ½ a cup every 10 minutes) to minimise the effect of fluid loss from the burnt tissues. Do not give alcohol. Seek medical aid urgently.

## Deep Shock
Shock can range from fainting (nervous shock) to deep shock following serious injuries and illnesses, especially where there is severe bleeding, pain or loss of fluid from burns. Deep shock can be a life-threatening condition. Insufficient circulation of blood to the brain and other body tissues may lead to a collapse of the circulatory system and death.

Shock is progressive and may take some hours to become obvious, and the symptoms should be carefully watched for. A casualty experiencing shock may be faint or dizzy, restless and apprehensive, nauseous and thirsty. The pulse may be very weak and rapid. The face and lips may be pale and the skin pale and clammy, the extremities becoming bluish. Breathing may be rapid and the injured person may become dull, drowsy, apathetic, confused or unconscious.

To treat a person in shock:
- Increase the blood supply to the brain if possible by lying the patient down with the head low.
- Control any external bleeding, dress any wounds or burns, immobilise any fractures and loosen any tight clothing.
- Keep the casualty warm, but do not overheat as this draws blood away from the vital organs.
- If thirsty, moisten the lips or allow the casualty to suck an ice cube.
- Monitor breathing and pulse.
- If breathing is difficult, or vomiting likely or if consciousness is lost, lie the casualty on the side with the mouth slightly down.
- Seek urgent medical assistance.

## First-Aid Kits
Although aeroplanes flying for a purpose other than public transport (e.g. for training or for private flights) are not required to carry a first-aid kit (whereas public transport aircraft are required to do so), it is good airmanship for the operator of the aeroplane to provide one.

# Afterword

We've now seen deep inside our inner human selves – as a generic group. We have seen how the human body and mind have certain abilities and certain limitations. We can recognise and accommodate these by checklists, back-ups, procedures and systems design. That is why we have more than one pilot in RPT aircraft.

But let's think about what we are trying to achieve. Ultimately this whole program of study is designed to make us safer pilots. To our passengers an accident is intolerable and unthinkable – and quite rightly so.

The intent of this manual was to make us aware that the accident chain is complex and prevention requires a team effort well beyond the flight deck.

More importantly none of us is an average human being. There is no such thing. Let's be absolutely honest and stop pretending. Let's recognise and accept our individual characteristics – our strengths and weaknesses. They are not really strengths and weaknesses but slight variations from the mythical norm. We each have such individual variations, in appearance and in physical and mental skills, attributes, characteristics and behaviour that we bring to our lives, our profession and our relationships. Let's take a moment to consider what those individual strengths, weaknesses and peculiarities are and then let's further change the patterns of our individual behaviour to ensure that our personal safety shields remain intact.

If a tennis player has a weak backhand, she will place her shots to encourage returns to her forehand side. The profession of aviation is no different. It is about achieving the best possible performance from the tools we have been given. It is to take advantage of our strengths and to compensate for our weaknesses, and within a crew we can do this for each other. That's what CRM and good management should really be about: recognition of individual strengths and weaknesses in members of the crew, or the team, or the company and placing them in a situation which exploits, and rewards, their strengths but never exposes, nor has to punish, their weaknesses.

Individually we also have good days and bad days, whether it be due to fatigue, stress, health and moods. Again the advantage of a positive team environment is the ability to carry that temporary vulnerability and still ensure a safe flight.

Armed with this information about ourselves, and ourself, on a particular day, we can see how we must change our behaviour to allow for the inherent design characteristics of this, generic and individual, fascinating human machine.

If we have reached this point we can now look back outside – safely.

# Index

hyperopia
    *See* long-sightedness
hyperthermia 107–108
hyperventilation 16
    treatment 16
hypoglycaemia 88
hypothermia 108
hypoxia 11–13
    anaemic 12
    hypoxic 12
    hystoxic 12
    stagnant 12


**I**

IAS
    *See* indicated airspeed
illusions 62–74, 143
    spatial orientation 64
    visual 34–47
ILS
    *See* instrument landing system
incapacitation 98–100
    gastroenteritis 99
indicated airspeed 235
information processing 135–156
    adaptation 139
    attention 142
    control loop 148–149
    divided attention 142
    levels 147–150
    memory 144–147
    mind-set 141
    perception 140–143
    precoding 142
    reflexes 154–156
    sensation 139–140
    sensory threshold 139
    skills 150–153
    stimulation 138–139
    stress 142–143
    time-sharing 142
insomnia 124
    situational insomnia 109
instantaneous vertical speed indicator 238
instrument landing system 241
instruments
    analog displays 237
    basic-T flight instrument layout 230–231
    display 229–246
    electronic flight instrument systems 243

International Standard Atmosphere 7
ISA
    *See* International Standard Atmosphere
IVSI
    *See* instantaneous vertical speed indicator


**J**

jet lag 130–133


**L**

leans 69–72
lifejackets 254
life-rafts 255
linear acceleration
    sensing 62–63
load factor 75–78
    a-loc 78
    blackout 76
    *g*-loc 77–78
    greyout 76
    negative *g* 76
    redout 76
long-sightedness 48–49
    presbyopia 49


**M**

magnetic compass 234–235
Maslow's pyramid 194–195
medication 90–91
memory 144–147
    action slips 167
    amnesia 147
    echoic memory 139
    environmental capture 167
    episodic memory 147
    event memory 147
    iconic memory 139
    long-term memory 146–147
    meaning memory 146
    reversion 167
    semantic memory 146
    sensory memory 139, 144, 171
    short-term memory 145, 171
    working memory 144
migraine 97
motion sickness 74–75
    simulator sickness 75
myopia 47–48
    empty field myopia 21, 28